THE

CHANGING CURRICULUM

OF THE AMERICAN

HIGH SCHOOL

PRENTICE-HALL INTERNATIONAL, INC.
London • Tokyo • Sydney • Paris
PRENTICE-HALL OF CANADA, LTD.
PRENTICE-HALL DE MEXICO, S.A.

KIMBALL WILES

College of Education/University of Florida

THE
CHANGING CURRICULUM
OF THE AMERICAN
HIGH SCHOOL

PRENTICE-HALL, INC., Englewood Cliffs, N.J.

PREFACE

If you were to ask what is meant by high school
curriculum you would get many different answers.
A sophomore boy might reply aggressively: "The things the
teachers make us learn."
The teacher might say meekly: "The courses of study provided
for us to follow."
The principal might say: "The courses for which units of credit
are given."
A parent could venture: "The facts that are in the textbooks."
If you asked if the band is a part of the curriculum you probably
would get hedging answers.
The principal would say: "A student can get a unit of credit for
it if he takes band for four years."
The teacher, if not a band director, would complain: "It
interferes with the real classes."
The parent would probably deny band a place in the curriculum:
"It is one of the frills you find in modern schools."
The pupil would state categorically: "It is extracurricular; you
don't get full credit for it even though it takes as much time as
general science."
What would be the result if you asked about football, square
dances, the school paper, the way the library is operated, the
food in the cafeteria, the assembly programs, the school plays,
the student government? All of these are under the supervision

v

of school authorities; all are supported by the taxpayers' money; all require expenditure of staff time and effort.

The word curriculum is an abstraction. It means different things to the child, the parent, the teacher, the college professor, the lay community member. Much of the difficulty encountered when people discuss curriculum lies in the fact that they are discussing different aspects of it. Some think of the formal curriculum of the school; others visualize the informal happenings in the school situation; a third group focuses its attention on what happens to children and teachers. The formal curriculum consists of the units of credit that are offered, the courses that are made available to students, the syllabi for these courses, the bibliographies and materials used, and the evaluative devices that are selected. The informal aspect of the curriculum includes the unplanned things that happen in classes, in the hallways, on the playground, in the cafeteria, and on the way to and from school.

This book has been designed to help teachers, administrators, and parents see the school program and its development more realistically. The curriculum is presented as a dynamic program, not a fixed abstraction. It is recognized that the curriculum becomes what it is in any school at any given moment because of the social setting; the ideals and commitments of individuals; and the skill, understanding, and strategy of those concerned with change. It is assumed that the curriculum consists of all the experiences pupils have under the supervision of school authorities and that it is necessary to have consistency in the way the student is treated in both formal and informal situations.

It is my hope that this book will help students who wish to become teachers to understand the operation of the institution in which they expect to teach and show them the best ways of working in it, stimulate teachers and administrators to more effective curriculum improvement, and challenge parents and lay citizens to make a greater effort to secure better secondary schools.

KIMBALL WILES

ACKNOWLEDGMENTS

Any author is deeply indebted to many individuals for their contribution to his product. Students, colleagues, teachers, other writers, all have affected his thinking and ideas. As the reader progresses through this book it will be easy for him to see the impact on my thinking of Art Combs, Earl Kelley, Doug Blocksma, and others. To each I acknowledge my debt and trust that I have interpreted his contributions accurately.

Although it is impossible to be certain about the assistance provided by all, it is easy to be specific about the major influence of many. I am happy to acknowledge my debt to:

1. The members of the departments of secondary education at New York University (1946-1950) and the University of Florida (1950-1955), who, in department meetings and action research projects, joined me in testing hypotheses designed to secure a more desirable secondary school curriculum.
2. The members of the Commission on the Education of Adolescents of the Association for Supervision and Curriculum Development, who for six years sought agreement on the nature of the high school we need. Franklin Patterson, for his assistance in helping to crystallize ideas as we prepared the final draft of the report of the commission.
3. Derwood Baker, for stimulating me as a graduate student to question existing practices and envision broader horizons.
4. Ted Rice, for sharing his faith, vision, and humility as we taught together.
5. Forrest E. Long, for challenging me by his constant insistence that an idea or procedure be practical.
6. Clara Olson, for inspiring me by her constant demonstration of concern for the education of all students.

TABLE OF CONTENTS

III THE PROCESS OF CHANGE

THE

CHANGING CURRICULUM

OF THE AMERICAN

HIGH SCHOOL

Present institutions are products of the past. To understand their nature, structure, and intended function it is necessary to know the decisions that have determined their development.

1

DECISIONS
THAT DETERMINE
THE CURRICULUM

The American high school curriculum is in transition,
and it is necessary to see it as a moving force with a past, a
present, and a future. It is important also to recognize that it
is a product of choices in which teachers, administrators,
parents, college professors, the lay public, and even pupils
participate. It is a unique institution. For the most part, it is an
institution provided by the state for all youth. It is not selective.
Almost every American child enters a high school. For seventy
per cent of the people who enter, it is a terminal education.
The size of the secondary school population has increased
enormously. As late as 1890 only three hundred sixty thousand
youths were enrolled in secondary schools. By the end of
World War I two million youngsters were enrolled in secondary schools. Seven and one-half million were in the
secondary schools in 1945; over ten million were in the upper
four years of the secondary schools by 1960.
And the nature of the population has undergone a drastic

change. In the early part of the twentieth century the high school was providing experiences for a very select group, most of whom had a definite vocational objective. They were getting ready for college or getting ready for a type of occupation to which courses that were then in the curriculum made some contribution. In the high school today many youngsters lack any real vocational purpose. Many are enrolled because it is required that they be there.

The curriculum of the high school is not and never has been fixed and immutable. It has been the subject of continuous debate, and decisions have been made which have greatly modified its nature.

Since Sputnik was sent into orbit the rate of change in the secondary school curriculum in the United States has been vastly accelerated. Many persons who ignored secondary school programs in the past have now become concerned. They want to become a part of the decision-making process and help to determine the content of the curriculum. In place of being a concern of only professional educators, teachers, pupils, and some parents, the quality of the secondary school has become of major interest to military men, statesmen, publishers, columnists, and scholars.

HISTORICAL DECISIONS

Although recent widespread public anxiety has increased the rate of change, the secondary school curriculum has been in transition throughout its history. No curriculum was ever legally established. It has evolved through a continuous series of decisions. Each person involved has been attempting to make the choices that will promote social or individual welfare.

The original secondary schools in America, first established in 1635, were the Latin grammar schools, designed to prepare boys for college. Latin, Greek, religion, and the tool subjects necessary for success in the colleges of the day comprised the curriculum. But by the middle of the eighteenth century many people in America felt a need for a different type of education beyond the elementary school. As a result the academy was formed. High hopes were held that it would provide a more practical type of education for the youth who did not expect to enter the professions. Surveying, mathematics, and other subjects needed in conducting day-to-day affairs were included in the curriculum.

But the influence of the headmasters changed the curriculum of the academies. To secure the best trained educational leadership for academies, headmasters were chosen from among men who had graduated from college. These men, as a result of their background and experience, felt that the academy should provide an education which would develop a cultured person. It is not surprising, therefore, to find that the curriculum of the academy was gradually changed to put a major emphasis on college preparatory subjects, and the practical, utilitarian aspect of the academy diminished.

In 1821 the first high school was established. Its curriculum consisted of English, rhetoric, and mathematics. As this new type of school spread throughout the country it began to take the place of the academy as an institution for the training of people not going to college. Its curriculum was expanded to include United States history, geography, natural history, intellectual philosophy, and natural philosophy. A demand emerged for Latin, Greek, and other subjects required for college entrance, and the high school followed the path of the academy. The persons selected to head the high schools had backgrounds which led them to insert more and more college preparatory education into the high school curriculum.

By 1890 a committee called the Committee of Ten was formed to study the high school program and to make recommendations for its improvement. This committee came to the conclusion that the high school did not exist primarily to prepare for college and recommended that the main function of the secondary school should be to prepare for life. Only three hundred sixty thousand pupils were in the secondary schools at that time.

Boys and girls left school at all grade levels at the beginning of the twentieth century, but so many left at the end of elementary school that it seemed necessary to attempt to provide a transition between the elementary and the high school. In 1909 the junior high school was instituted. Combining some of the qualities of both the elementary school and the high school, it was designed to give opportunity for exploratory activities so that students could make a more satisfactory decision about entering high school. In the beginning it differed drastically from the high school program, but through the years there has been a gradual tendency for junior high school staffs to copy the program offered by the senior high schools.

Again in 1918 a national committee was established to study the high school program and to make recommendations for its improvement. This committee, the Commission on the Reorganization of Secondary Education of the National Education Association, also placed

States he came involved in education about 1920.

emphasis on preparing for life rather than for college. It recommended that the secondary school attempt to promote seven types of pupil growth: health, worthy home membership, worthy use of leisure time, command of fundamental principles, vocational training, civic education, and ethical character. (See *Cardinal Principles of Secondary Education*, U.S. Bureau of Education Bulletin No. 35.)

Ten years elapsed before the Department of Superintendence of the NEA made recommendations to guide the secondary school program. In their 1928 yearbook, *The High School Curriculum*, they recommended that the high school promote in each pupil an understanding and evaluation of self, an understanding and appreciation of the world of nature, of organized society, and of the forces of law and of love that are universally operating.

But despite the recommendations of the committees that have studied the high school and recommended increased emphasis on preparation for living, the program has continually drifted back to a primary focus on college preparation, with additional courses for other students when staff and student body were sufficiently large to permit a more comprehensive program.

In the mid-thirties the General Education Board underwrote an eight-year experiment to determine the effects of modifying the curriculum of the secondary school. This study, conducted under the auspices of the Progressive Education Association, sought to discover a program that would both meet the needs of youth and also prepare them for college. The school staffs involved in the study agreed that the high school program should produce the following types of growth in students: improved study habits, ability to collect data and interpret them, skill in applying facts, socially desirable attitudes and interests, social sensitivity, the power of critical thinking, initiative, resourcefulness, and self-reliance. Agreement was reached with colleges to accept the graduates of the schools involved in the experiment, and each school faculty was encouraged to change its program in any way that seemed desirable. Careful follow-up was made of the graduates of the experimental high schools who went to college. Their records were compared with those of a control group of students who had graduated from regular high school programs. The students from the experimental schools were as successful academically as, and more successful in nonclass activities than, graduates of regular programs. It could be concluded that a curriculum designed to promote the qualities that enable a person to live successfully could also prepare students for college. In fact, in this study (the Thirty Schools

Study) it was found that the schools that deviated most from the traditional college preparatory curriculum produced the students who were most successful in college.

In 1937 the Educational Policies Commission advocated in *The Unique Function of Education in American Democracy* that

> Education must keep alive memories, linking the past with the present and tempering the sensations of the hour by reference to the long experience of the race. . . .
>
> Education must foster aspiration—the desire to be more, to acquire skill and knowledge, and to create. . . .
>
> Education now lays emphasis on its social obligations and must serve an associational economy, prepare youth for an associational life and activities, prepare citizens for participation in associational government, and aid in upholding social values. . . .

Contrast this statement with the viewpoints advanced three years later by the American Council on Education in *What the High School Ought to Teach:*

> The program of schooling at the secondary level should be more functional, much less formal and academic than is the conventional program. . . . Some way must be found to provide work experiences for youth while they are in high school.

The recommendations of the council called for modification to make the program more functional in fulfilling the following needs of youth:

—friendship, respect, and admiration of fellow youth
—experiencing the satisfaction of achievement
—economic independence
—instruction in family living and family relations
—understanding political and economic conditions
—physical and mental health
—ideals which serve as goals and inspiration.

Throughout its history the American secondary school has been subjected to contradictory pressures. On one side are those who want the school for adolescents to prepare all youth for practical day-to-day living, while on the other are persons who expect the secondary school to get pupils ready for college work. New developments in the program have been a departure from the existing college preparatory curriculum. Each break with tradition has been followed by a movement back toward the college preparatory offering.

Each new thrust has resulted in the inclusion of new courses and activities in the program. The persons wanting emphasis on preparation for college have gradually expanded their idea of what prepares for college. In the beginning, it was Greek, Latin, and rhetoric. Later it was extended to include mathematics, English, science, history, and foreign languages.

Within the past three decades some educators have taken a position which would make possible even greater elasticity. They have contended that the school's primary function is to aid youth in solving their present problems and that in the process they will learn the techniques of problem-solving which will enable them to deal competently with any problems that the future may bring. They have challenged the basic assumption that there are portions of the culture that must be studied by pupils as preparation for living. These persons believe that in the process of solving his problems a pupil will acquire the essential understanding of his heritage plus the skills which will enable him continually to acquire information from the record of the past while living in the present.

Attempts to restrict the high school program have centered in the colleges, where entrance requirements have been controlled either by those who sincerely believe that their fields are at the heart of living and culture or by those who wish to maintain a vested interest. During the thirties, forties, and early fifties, however, many colleges, particularly state universities, accepted high school graduates without specifying particular courses that they had to have completed. Since Sputnik, some of those institutions have returned to a more restricted concept of the high school courses that prepare for college.

Meanwhile, the high school curriculum has continued to expand. New courses have been added; relatively few have been dropped. Requirements for graduation have become more elastic. Students have greater opportunity to select courses which they feel will help them.

At the present time secondary school faculties still find themselves facing the dilemma that has confronted them throughout the history of the secondary school in America. What shall be the major emphasis in the high school program? In some faculties there is strong sentiment for emphasizing qualities that will enable a person to live successfully. In others there is the insistence that high schools focus their attention on preparing students for success in college by traditional methods.

ə

STATEWIDE DECISIONS

When the second-ary school was established as a state institution the curriculum was not defined. Although it was assumed that the product of the secondary school would be a good citizen, no statement as to content or organization of the school was made. The nature of the secondary school program to be provided was left to the educators. Thus educators are expected to produce good citizens, but the description of a good citizen has not been provided for them. They find themselves faced by the problem of making that definition and are as disturbed by the responsibility as any other segment of the population would be. Some of the problems they face in executing their responsibility follow.

A good citizen should believe in American values. On some values—honesty, truth, fair play—there is widespread agreement; but what about states' rights, government planning, provision for housing and necessary medical care? Where is the school to get its answers as to which of the many conflicting values held by American society it is to teach to youth?

A good citizen should have basic citizenship skills. What are these? Ability to read and write? Skill in defining problems, collecting data, forming generalizations, taking action to test conclusions? Skill in organizing groups? Skill in sifting evidence to select facts and discover distortions? How much should a good citizen question? How much should he obey? Does good citizenship extend to the way a person lives in a family? Does it include his knowledge of economics and his vocational skill? Does it involve teaching him to drive so he will not kill other persons on the highway?

All of these questions and many others have been left to educators. Some state legislatures have required that certain subjects be taught. Driver training, conservation, temperance, and state and American history are samples of curriculum content that have been mandated by legislatures. In 1961 one state legislature ordered that each high school must include a six-week unit on Communism versus Americanism. When politically powerful groups in states have become anxious or crusaders for specific causes, legislatures have enacted laws that require specific content to be included in the high school curriculum. But such action is atypical. For the most part funds have been provided and laymen have let educators select the experiences children should have.

How have educators decided what to teach? The basic decisions have been made on a statewide basis. State departments of education have established an approved curriculum. Local schools have then had to adopt it in order to be on the state's list of accredited high schools.

Some state departments have made their decisions on the basis of tradition. State department members have checked with friends in other state departments. Representatives of the colleges and universities have been consulted. If a regional accrediting agency had been established, its regulations were considered. After the examination of these sources, the state department has issued an official course of study.

Some state departments have engaged experts who came to the state, studied the situation, and then recommended a program that in their opinion would meet the needs of high school pupils in the state. The experts may have been influenced by the same factors as the state department people: other courses of study, leaders on local college faculties, accrediting agencies. Or they may have made an analysis of living in the state and recommended a set of experiences designed to get people ready to follow the activities normally pursued in that state. Or they may have decided that, based on their personal interpretation of the American heritage and culture, man today needs to know certain facts.

A more common procedure has been for the state department of education to call together committees composed of public school and college teachers to discuss and decide together what should be taught. Some have undertaken the task seriously. Others have used the scissors-and-paste technique, lifting from other courses of study and from writings in the field. Numerous curriculum bulletins have been produced which are supposed to guide teachers.

In a few states committees of laymen and parents have been assembled to state the kinds of growth they hoped the school would produce in children. The framework thus developed has been used as a guide in determining the courses to be offered in the high school.

Although in some states little responsibility for determining curriculum content is left with the local school unit, the trend in curriculum development is in the direction of putting responsibility on the local staff. Where this procedure is followed, each principal and faculty is held accountable for the quality of curriculum that exists in the school. Much can be said in favor of this trend. Schools have different needs to meet. Faculties should be able to use all of the insight they possess. Local school units should not be held back because of lack of progress in the state as a whole. Furthermore, responsibility should be fixed on a staff so it cannot hide behind state regulations or blame lack of progress on outside forces. If the staff makes the curriculum decisions, it assumes responsibility for implementing them.

However, at the local school level the common way of determining the curriculum content for the school has been to follow the state course of study and use the approved texts. Although some states permit exceptions to the approved program, the typical school does not take advantage of the option. It is easier and less dangerous for local staffs to leave to someone at the state level any necessary decisions about what experiences produce a good citizen.

Most observers would agree that textbooks have also determined in large measure what has been taught in the secondary school. Despite efforts by some supervisors to encourage teachers to depart from a text, most teachers select and follow a single book. Statewide textbook committees have selected approved texts, and their decisions have in large part determined the curriculum content.

Thus the framework for the curriculum of any high school consists of the state laws, the regulations and courses of study established by the state department of education, the textbooks approved for use in the state, and the decisions concerning curriculum made by the local board of education and staff.

FACULTY DECISIONS

How can a staff make decisions concerning the program that will be best for boys and girls in that school? How does it know what to teach? It is impossible to teach all the information in the world; the secondary school program is not long enough. A staff is faced with a choice as to what information should be included.

What are the bases of choice?

One basis has been *tradition*. The things that have been taught are good; therefore, keep on teaching them. The knowledge and the culture of mankind have been incorporated into the curriculum by previous decisions. If the purpose of the school is to produce cultured citizens, it should continue to teach the same content that has been taught. Such an approach, however, does not take into account that new conditions and new times may call for new knowledge, or that different kinds of knowledge are needed in different kinds of communities, or that knowledge is multiplying each decade.

Another basis has been *prejudice* or *hunch*. The faculty sits around the table at a meeting and decides that a particular kind of information is desirable for all pupils to have. The person who speaks first or loudest or with the most emotion will probably have the greatest influence on the decision.

A widespread basis has been *keeping up with the Joneses*. One high school faculty finds that another high school has introduced a new activity or class into the program, and it feels that it should do the same. This practice has been one of the reasons why some high school curricula are such hodgepodges without logic or consistency. Faculties have added new courses without studying how they fit into the total program or deleting contradictory courses.

Another basis of choice has been *college entrance requirements*. If a staff believes that the function of the secondary school is to get people ready to enter college, it can determine the content that should be taught in the high school by looking at the college entrance examinations. If youngsters succeed in passing their college entrance examinations, the staff can rest assured that it has taught them the right content and that the high school curriculum has been satisfactory. Such a basis overlooks the seventy per cent who do not go to college and assumes that the content needed for those going to college is good for all.

A further approach has been to look at the *vocations that students will enter*. If a staff takes this path, it can decide by job analysis what is needed to be successful as a bricklayer, a barber, a farmer, or in any other vocation that is widespread in the community in which the high school is located. After the analysis is completed, it builds the high school program in terms of the kinds of skills, knowledge, and attitudes that it takes to be successful in the vocations for which the school hopes to prepare students.

Another basis of choice has been the *interest of pupils*. If it is assumed that the students will learn more by examining the problems in which they are interested, the curriculum content can be chosen by planning with students investigations into the areas which they find interesting or challenging. Under this approach there is no assurance that any area will be covered by any particular group of students. Certain interests, however, seem to be fairly common at certain age levels, and the pupils will probably select problems in these areas.

A seventh approach has been to base the selection of curriculum materials on the *needs of the community*. A high school may take as its basic assumption that its function is to improve living standards in the community. By an analysis of the community, its occupations, its institutions, and its activities, teachers, or parents and teachers planning together, can decide the kinds of experiences and knowledge that people in that community need. When this answer has been reached it is the staff's job to plan the experiences through which boys and girls will acquire these skills and knowledge.

An eighth basis has been the *needs of pupils*. Studies made of the concerns and needs of adolescents have indicated the areas in which adolescents want help. It is possible to select subject matter which provides answers to the concerns of adolescents and to let that information constitute the basic curriculum content.

A ninth way has been to accept the *insistence of pressure groups* in the community that certain ideas and certain materials be taught in the school. These pressure groups decide what they consider to be right and then use legislation or other means to enforce their desires on the school program.

The most accepted answer to this dilemma, philosophically at least, has been a combination of these approaches. Verbal allegiance has been given to a curriculum based on a study of the social conditions, the goals, and the nature of the adolescent. Under this approach a faculty looks at the world today, the national and international scene, and gets some cues as to the topics or problems that children should study. By looking at the local community the faculty gets an indication of the kinds of skills and attitudes and information that people need in that community. Further, they study the nature of the adolescent to discover his concerns, his physical and emotional needs, and then begin to select the kinds of problems and experiences which will be of benefit to him. As the third prong of the analysis, they examine the social goals of the society in which the school exists. What point of view has been advanced by the founding fathers? What have the poets, writers, philosophers, statesmen, politicians, and ministers had to say about values and direction? What are the agreements and conflicts that should be known to adolescents? On the basis of these three analyses, the faculty makes judgments concerning the kinds of attitudes, skills, and knowledge boys and girls need and the experiences that will make possible the development of these attitudes, skills, and knowledge.

STUDENT DECISIONS

Recent studies in the field of perception indicate that each person perceives in terms of his background, his purposes, and his needs. Studies conducted at Dartmouth, at Princeton, and at Ohio State explored this hypothesis. (See Earl Kelley, *Education for What Is Real.*) Situations were presented in which persons looked at abstract objects and told what they saw. The results indicate that persons looking at the same object do not see the same things. What a person sees is determined by his past experiences and by the motivations that he has.

The implications of these and other studies in the area of perception do not stop with interpretation. Not only does the individual see the items in his environment in terms of his past experiences, needs, and purposes, but his behavior is in turn controlled by the way in which he sees the situation and the factors in it. Combs and Snygg, in *Individual Behavior,* state the position bluntly:

> People do not behave according to facts as others see them. They behave according to facts as *they* see them. What governs behavior from the point of view of the individual himself are his unique perceptions of himself and the world in which he lives, the meaning that things have for him.

If these conclusions are accepted, it means that the interpretation a pupil gives items he encounters in his classroom varies from the interpretations that other children give to those same things. If a teacher uses a word such as Republican, it has an entirely different meaning for the child from a Republican family than for a pupil from a strong Democratic background. The books that children read have different meanings. Many Negro families have objected strongly to the use of *Little Black Sambo* because it has a significance which they cannot accept for their children or which their children cannot accept as a result of discussions that have gone on in their homes. The picture of an automobile wreck in a safety lesson is entirely different for the child whose mother was killed in an automobile accident than it is for a child who has had no experience with the results of traffic accidents. In other words, the curriculum for each child is an individual affair. He interprets the environment which the school provides for him, and that becomes his individual curriculum.

Although thirty children are in the same classroom and go to the same cafeteria and ride the same bus, they do not experience a common curriculum. Each individual child has his own curriculum in the environment that is provided by the school authorities. Each perceives the adults in a situation differently. They may be a threat, or they may be persons to trust. Each sees the classroom differently. For one it will be a place of restriction and confinement. For another it is the spaceship in which he explores his universe. Each will see arithmetic differently. For one it will be utterly meaningless and useless. For another it will be a new language, a set of skills that will open the door to the kind of goal that he wants in life. Each will see the social environment of the school differently. Some will see it as a place where they are ostracized, where they do not have the opportunity to belong, where people look down upon them because they are inadequate, where they are infrequently chosen, where they do not have friends. Others will see the school as a place where they achieve easily, where they receive a great amount of recognition, where their company is sought, where they are happy in their relationships with adults.

The curriculum for each pupil is determined by what he brings to the school. His concept of himself and his world provides the basic orientation of the curriculum for him. His immediate purposes and needs decide which of the experiences that are available in the school will be used by him. His past experiences will determine how he interprets the many facets of his school environment with which he must interact.

The organization of a child's experiences at school is done by the child in spite of all the things that adults do to attempt to control the child in his environment. The organization of knowledge that a child makes does not follow the outline that the teacher puts on the board or that he finds in a textbook. It is made by the student and consists of the facts that he comes into contact with, the data he chooses to incorporate in the body of knowledge that he possesses, and the new fields that he picks to stake out for himself as future areas of exploration. The organization of content is something with which the child emerges as a result of his experiences rather than of a course syllabus or outline that the teacher makes before the child enters a situation. Each youngster analyzes his experiences and creatively develops his own application to the succeeding situations at school and at home.

The teacher who seeks to promote creativity does not expect students to emerge with the perceptions, interpretations, or applications that he has. In fact, he is disappointed if they do. He begins to question his procedures to see what he has done to block the creativity and insight of pupils. In his role he does what he can to stimulate and promote creativity in interpretation, in generalization, and in application.

Even when teachers attempt to force conformity, they can make sure only of outward conformity. When students are in a situation where they are expected to conform and the teacher has the power to make them do so (in appearance, at least), they give the answers that are expected. But inwardly they draw their own conclusions, and these conclusions may be the exact opposite of those which the teacher forces them to voice. They behave in the classroom situation as the teacher has told them that they must, and in out-of-school situations they behave in terms of their own creative interpretation of the experiences that they have had in school.

Schools staffs must recognize that the curriculum provided is not the idealized version that they have in their mind and which they have expended energy to produce. Rather, the curriculum in a school is the one that the child feels and sees and hears there. Even though the staff has taken endless hours to formulate good courses of study and to secure the materials of instruction which meet its goals, if the child, as a result of contact with teachers and with the materials that they have collected, is formulating the type of conclusions about himself and others in our society which will operate against his becoming a worthwhile member of the society, the curriculum is not good for him.

Viewed in this light, the curriculum cannot be described as a set of textbooks or as courses of study provided by a state or city curriculum department. The curriculum for a child consists of all of the experiences that are provided for him by the school—all of the factors in his environment which are a part of the school day. It is more than the school environment. It consists of his out-of-school experiences which the school uses in developing understandings and skills. In this sense the curriculum may consist of fights on the school ground, of smiles from the teacher, of the kind of spirit that prevails in the school, of the cafeteria and the way food is served, of the art in the school hallways, of the color in the classroom, and of all the things that go to make up living in the school. Any attempt at analysis of curriculum cannot be restricted to a course content outline or to textbooks that are used. Any attempt to improve the curriculum will have to be an attempt to improve living in a particular school.

From the point of view of the learner, the curriculum of the secondary school is the environment provided by school authorities for pupils in grades seven to fourteen or for pupils from eleven years of age to those of nineteen or twenty. No sharp break in subject matter exists between the elementary and the secondary school. If a fourteen-year-old is learning to read better, then reading is a part of his curriculum in the secondary school. If a fifteen-year-old does not know his multiplication tables and finds it necessary to work on his multiplication tables, then multiplication tables are for him a part of the content of the secondary school. If a student of sixteen years of age has learned to despise people of another religion, then the process of learning how to understand and live with others is a part of his curriculum. Other youngsters may have learned all of these things during their elementary school experience. It is possible to make some guesses as to where most youngsters will probably acquire certain skills, certain understandings, and certain values that it is hoped American citizens will have; but no staff can guarantee that each child will acquire them at precisely the moment when it is hoped they will be acquired. No staff can tell a child he must make this growth at this time. No staff can guarantee that a child will reach any level of achievement by insisting that he reach it. Children grow at their own rate. All a staff can do is to provide the kind of environment which will be conducive to the type of growth sought and the kind of emotional climate in which students will develop into wholesome, healthy individuals.

NATIONAL DECISIONS

The federal government has never established nationwide requirements of curriculum content for all secondary school youth. During World War I Congress enacted the Smith-Hughes Act (1917), which provided federal funds for high schools that would offer certain types of vocational education. But the legislation was permissive, not mandatory. Since Sputnik, national funds have been provided for the improvement of instruction in science, mathematics, and foreign languages. The monies are being used to develop what it is hoped will be a more useful organization of content in these fields and to provide in-service education for teachers. But no decisions to require certain content of all students has been made at the national level.

Within recent years there has been an occasional demand from some lay and some professional sources for a national curriculum, but few people have as yet accepted such proposals as desirable or necessary. In 1960 the National Education Association, as a partial step, established an Instructional Program Project to investigate the degree of agreement that exists concerning curriculum content.

On the other hand, some authorities claim that a national curriculum already exists. One man cites the following experience: He left Boston by plane, stopped in Cincinnati, St. Louis, and Denver on his way to Los Angeles. In each city he visited high school chemistry classes, and in each location they were studying a unit on oxygen. On the way back he visited twelfth grade English classes in Los Angeles, Phoenix, Dallas, Knoxville, Washington, and Boston. He found each class studying *Macbeth.* He believes that the textbook publishers have provided a national curriculum whether school people recognize it or not. Officially, however, decisions concerning curriculum content are not made at the national level except through permissive legislation and commissions and committees which influence by their advice.

FORCES AFFECTING DECISIONS

Many people are attempting to work out a more satisfactory curriculum for the secondary school. It is a difficult proposition because of tradition, because of the attitudes held by some members of the staff, because of the vested interests of certain college groups who wish to see the subject that they teach continued, because of certain pressure groups within the community who feel that any change is one that will affect them adversely, because of accrediting associations which have built rules and regulations designed to help them make judgments about types of high schools that now exist, because of textbook materials that have been prepared which are designed for the present curriculum, and because of lack of understanding of the nature of the learning process. An understanding of the background of the secondary school, the levels at which decisions have been made, and the bases on which they have been made provides the necessary orientation for an intelligent approach to the task of improving the high school curriculum.

SELECTED READINGS

American Youth Commission of the American Council on Education, *What the High School Ought to Teach.* Washington, D.C.: The Council, 1940.

Report of the Special Committee on the Secondary School Curriculum.

Combs, Arthur W. and Donald Snygg, *Individual Behavior*, rev. ed. New York: Harper and Row, Publishers, 1959. Advocates a perceptual approach to the understanding of human behavior.

Kelley, Earl, *Education for What Is Real*. New York: Harper & Row, Publishers, 1947. Presents early research in perception and the implications of the findings for the school program.

National Education Association, *Cardinal Principles of Secondary Education*, U.S. Bureau of Education Bulletin No. 35. Washington, D. C.: The Association, 1918. Proclaims the major objectives of secondary education in the most famous declaration in the history of secondary education in the United States.

——, *The Unique Function of Education in American Democracy*. Washington, D. C.: The Association, 1937. Attempts to clarify the role of schools in the United States.

I
THE BASES
OF DECISIONS

Although the bases of decisions are not always recognized, individual and group decisions are affected by social goals; the world situation; the condition of the nation; the community setting; the needs, concerns, and wishes of youth; and the vision of teachers, administrators, and laymen. From the consideration, formal and informal, of these factors, there emerges an image of what the school could be. A study of the contrast between the present status of the secondary school and the ideal image provides the dissatisfaction that motivates change and progress.

2

THE SOCIAL NEEDS

Decisions concerning the secondary school curriculum
are determined in part by the values of the society in which the
school exists and by the quality of living in the community—
world, national, and local—in which it is located. What are
the implications of current social values for the operation
of the secondary school? What social conditions affect the
school curriculum?

SOCIAL GOALS

The secondary school
is accepted as a major instrument of society for
promoting the development of basic American values.
Through living and working in the school, it is hoped that
students will develop a concept of democracy and a belief
in democratic values and will gain new insights into the
application of those values.
What are the essential ideals of American democracy? Although there are many issues and ideas on which the people
disagree, the following values run throughout the American

23

political and social heritage. They constitute the ideals to which Americans give verbal allegiance and which they strive to attain in actual practice.

Belief in the worth of the individual. Each individual has value and a unique contribution to make.

Belief in the use of the intelligence of all. Problems should be solved by the intelligence of those involved. Individuals and groups should be free to reject the answer of authority unless they believe that it contributes to the solution of their problem.

Belief in keeping the channels of communication open. Each individual may have access to information and use his intelligence to arrive at a wise decision. He may have freedom to express an opinion about what needs to be done.

Belief in flexibility. Those involved should be free to change the structure and procedure in any way that will still maintain the free flow of information and the participation of all in decision-making.

Belief in the freedom of the individual to think, speak, listen, worship, and take action that seems desirable to him. Minorities and members of minority groups are entitled to the same privileges as majorities and members of majority groups.

Belief in respect for the rights of others. Freedom must never extend to the point where an individual's actions invade the rights of others.

Belief in the responsibility of the individual. Each individual may use his intelligence and his energy to define, maintain, and implement his rights and freedoms.

That the society does not fully achieve its ideals is recognized by all. Many times even those ideals to which common allegiance is given are denied in actual practice. Sometimes the freedom of individuals is curtailed and opportunities are not equally extended. But the society is one with high ideals. Any discrepancy between practice and ideals is one that involves much soul-searching on the part of the total population. Cynicism is present in some, but, in general, members of the society attempt to achieve their ideals more fully rather than to rationalize their present shortcomings.

Americans differ in their interpretation of how some of these common values may be achieved. Authorities, politicians, and average citizens hold widely differing positions concerning desirable beliefs and courses of action. Various groups with vested interests attempt to influence thinking. Individuals many times find themselves in the middle of conflicts between two or more pressure groups attempting to get the total society to accept their particular interpretation.

Although within the society there are values held in common, there are also values that conflict with each other. The nation is composed of many different national and social groups with divergent cultural backgrounds and experiences. Not all believe the same thing with regard to the extent of participation in world government, the control of national resources, the necessary amount of government planning and of socialization of medicine, the place of labor, or race relations—to name only a few major issues.

Conflict of values is, therefore, a characteristic of the society in which the secondary school exists. But this difference is not a liability. In a society in which the bonds of common values are strong enough, difference of opinion is the area in which new insight is gained and progress made.

How shall the secondary school operate to promote the social goals? Values are learned by experiencing them. They are not taught by reading them in a textbook or being required to memorize them for a test. If the staff does not make it possible for students to experience democratic values in school, they have very little possibility of convincing the pupils of their importance. If teachers want pupils to believe that each individual is important, they develop a program in which each pupil finds an activity in which he is successful and makes a contribution that is recognized. They revise the curriculum if they find that half of the students cannot be successful enough to continue in the present one.

If teachers value the use of intelligence, they recognize that problems which arise constitute one of the most important phases of the school curriculum. Bringing all of the students involved into participation in making decisions concerning problems is the technique used to develop the fundamental skill of problem-solving. If a staff can help boys and girls to think together and to arrive at decisions in terms of the values that they hold, it is developing a basic democratic skill.

A staff helps to develop belief in the free flow of information by maintaining a school situation where all are encouraged to express their opinion about what needs to be done. Whenever barriers are established that prevent individuals in the schools—children, teachers, principal, or parents—from talking openly with one another, democratic practices are hindered. Unless there is opportunity for those involved to change the structure of the school and its program, the free flow of information is not too important. Unless pupils find that information is used as the basis of decisions about change, the free flow of ideas is meaningless. But when people live in a group in which they have the opportunity to make decisions that change structure and practice, the significance and responsibility of democracy are realized.

Pupils learn to value freedom by experiencing it. Are school publications censored? May students call an assembly to discuss the marking system? May a student express opposition to the school administration concerning the allocation of funds for sports activities? Are pupils free to disagree with a teacher's interpretation of history or economics and not suffer at marking time? Unless the school is operated in such a way that students experience the essential American freedoms, the school cannot be an effective instrument in promoting loyalty to these freedoms.

Are provisions made for minorities in the school organization? Minorities do not want to be just tolerated. They want to have their place and to make their contribution. Valuing of minorities is achieved through three steps: being willing to accept people who are different, understanding the increased richness of plural cultures, being willing to accept the contribution of those who are different. If youngsters have these three attitudes, the position of minorities within the school and within the society is assured. Secondary school administrators and teachers must hold these beliefs and demonstrate them in the daily operation of the school.

Another aspect of democracy is that of shared responsibility. Democracy does not consist of privileges and rights alone. It carries with it the responsibility for making a contribution to the development of that society which will provide those rights. As a staff helps youngsters work with one another, it is developing the shared responsibility that is the essence of democracy.

Democratic values are not taught by empty gestures and symbols. For example, a secondary school does not teach democratic values merely by having a student government. It may be a breeding ground for embryo politicians skilled in all the shabby tricks of winning at the price of honor. It may be an organization in which pupils are taught to accept the sham and hypocrisy of puppet government which has a democratic appearance but is manipulated by an authoritarian administration. Democratic values are taught when pupils are helped to discover that the essence of democracy is the application of the intelligence of those involved to the decision-making process and the assuming of responsibility for the implementation of those decisions.

Does the social scene emphasize, too, the need for a curriculum which stresses student government? Only fifty per cent of the adults vote because only fifty per cent believe that it is important. Must the

school government, if it is to meet the need of a democratically organized society, be organized in such a way that all have the opportunity to participate and that decisions made will be implemented? If
pupil effort is expended in reaching decisions, and then teachers or
administrators veto the action or otherwise circumvent it, youth learns
quickly that voting is a farcical pastime. If teachers want youth to take
civic participation seriously, the areas in which decisions may be made
must be clearly defined and the decisions reached put into effect.

THE WORLD SITUATION

During the first
half of the twentieth century the balance of power in the world shifted,
and because of its industrial might and financial wealth the United
States found itself thrust into a position of world leadership.

The American people lack agreement on what they want for themselves or for the rest of the world. They are divided as to the type of
leadership that they should exert and the function they should perform. Some want to give our American values and way of life to the
rest of the world. Others want to plan with the rest of the nations the
way of life that will be best for all. Some hope it will be possible for
the United States to withdraw and lead its own life without interference from the remainder of the world. They would like to say: "Let
Americans look out for Americans and the rest of the world look out
for itself." But that is impossible. At this stage of technological development there are no insurmountable physical barriers to communication or transportation. The people of the world are so close in time,
space, and communication that working out a way of living together is
essential. Although Americans are not quite sure what kind of a world
they want, their wealth and military might make a return to isolation
impossible. They must succeed or fail in their world role.

Americans have devoted money, energy, and lives to achieve worldwide cooperation. They have been idealistic and optimistic. They are,
however, realistic about the forces in the world that make unity seem
impossible and are developing deep cynicism concerning the success
of these efforts. A portion of the difficulty has come from their concept
of cooperation. They have been willing to spend freely of the economic
wealth of the United States in order to help other people grow and
develop, but they find it hard to cooperate to the extent of giving up

some of their sovereignty in decisions which vitally affect their national welfare.

The failure to achieve world unity is highlighted by the destructive power that scientists have developed. Weapons of war possessed by several nations are able to destroy entire regions of the world. Many do not yet fully realize how devastating these forces can be, but the men who perfected them warn that, if used, the weapons can wipe out our present-day civilization. As a result of failure to achieve unity, the world exists as an armed camp. Nations live in an uneasy truce, suspicious of the motives and actions of one another.

The United States is influenced by this world pressure. It wants peace. Citizens would like to cut down the armament program but would not feel safe in doing so. It is widely believed that it is necessary to maintain military strength and to devote by far the major portion of the national budget to getting ready for a possible future struggle.

The lack of world unity or of a structure through which disagreements can be settled has led to fear of armed conflict and competition to produce weapons powerful enough to insure supremacy. This threat of conflict and destruction has an impact on the thinking and planning of youth. Fears are increased. A sense of futility engulfs some; purpose is strengthened in others because they feel that they can contribute to success in the competition. Faculties are confronted with the task of helping pupils understand and live with the reality of the situation and with thinking through their roles in achieving greater world stability.

Not only world disunity, but also population expansion causes concern. The world population continues to grow. Since the end of World War II productive capacity for food has been increased by nine per cent, while the population of the world has increased by thirteen per cent. Food production is falling steadily behind the population increase, and something must be done if there is not to be less and less food for more and more people.

In light of the world situation, what is the responsibility of the secondary school for helping students learn about the entire world, its peoples, its resources, the qualities and values the peoples hold in common, and the basic issues which divide them?

Understanding and intelligent action cannot come without knowledge. High school students need the opportunity to learn about other people of the world, to meet them, to know them, and to appreciate their cultures. Is a high school program that restricts its offering to the history and literature of a few Western European nations preparing youth for leadership in a world in which five persons out of every six are non-Caucasian?

One of the major questions adolescents face is what it means to be both a citizen of the world and a citizen of a particular homeland. How much world organization is desirable? What loyalty is due it? What position should be taken when national interests conflict with world interests? Adults face this dilemma and find themselves filled with doubt and confusion. Youth do, too. No one can give them a ready-made answer. What should the secondary school do to help them examine the implications of various courses of action?

To accomplish its task successfully, the secondary school must help pupils acquire a deep understanding of the values for which America stands. What are the basic beliefs, what are the essential elements of the society that citizens must be willing to make sacrifices to preserve? Schools have the responsibility of helping youngsters not only to look at themselves and at the national ideals and way of life, but also to learn about the ways of life, ideals, and ambitions of the rest of the world, and the role that the United States can play in helping others achieve the kind of society from which all may benefit. Unless the school helps students acquire an understanding of the many possible choices, the nation will not be able to fulfill the role which has been thrust upon it.

THE CONDITION OF THE NATION

The United States is not an island. It is interacting with the rest of the world and it is constantly changing through that interaction. Many citizens feel the pressure from abroad in the area of ideas. Some have become afraid for America to continue to be an open market place of ideas. They want to control what can be said and thought and read. They give as their reason the fact that the Communists do not play fair, that they use every technique at their disposal to subvert the minds of men. Once again the nation is confronted by an issue that has appeared variously throughout its history: "How much freedom of thought and expression can be allowed?" Despite all the previous tests and trials, the belief in freedom of ideas has continued to be an essential element of the American scene. But never before have nations of the world been so close or the pressures from the outside been so great.

Freedoms have not been forfeited. Freedom of assembly, speech, and decision are the common practice. Exceptions are so rare as to be newsworthy. Although the number of instances in which they have been challenged has increased, each attack has been answered and the battle lines clearly drawn. Those who value basic American beliefs are alert to the peril and have increased their vigilance in protecting our heritage. Certain groups within the society have attempted to foment suspicion, particularly suspicion directed at members of the mass communication media, the teaching profession, the ministry, and certain branches of government. Rumors, accusations, and investigations have tended to decrease trust in one another. These have been attacks on the freedom of ideas made in the name of preserving American liberties.

Honest differences of opinion on basic policies do exist among segments of our population. Management and labor are still attempting to work out a more satisfactory division of the income. The relationships between members of different races are not yet settled. Minority racial and religious groups have problems of lack of understanding and acceptance on the part of majority groups. But of greatest concern to many is the lack of action by large numbers of the citizenry on any issue. Although the greatest number of citizens vote in a presidential election, even then no more than fifty-five per cent of the qualified voters participate. Elections which deal only with local community issues are ignored by most. Verbal allegiance is given to the value of voting and the participation of all in government, and yet one-half of the population does not take the necessary time to cast a ballot.

Unity and difference are the essential ingredients of progress, and the secondary school can contribute to both. In addition to helping students understand and accept the common values that bind the nation together, it should help youth analyze the issues on which it is divided. When agreement exists on enough common values to hold the group together, disagreements are assets which should be used to deepen understanding and increase insight. Issues are the cutting edges, the frontiers of a society, the areas in which new truths are being hammered out. Issues define the data that should be collected, and it is in the study of issues that adult learning occurs.

Youth is excited about the learning their parents and other adults are doing. The undecided issues of the day are the areas where learning is important. Not only do secondary schools increase the interest of pupils in school work if they deal with the unsolved problems of the day, but they also provide the major preparation for living. In a society that is changing rapidly the one certainty is that people will be confronted constantly with new problems or with old problems under new conditions. The essential need of every citizen is skill in problem-solving. A high school's contribution to the national society should be judged by the extent to which it has developed in students the ability to define and solve problems. To do this, the school curriculum must include opportunities to study the controversial issues of the day. Pupils cannot be shut off from certain issues with the dogmatic statement that they are too young and their minds may be perverted or distorted. If a pupil is old enough to be interested in a problem, he is old enough to investigate it. If he comes out with what teachers think is the wrong answer, they need not be disturbed so long as he is developing skill in problem-solving. If the student is acquiring this ability he will continue to collect additional data and revise his conclusions as he grows older.

One phase of problem-solving is skill in analyzing data. In a society where only a small percentage of data comes from the written word, how can high school teachers aid pupils in examining what they see and hear? Television, movies, and radio present data in a variety of ways. Sometimes it is enforced or colored with music. At other times it is given quickly, with no opportunity for checking. Frequently it is repeated and repeated. In advertisements, everything is said with all the persuasiveness the announcers possess. The degree of emphasis has no positive relationship to the importance of the statement. How can the secondary school help pupils to analyze books, newspapers, magazines, talks, radio and television programs, advertisements, and everyday conversation in order to discover the assumptions, facts, and distortions?

If the secondary school is to serve its purposes, it must be open for ideas, all ideas. Censorship cannot be applied to materials or certain areas of information. If pupils are to be prepared as citizens to deal with the powerful ideas of the day, the school cannot restrict their experiences in class to contact with safe or weak ones.

Modern means of communication offer tremendous possibilities for increasing understanding and agreement. Ideas expressed in one part of the country may be heard instantaneously in all other parts of the world. Through television, millions watch the same event. Speeches of leaders, discussions of issues, and evaluations of new developments can be shared by all. The opportunity exists to develop a common culture that promotes individuality or one that forces conformity.

The society is in a process of rapid change. The population has become extremely mobile. From 1940 to 1950, one out of ten families moved across state lines, and in 1957 one out of eight children moved from one community to another.

Communication and transportation have created a delicate balance in the relationships between people. They have led to the development of increased specialization. People produce single products and depend upon the rest of the society for the other products needed for life. Interdependence has increased and people must now be able to live with one another and depend upon one another.

In many types of work neither workers nor their children see the relationship between the type of work done and the outcome and use of the product. Seeing one's place in society and the worth of one's contribution is a problem for many individuals.

Another aspect of interdependence is the growth of large industries and organizations, with a decrease in individual enterprises. In each succeeding generation more and more people in the United States work for someone else. Eighty-two per cent of the population works for someone—an agency, a corporation, a person, or a company. As more and more people cease to direct their own efforts, individuals have less of a sense of the relationship between the quality of product they produce and the way they live. Their main concern becomes earning a living. Their wages are their primary consideration. The product has a trade name other than the workers'. They move further and further from the craftsman who has pride in his work, and take less and less pride in the quality of the product. Their paycheck, not their creativeness or the quality of their product, becomes the important factor. Some companies are attempting to combat this by building, as far as they can, a tradition of pride in craftsmanship among their workers and by stressing the fact that their workers have stayed with the company for a long time building their craftsmanship into the product. But this is not as widespread as it might be. The result for many people is the establishment of increased income as the criterion for measuring success.

What should the secondary school do to stress pride in craftsmanship and creativity? As the individual becomes a part of a huge organization and loses a sense of identity with the product, his sense of worth decreases. He cannot point with pride to something he has produced. Wages become more important than the product. Should schools provide the opportunity to produce? Should creative action take the major portion of the school day? Should the relationship between the individual and his product, rather than the mark given him, be stressed? Should schools put high priority on the feeling of wholeness and worth that comes from being able to produce something that can readily be accepted by the producer and the consumer?

Throughout American industry automation is increasing. More and more machines are replacing men in producing the necessities of life. As this trend continues, men will need to find new ways of feeling useful and valuable. If their efforts are less and less important in securing food, clothing and shelter, what are the contributions they can make as individuals? The problem is greater than finding a worthy use of leisure time. It is discovering ways of feeling important, worthy, and needed. As automation increases, the secondary schools must face more and more the task of assisting youth to gain a sense of meaning and purpose in their lives. As more and more people work for others, the necessity of learning to work with others increases. Eighty per cent of the people who are fired from jobs are fired not because of lack of skill, but because of inability to get along with other people.

If the schools are to develop persons capable of functioning effectively in present-day society, must they stress improving skills in human relations? With increased interdependence, increased mobility of the population, and decreased stability of homes, must the school assume greater responsibility for helping pupils accept themselves and each other? Is it satisfactory to say that someone else should teach how to get along with others and that schools should teach subject matter? If a student has not learned from other situations how to live and work with other people, can he live up to his productive capacity in school or in society? Development of the ability to work with others is basic to other civic, social, and economic competencies.

On the economic side, the society has a productive capacity far beyond the level of goods used. Means of distribution which make it possible for all people to have the results of the potential productive power of the country have not been devised. Some are still underfed; some are without adequate housing; some are not sufficiently clothed. To a great degree there is scarcity in the midst of plenty. But the economic prosperity in the United States is great. The standard of living is the highest of any people at any time. More people are employed than ever before. But some are not sure of the stability of the economic structure. Past fluctuations in the business cycle are well remembered, and doubt still exists. Economists and the government are constantly seeking ways to stabilize our economy.

The productive power of the United States is so great that it is supplying many of the needs of the rest of the world. Not only are products made available, but money is also provided to develop production in other countries (while tariffs are established to make it impossible for those countries to sell their products to us). Help is given to aid other countries to become self-sustaining, but it is hoped that these countries will continue to buy our products. Americans want contradictory things in international relations, and the foreign policy reflects our conflicting values.

One of the liabilities of high production is a rapid depletion of natural resources. Many believe that new natural resources will be found to take the place of the ones that are exhausted. Others, however, believe that through the process of producing at a high rate to maintain a high present-day standard of living natural resources will be depleted in such a way that future generations will not be able to have the standard of living now available.

How should the secondary school further economic literacy? It is no longer enough to know how to budget or how to buy intelligently. Each citizen is asked to vote on economic issues. Due to the economic position of the United States, these decisions affect not only the individual, the state, and the nation, but the world as well.

THE RELATIONSHIP WITH THE COMMUNITY

In the sixties very few high schools have attempted to adapt their program to the needs of the community they serve. But the issue is not dead. During the thirties much was written about the community school (see Everett, *The Community School* and Olson, *School and Community* for the thesis that schools should contribute to living in the community), and some high schools made real contributions to community living (see Wallace, *The Story of Holtville* and Carter and Ogden, *These Things We Tried*). World War II came, and the international crisis forced local issues into the background. The atom bomb, the cold war, and Sputnik and his cousins keep them there. Curriculum thinking has been devoted to how to promote academic excellence that will enable the United States to keep abreast of the rest of the nations of the world in scientific develpment. (The failure of one type of high school curriculum to meet the needs of the children of all communities has been forced upon the attention of all persons concerned with education and the future of the country by Conant's *Slums and Suburbs*.)

In a society with a mobile population, how much should the conditions of the local community determine the content of the high school curriculum? What proportion of the program should be built around the problems of the community? What adaptation of the program to the purposes and vision of the community members should be made?

If learning starts with the known and moves to the unknown, the community is the center of focus in the lives of its youth. Boys and girls grow up in a community and know its activities, institutions, and mores. All learning that they do about other situations is interpreted and perceived in terms of their knowledge of their local community. The school is only one of the educational forces affecting youngsters, perhaps a minor one. Youngsters live in the community for a greater portion of the day than they do in the school. The beliefs, the customs, the ways of thinking, the ways of acting, the manner of speech of the community all educate the child. The community educates whether the schools operate or not.

How should the secondary school relate to the local community? The most common relationship with the community is for the staff to seek ways in which it can use the community to enrich the existing curriculum. Local citizens are brought into the classroom to describe the community and to illustrate concepts that students are exploring in their courses. The backing of adult groups is sought for existing programs. Local papers, movies, television and radio materials are used in the classroom. Students make excursions to visit community libraries, industries, and museums. Students in such schools learn about their community as they are following their regular courses.

The school faculty also attempts to involve students in community activities and bring adults into the school program. Where community activities complement the school program, opportunities are created for students to participate in community drives, festivals, and planning. An attempt is made to coordinate youth services in a community. If a youth council exists, representation of the school is sought on the council. If no community coordinating agency is in operation, the school initiates its organization and helps keep it going during its initial stages. When the school undertakes a project, it brings community members into the planning and involves them in its execution. The community is invited to utilize the school as a community center, and the school facilities are kept open as they are needed. Adult education classes are considered a regular part of the secondary school curriculum.

A third type of community relationship is based on the assumption that the school should seek to improve living in the community. Classes study the community to determine its problems and to determine what should be done about them. With adult cooperation where possible, students undertake projects to improve the recreational, cultural, social, political, and economic well-being of the community. Activities go beyond cooperation with existing community agencies. The school group takes the lead in initiating projects it feels are desirable and enlists support of community groups interested in the same goals.

When a school accepts a responsibility for working for improvement of community living, the school program is obviously reoriented. The school faculty serves the total community, the young and the old. As the program of the school is planned, the offerings of the school are made available to adults as well as to youth. Plant and facilities are available for community use. No longer is the investment of the community in a school building restricted to use from nine to four each day. Playgrounds, gymnasiums, shops, auditoriums, and classroom facilities are used by community work, play, and study groups. The school building is considered a resource to be used sixteen to eighteen hours a day if needed.

Thus a highly flexible school building is required. Classrooms are equipped to provide for different types of activities. Meeting rooms and lounges with adjoining snack facilities are desirable for both youth and adults. A playground area that includes picnic space brings more people to the school grounds. Combining the school and community library increases the resources available to youth and adults.

A community secondary school becomes a cultural center for the community. In addition to the library and recreational facilities, the school auditorium and workshop are places where community dramatics and music groups function after the regular school day. Glee clubs, symphonies, little theatre groups are available to both youth and adults. The school auditorium is a location for forums, lectures, and discussions of community issues.

Such a program requires a different type of custodial service, teacher and administrative leadership, and scheduling. As custodians are hired, it is recognized that their services are for a longer day, and different shifts are planned. It is recognized that it is false economy to have the use of a million-dollar plant denied to the community because it will add the cost of additional custodial service to keep it open for an additional eight hours a day. Teachers and administrators must be able to deal with adults as well as with children. They see themselves as group leaders and coordinators of activities, rather than as persons making assignments and checking on how well they are done. The school staff is also scheduled to work on different shifts. Not all teachers start at nine o'clock in the morning. Some work from nine to four, others from twelve to seven, others from four until eleven. Schedules are viewed as a device for keeping a flexible program rather than a prescription of rigid limits.

The schools in Flint, Michigan, are representative of this idea. Working with the Mott Foundation, the board of education has developed adult education programs which include clinics, study groups, an athletic program, children's theatre, health centers, a cooperative safety program, leadership training program, physical fitness programs, science fairs, and work experience. Community activity directors are included on the staffs of schools.

Few secondary schools have moved to this type of program. Is this the direction they should take to help youth become effective citizens?

SUMMARY

Decisions concerning the role and the curriculum of the high school cannot be made on the basis of tradition or expediency. The secondary school is a social institution with the function of preparing citizens who can participate effectively in the world in which they live. The types of competency sought in pupils must be determined by consideration of the nature of the present world and of the future that it is hoped will emerge. Content must be selected for the curriculum from the existing cultural heritage to produce the competencies deemed desirable for living in such a world. Curriculum workers, teachers, parents, school boards, legislators, and all citizens concerned with improving the secondary school must face the questions that arise from an analysis of the school in its social setting.

SELECTED READINGS

Association for Supervision and Curriculum Development, *Forces Affecting American Education* (1953 Yearbook). Washington, D. C.: The Association, 1953. Presents an examination of various forces—

cultural, social, political, and economic—that are influencing American education.

——, *Fostering Mental Health in Our Classrooms* (1950 Yearbook). Washington, D. C.: The Association, 1950. Discusses in detail the relationships among child growth and development, motivation, and mental health as they pertain to school experiences.

Barker, Roger G. and Herbert F. Wright, *Midwest and Its Children: The Psychological Ecology of an American Town.* New York: Harper & Row, Publishers, 1954. A study of life in a small midwestern city.

Conant, James B., *Slums and Suburbs.* New York: McGraw-Hill Book Co., Inc., 1961. Discusses the educational problems arising from two contrasting socioeconomic areas of modern cities.

Everett, Samuel, ed., *The Community School.* New York: Appleton-Century-Crofts, Inc., 1938. States the philosophy of the community school.

Ogden, Jean and Jess Ogden, *These Things We Tried.* Charlottesville, Va.: University of Virginia, Extension Division, 1948. Describes attempts of schools in Virginia to improve living conditions in the communities in which they exist.

Olson, Edward, *School and Community,* 2nd ed., Englewood Cliffs, N. J.: Prentice-Hall, Inc., 1954. Contains many examples of school-community cooperation.

Wallace, Whilden, James Chrietzberg, and Verner M. Sims, *The Story of Holtville.* Nashville, Tenn.: Cullom and Ghertner & Co., 1944. Presents a vivid picture of the activities and program of a rural consolidated school working for improvement of living conditions in the community.

3

THE NEEDS OF YOUTH

The secondary school was not organized to meet the needs of all youth. Its original function was to prepare students for college. When the academy and the high school opened their doors, they attempted to offer content that would prepare for adult life. No effort was made to build a program that dealt with the immediate needs of youth. The secondary school was an institution which offered specialized training either for college or for a vocation.

As the belief of the American people in the value of education for everyone increased, compulsory attendance laws were passed. The age of required attendance was gradually raised until today most pupils must attend school until they are sixteen. Over ten million students are enrolled in the upper four years of the secondary schools. Hundreds of thousands of these pupils have no intention of going to college or of using the school as preparation for a job. Many are in school only because the law requires their attendance. Does the school that was designed to prepare for college or for certain limited occupations meet their needs?

39

CHARACTERISTICS OF YOUTH

During the past seven decades, the high school in the United States has become a school for all youth. Almost every youngster enters the high school. Although at the present time one out of three who enroll fails to graduate, the children of all social groups attend. The high school student body is composed of every racial, economic, religious, and national group in the country, each with its particular beliefs, customs, values, patterns of living, and talents.

The students in the high school differ. They are different in size and physical well-being. The high school period is the one in which there is the greatest amount of physical differences among pupils; some are tall, some short; some have developed full physical maturity, others are still in late childhood physically. Not only does the school population contain all of the gradations observable in the adult population, but they are accentuated due to the rapid growth and varying growth patterns of adolescents.

Adolescents in high school differ in ability. Their IQ's range from seventy to one hundred seventy. Their reading ability extends from the fourth grade level to that of college seniors. Some high school students are as intelligent and able as adults. Some with special talents may even surpass adults in the field in which they are talented. Still others lack the fundamental skills necessary to participate with contemporaries of average ability.

They vary in social maturity. Some are skilled in participation in social activities, while others lack the knowledge and the manners which would enable them to be at ease with younger children, adults, or their own peers.

They differ in age. The secondary school serves youth from twelve to twenty.

But although the range in size, ability, and social maturity is great, adolescents do have some qualities in common. The high school student seems to be inconsistent in his behavior. He is leaving childhood and moving on toward adulthood. As he assumes the adult role he finds himself confronted with the need for behaving in a different way, and it is confusing. On one occasion he exhibits childish behavior; on the next he behaves like an adult. He pushes toward adulthood and in the process must by trial and error discover the kind of behavior most satisfactory to him. He is experimenting with different types of behavior to see which most nearly satisfies the goal that he has set for himself. To the adult observing this behavior it appears to be inconsistent.

The adolescent is idealistic. He knows what the world should be like and wants to make it that way. He is disappointed when he finds that persons or events do not live up to his expectations. Although some become more or less cynical as a result of their experiences in the more adult world, the majority of students who are successful in high school continue to be idealistic.

Adolescents, although they seek to give the impression of knowing all the answers, have many feelings of insecurity. As they change physically, seek different status, become aware of multiple sets of values, and enter new social situations, adolescents face more new problems and more difficult situations than an adult normally encounters. The adolescent is confronted with the necessity of seeking to understand himself, his physical changes, his emerging role, as well as the routine problems of living and attending school.

PRESSURES ON YOUTH

Youth is subject to many pressures. One of the most important is the pressure of parental expectation. Parents see within their children the opportunity for the realization of their own unfulfilled dreams and attempt to influence their children to achieve them. They are disappointed and vaguely resentful when they find that children do not have the same desires they have and do not make as rapid progress as possible in the direction of the parents' hopes.

According to Wood, forty-seven million Americans live in suburbia. Between 1950 and 1956 the suburbs grew nearly three times as fast as the population of the entire United States and over six times as fast as the population of the cities around which the suburbs were springing up. Suburbs have been called an antiseptic way of life: nice families in nice homes are located away from the pollution of both industry and the heterogeneous masses. Suburbs have been largely segregated by races, other ethnic differences, socioeconomic status, and age. Families living in a suburb tend to be homogeneous in age and social values.

The youth who live in a suburb do not get a chance to see an age range in the population; neither do they see a social range. All people in their area have relatively the same income. If the income becomes greater, the family moves to a more expensive suburb. If the income decreases, the family must withdraw to a less expensive area. Youth in suburbia find themselves in a society in which it seems all people are much like them. Their schools are composed of youth from homes much like their own. *They do not learn to live with diversity.* Instead they feel a great need to conform in order to be accepted.

As he lives in a suburb, the youth gains an unrealistic picture of the role of work. The income earners go to another section of the community to earn their living. Aside from housework, the only real work the child sees being performed is done by the service and maintenance personnel. So many services are provided that there is little the child must do to enrich his everyday life, and he grows up in a situation in which the tasks assigned to him seem more a social requirement demanded by his parents than a practical action to meet an economic or social need. Work is either something done by less fortunate people or something assigned for disciplinary purposes. He does not see a work role for himself that contributes to the improvement of living in the home or community.

Life in the suburbs is centered around the child. Securing desirable recreation and a good education for the children has been a prime reason for moving to the suburbs. Certainly it is not to make the breadwinner's role easier. Other interests give way to efforts to promote the child's upward progress. While the focus of interest on his happiness and success gives the suburban youth some advantages, it places him under tremendous pressure. He must succeed. If he fails, the family loses status and prestige because it is not attaining its primary goal.

Many youth today are also subjected to the pressure of being a part of a mobile population. In one twelve-month period (1957) one million children moved from one geographic area of the country to another, two million more from one state to another, another two million from one county to another. Five million children moved from one community to another in twelve months! Seven million additional children moved from one house to another. In one year, twelve million out of the forty million children in school moved, and five million of those changed from one community to another! If all children were moving equally, in a little over three years the entire forty million children in school would move. But the shifting of homes is not distributed equally throughout the population. Youth growing up in families with lower incomes, belonging to minority groups or nonwhite groups, move much more frequently.

Changing from one house to another has its effect on youth. If the family unit is a secure one, the impact is less. Youngsters who move lose some of the support that children in a less mobile society have. When a youth grows up in the community in which he and his parents were born, surrounded by grandparents, uncles, aunts, cousins, he has many sources of support. If he does not get help and love from brothers, sisters, or parents, he can turn to other members of the family of which he is a part. He feels that he belongs. He can see the place that his family holds in the community, and he knows he is a valued part of the family.

But when a youth moves to a new community in which his father and mother have no family connections, he runs the risk of losing his sense of identity. He may not feel that he belongs. There may be no one in the community who values him or his family. They have not yet won a place. He may be ridiculed or ostracized because of the geographical region from which he came. He is without roots, a stranger in a strange land.

The youth in a new community feels the compulsion to conform in order to become accepted. One child who moved from the North to the South came home at the end of his first day in school with an attempted thick southern accent. When asked why, he said: "I want them to like me." In many more dramatic ways the necessity to conform plays a part in shaping the personalities and values of youngsters who move.

Another facet of the impact of mobility is that the nature of some communities changes rapidly. As a community changes, the tensions in it increase. Those who have been there and must stay attempt to hold on to the kind of life that they have had. Those who are new attempt to gain status in the community and thus develop a different pattern of living. Social agencies and institutions that have served the needs of the population cease to be adequate. Members of the community begin to blame each other for the difficulties of the situation. Youngsters living in such communities find themselves torn by the tensions that divide the adults. They seek identification with individuals like themselves who can join together for self-protection against people who are different. Violence and aggression occur. Organization of gangs and gang warfare are sensational manifestations of this tension.

Other youth in the United States do not have a complete relationship with both parents. Two million school-age children are not living with either parent. They not only lack the support of a family, but they do not have the affection and security that comes from association with even one parent. Four million children live with only one parent. One mother out of five works outside the home. Add the number of men who are separated from their families by duty in the armed services, and it is easy to see that this generation of school-age youth needs a kind of support that the school has never before been asked to provide.

Communication which makes it possible to know what is going on in all portions of the world has many advantages, but it has also served to increase the pressures on youth. They are made aware of worries and problems and concerns that in a time of less adequate communication would never enter their consciousness. Read the front page of the local newspaper. Most items deal with a world, national, or local problem or with a crime. Read the statements that are quoted from national and world leaders. Many are dire predictions about foreign policy or domestic economics. Listen to the news commentator. Does his news increase a youngster's feeling of security within his society? Read the funny pages. What percentage of the comics deal with individuals in a crisis situation?

Today's youth constitute the world's first television generation. For the past decade children in most communities have watched TV almost as many hours a week as they were in school. (Twenty-two hours was the weekly average in the Chicago area in 1959.) Students have become better acquainted with western marshals than with the policeman on the corner, and have seen and listened to the President more than they have to their local mayor. Millions have been barraged by the same stereotypes of people, behavior, and speech.

What has been the effect of this phenomenon? Youth read more, and the reading choices are influenced by TV. Ask any librarian. Students know more facts about more things than any previous generation. They think of worldwide and even interplanetary explorations in matter-of-fact terms. Nothing surprises or overwhelms them.

During the fifties TV gave certain persons vast influence over our children. They watched contests of the intellectuals in which persons strained and sweat to come up with answers they had been told beforehand. A Van Doren became a new type of hero before it was revealed that he had feet of clay. Disc jockeys told teenagers what songs to like and convinced many that "Hound Dawg" and a pitching pelvis was their culture—until it was revealed that some of these custodians of the culture were handsomely paid perverters of taste.

But D. W. Dodson's report on children of suburbia raises questions as to the positive nature of their interest. He found that youth in suburbia were not much concerned with social issues, which are mainstream problems of democracy. They are content with their present life and want to "get ahead." But they are not concerned with the problems of others and are unwilling to get involved in causes that demand action.

Pressure on youth is further increased by the confusion with regard to morals. The church no longer plays the role that it formerly did in establishing a value pattern for youth. In a recent survey in New England it was found that only one out of three children goes to any church. Youth today is confronted with many value patterns. They hear one type of behavior praised in the church. Books and magazines portray many ways of living. So do the movies and television. Families within the community believe differently. Even parents in the same family may have conflicting values. Students are forced to work out their own decisions as to what is acceptable.

The March 29, 1960, issue of *Look* contained an article based on the interviews of twelve *Look* reporters with hundreds of people in small towns and cities in all parts of the country. They arrived at conclusions that can hardly contain hope for persons concerned with youth. They found that "in one southwestern town hardly any children could recall their parents teaching them anything about right and wrong. Many parents claimed they had, yet half of them admitted they did not punish their children for lying."

In an eastern city where the juvenile crime rate rose sixty-seven per cent in 1959, a discussion of Van Doren's pretending scholarship on a quiz program where he had been given the answers elicited these comments from teenagers: "After all, he didn't hurt anybody." "Basically he was wrong, but those who enticed him were more wrong." "Once he took a wrong step he couldn't stop."

Attwood, the author of the article, interpreted the results of the survey as follows:

> Lacking a clear-cut code of ethics, people are falling back on a kind of personal relative morality, which justifies most actions— even illegal ones—that don't actually cause harm to another person (p. 41).

> Out of the confusion, a new American code of ethics seems to be evolving. Its terms are seldom stated in so many words, but it

adds up to this: Whatever you do is all right if it's legal or if you disapprove of the law. It's all right if it doesn't hurt anybody. And it's all right if it's part of accepted business practice (p. 36).

It was a rare American who thought the change in our moral standards was for the better. Some detected no change, but a majority of those interviewed said our standards were deteriorating (p. 35). (W. H. Attwood, "The Age of Payola," *Look*, March 29, 1960. Quoted with permission of the publisher.)

Pressure on youth is increased by indecision and uncertainty on the part of adults. Youth hear their parents and other adults in the community talking about national and world government. They hear arguments about human welfare versus free competition. Dinner table conversations deal with what to do about "the bomb." They see that their parents have conflicts within their thinking, and sometimes their parents' actions totally contradict the values to which they give verbal allegiance.

The interdependence of our society also acts as a pressure on youth. They see their way of life threatened by actions of persons they do not know. For example, the defense effort of an entire nation may be stalled by a strike in an industry or by a small group's demand for a certain amount of profit. They see a city forced to shut down its schools and places of amusement, to allow garbage to pile up in the street and endanger the health of the whole neighborhood because of strikes of small minorities. They find themselves wondering whether what they do as individuals really counts for as much as their parents and teachers say it does.

They find themselves subject to the pressure imposed by their status in the community. If they come from the upper classes they attempt to keep up with their neighbors, to engage in as many activities and to achieve as much as other youngsters in the neighborhood. In the lower classes they find themselves subject to real economic and social pressures.

To add further to the confusion, adolescents read in the newspaper and hear over the radio attacks on their schools. They hear their teachers' loyalty and patriotism questioned. They read that schools are being used to promote creeping socialism, that schools no longer teach boys and girls the fundamentals. So another source of security is challenged and threatened.

Pressure on youth was increased when Sputnik went into orbit and dramatically announced the arrival of the Space Age. The complacency of the United States was jolted, and its way of life was challenged in all its phases. Youth were no exception. Their naïve assumption, held in common with most of their elders, that the United States could not be equaled in engineering and industrial skill was devastatingly shattered. They found themselves in a world in which their sense of personal and societal superiority could no longer go untested. They were forced to face the fact, after years of self-assurance, that they were on trial.

Some Americans, frightened by the spectacular display of Russian progress, began to criticize their schools and their teachers. School personnel were publicly chastised for making school too easy and too much fun. Teachers began to react to this prodding by increasing the pupils' workload. The week's schedule began to include five to twenty hours of homework. The reaction of youth was, for the most part, positive, a clear acceptance of the challenge. The more able students began studying harder to live up to the expectations of their parents and teachers and to the demands of the crisis. Scientific experimentation ceased to be a bootleg operation in the bedroom or basement and became a rewarding, praiseworthy activity. The ceiling on imagination was lifted. Unlimited frontiers were again available. Talk of going to the moon or Mars was transformed from wild fantasy into a respectable activity. Since Sputnik, more youth are experimenting, thinking creatively, challenging the unknown, than in any previous period of United States history. A space frontier is once again a reality for American youth.

But the results of entering the age of nuclear fission and space travel have not all been positive. Pressure on youth has increased. After the production of the atom bomb and all that has followed, children and youth live with the constant possibility of no tomorrow. After reading Nevil Shute's _On the Beach,_ a fifteen-year-old asked: "Why plan? It doesn't really matter what one person does. Why not live as much as you can before it's too late?" His parents may have reacted this way in the late forties and recovered, but it is still a commonplace reaction for youth in the 1960's.

The post-Sputnik emphasis on increased effort has enabled colleges to raise entrance requirements. Opportunity to go to college now depends upon hard work and correct choices throughout high school. Some parents and children begin worrying about the children getting into college by the time they reach the third grade, because a college degree is a status symbol and the key to upward mobility.

The pressure to get into college is affecting what pupils study in high school. With college entrance conditioned by scores achieved on tests, pupils are choosing the courses that will increase their chances of being successful on the tests. Science, mathematics, English, and social studies are being emphasized, and art, music, and less traditional disciplines are being neglected.

Conant's report, *The American High School Today* (1959), recommended putting the brilliant pupils in science, mathematics, and foreign languages. The author defended his recommendation by saying that in 1959 he felt a national emergency existed. But if the nation follows his advice it runs the risk of not providing the social scientists, the philosophers, the poets, the artists who will be able to deal with the social problems it encounters and to express the values it envisions. Spiritual power may be lost in the race for scientific power.

The self-styled experts who are advocating educational reform that will make the school offering more rigid and more rigorous do not take into account that even the present program is not suitable for one-half of the population. Approximately one-half of all fifth-graders will not finish high school. Less than two out of three ninth-graders will finish high school.

Juvenile delinquency is ten times more frequent among drop-outs. When a nation does not provide the kind of school that makes it possible for all children to feel worthy, wanted, and adequate, it increases the number who must turn to socially unacceptable out-of-school activities to maintain their self-respect. If increased rigidity and rigor of the school program are demanded for all, an increase can be expected in the drop-out rate with a consequent increase in juvenile delinquency.

The United States has been termed an affluent society. Family income has risen steadily during the past decade. Housing is better and food and clothing more abundant than never before. More jobs are available. Material benefits once only dreamed of are now to be had. For children, greater material wealth has meant better food, better housing, better clothing, better medical care, and more opportunity to develop talents and hobbies. But some high school counselors say that the psychological results have not all been good. They say that more children feel that the world owes them a living, that a good job is not something that must be earned by effort but may be attained through personal influence or pressure, that youth sees little connection between effort and economic attainment. Some children say bluntly that the organization they belong to will insure their continuation on the job and that promotions will come on the basis of seniority no matter what their effort or ability.

49

The fact that boys go into the military service as they finish their school program is another pressure. They cannot make long-term plans. Girls, too, are affected by a similar problem. Many are not sure that they will find someone to marry. At the very least, a period of waiting and uncertainty is in store for many girls as well as boys.

Other pressures bear on some youngsters. Lack of acceptance and security, lack of home care, and poverty accentuate the universal pressures. The burden may become so great that these youths will drop out of school. Children who come from homes where they have lost one or both parents through divorce, death, or desertion, and children without friends in school drop out most frequently. Dillon (*Early School Leavers*) found that if a pupil is retarded one year, it decreases by fifty per cent his chance of successfully completing school. The social stigma of failure is more than he can bear. And grade retardation for impoverished children is ten times as great as for middle-class pupils.

The attitudes of some teachers places pressure on many children. Because of their middle-class background and values, many teachers are unable to understand or work with pupils who hold values and behave in ways they consider unacceptable. They belittle and berate them. They consider pupils discipline problems if they will not behave and act in a middle-class manner. They punish them. They fail them. They resent working with pupils they feel are beneath them, because they want to better themselves, to climb socially. Teachers who cannot accept pupils from the lower social groups put additional pressure on the very pupils who already must withstand the greatest pressures. Many of these students leave school as a way of escape.

STUDIES OF THE NEEDS OF YOUTH

Since the early thirties, educators and social workers have attempted to identify the needs of youth. They have sought to discover what schools should do to serve youth and the nation more adequately. Youth have been asked by interviewers to state their concerns and their problems. Although this method is not valid for discovering the real problems of youth, it is a technique for getting a statement of the surface problems that concern them.

Some researchers have attempted to devise a questionnaire that would sample the needs of adolescents. Using the results of previous studies of adolescents, they have formulated lists of problems which seemed to be common for many adolescents. These problem checklists have been submitted to thousands of adolescents, and tabulations have been made of the concerns and problems checked.

In the late thirties Carolyn Zachary directed the Adolescent Study under the sponsorship of the Progressive Education Association. The procedure of the research team was to conduct intensive case studies on a number of adolescents. On the basis of the analysis of these cases, it was concluded that adolescence is a period of rapid body change with a definite need for understanding the change and adjusting to it. Adolescent concerns are:

Learning what is permitted, what is expected, and what is not approved of in the role of a given sex.

Identifying with one's own sex, and changing one's relationship with the opposite sex.

Seeking ways to relate oneself to adult society in a constructive and satisfying manner.

Seeking to learn one's own potentialities and abilities.

Seeking adult status.

Wanting independence and protection.

Seeking acceptance by peers.

Two of the most important studies of youth conducted to date are Bell's *Youth Tell Their Story* and Hollingshead's *Elmtown's Youth:*

In the mid-thirties Bell undertook to survey the concerns and needs of a representative sampling of youth in the entire State of Maryland. He sought to find what youth in that state, a representative state, did, what they were like, what their concerns were. He found that:

> At the time of the study, thirty-three per cent of the sixteen-year-olds had left school, twenty-five per cent of the seventeen-year-olds had left school, seventy-five per cent of the eighteen-year-olds had left school, eighty-five per cent of the nineteen-year-olds had left school, and ninety per cent of the twenty-year-olds had left school.

> Three factors affected how far a student went in school. They were the occupation of the father, race, and sex.

> Pupils left school because of economic need, lack of interest, desire to earn their own money, graduation, marriage, and poor health.

> Students received little vocational guidance.

Three-fourths of the youths interviewed believed sex education should be taught in the school. The chief source of sex information had been from contemporaries. Sixty-six per cent of the boys and forty per cent of the girls reported that what they knew about sex was more or less limited to what friends of their own age had told them. [Howard M. Bell, *Youth Tell Their Story* (Washington, D. C.: American Council on Education, 1938). Quoted with permission of the publisher.]

In the mid-forties, Hollingshead studied youth in a town in the Midwest. Using the system of classification developed by Lloyd Warner and others, he studied the academic and social experiences and activities of students from the upper upper (I), lower upper (II), upper middle (III), lower middle (IV), upper lower (V), and lower lower (VI) segments of a community. He studied their hobbies, their attitudes, their participation in the institutions of the community. He concluded:

The school, the job, and leisure time pursuits are the greatest competitors for the time and loyalty of adolescents in Elmtown (p. 155).

Enrollment in each course is related very significantly to class position; this is, each course acts either to attract or repel students in the different prestige classes. In 1941, the class I's and class II's concentrated on the college preparatory (sixty-four per cent) and ignored the commercial course. Fifty-one per cent of the class III's were in the general, twenty-seven per cent in the college preparatory, and twenty-one per cent in the commercial course. The class IV's entered the general (fifty-eight per cent) and commercial courses (thirty-three per cent) and avoided the college preparatory; only nine per cent were in it. The pattern for the class V's was similar to the class IV's, except that eighty-eight per cent were in the commercial and four per cent in the college preparatory course (p. 168).

. . . the higher an adolescent's class position, the better his chances are to receive high grades. Conversely, the lower one's position in the prestige structure, the more likely the adolescent is to receive low grades (p. 173).

A high school education is outside the experience of class V parents and beyond the expectancy of most of their children (p. 178).

Student attendance or nonattendance at athletic events is associated very highly with class position (p. 195).

. . . fifty-three per cent of the students do not attend any dances. Although some nonattendance exists in all classes, it is concentrated disproportionately in classes IV and V. No class V boy attended a single dance; only one girl reports that she went to one (pp. 197-198).

The attendance pattern for club parties and plays is very similar to that of the dances. Every class II boy or girl attends at least one party or play held in the evening, but no class V boy or girl attends a single one (p. 198).

Participation in all extracurricular activities, except boys' athletics, is biased in favor of some classes and against others. Moreover, each club is class-graded. For example, the Home Makers' Club is composed predominantly of class IV girls (sixty per cent). Class II girls avoid it; two, or four per cent of the membership, are in it. The French Club, in contrast, is essentially a class II group, sixty per cent, whereas only two class IV girls belong to it. The Library Club is weighted heavily with class III's, seventy-one per cent. The Future Farmers of America is its counterpart among the boys—sixty per cent from class III (p. 202).

As a boy or girl progresses in school, school class lines are crossed more frequently than prestige class lines (p. 212).

Mutual acceptance of best-friend status is general when the namer and the named belong to the same class. Rejection of the namer by the named occurs in each case when the namer belongs to a lower class than the named (p. 215).

Approximately ten per cent of the students list as best friend an adolescent in the out-of-school group. [All of those who named a person not in school as their best friend are in classes III, IV, V.] (P. 217.) [August B. Hollingshead, *Elmtown's Youth* (New York: John Wiley and Sons, Inc., 1949). Quoted with permission of the publisher.]

The findings of these studies of the thirties and forties coincide with the apparent needs and concerns of youth in the sixties. Even though the earlier investigations were focused directly on adolescents and their problems and the later research presented a broader sociological approach, the results were closely parallel. The adolescent appears to hold in common with all humanity the need for food, affection, and self-esteem. In addition, he has needs that occur as the result of his physiological growth and his changing role in society.

CONCERNS OF YOUTH

The most important concern of the adolescent is to be successful. In the process of growing up he is forming his own picture of what success is. He wants to achieve certain things. He wants to belong. He wants to become self-directing. He wants to have the qualities that other adolescents will admire. He wants to be accepted in the community as an adult. He rejects the kinds of motivation which are not tied in with his becoming successful in the situation in which he finds himself.

Not the least concern is the desire to belong. He wants to be a part of a group and will make many sacrifices in order to be accepted. School groups, community groups, state groups, national groups— all are a part of the society in which he wants to be accepted. The most important group to him is that of his own peers in his own school and community. Their mores, their ways of dress, their manner of speech, their attitudes toward themselves and toward other people all play an important part in his life. He is afraid to go against the prevailing pattern because of the fear that he will not be an accepted member of the group. He accepts readily and willingly kinds of behavior and dress that he would not choose for himself alone. He wants to be accepted by the members of his peer group. If other boys and girls wear blue jeans he feels that this is important for him, too. If they smoke or drive their own cars, these symbols become important to him. If other youngsters pet and stay out late he insists on doing the same. Adult objection and evaluation of such behavior is not as important to him as the desire to belong and to be accepted by other adolescents. Unless adults recognize this characteristic, whether they be parents or teachers, they find themselves increasingly rejected by adolescents.

He wants to acquire status. Desire to be recognized is basic in everyone. Children have it. In childhood one is given recognition because he is young. But this status is no longer acceptable to the adolescent. He is no longer content to be a family baby or the neighborhood pet. He must do the kinds of things that will win him recognition as a maturing individual. He begins to want to have a much greater part in determining his own course of action and his own goals. He wants to be recognized by the adults of the family and of the community as being a grown-up person. He shows his resentment of being excluded from certain places of amusement and adult governmental activities by making cynical or derogatory remarks.

The adolescent wants to be self-directing. Many times adolescents do not know how to achieve recognition. Some attempt to gain it by aggression. Others try to be funny. Others try to be the strong, silent type. Each adolescent is working out in his own way the techniques by which he can achieve the recognition and status that he wants.

Many adolescents desire help. They have questions that they cannot ask their parents or their fellows, and they turn readily to the kind of adult friendship that is willing to help them think through their problems.

The concern for status and self-direction can be seen in the way that adolescents behave in school. Within the school, students become more and more unwilling to accept direction and dictation from the teacher. The desire for school student government and increased pupil-teacher planning is a symptom of this concern for the achievement of status. Rebellion and aggression are increasingly apparent in the behavior of adolescents when they are forced to bow to adult wishes or are left out of the decision-making processes. They cry out not to be treated like children; they want to be grown up.

Another worry of adolescents is the conflict that their striving for status brings with their parents. Children do not wish to be in open opposition to their parents, but as they become more and more independent they find themselves confronted by new problems. Such questions as whether or not they should have a latchkey, be able to drive the family car, have no curfew, have an allowance that is greater than the one they have been getting are problems that all adolescents must work out with their parents. If the parents are understanding the task is not difficult. If they are not, conflict results. The parents may refuse to accept the fact that their child is growing up and should have a greater part in his own direction. Neither the adolescent nor his parents understands the other's point of view. If the parents do not accept the fact that their child is growing older, the adolescent usually finds himself forced to open opposition or subtle manipulation of the situation so that he does have an opportunity to become more mature.

A third concern of adolescents is the establishment of satisfactory social relationships with the opposite sex. In preadolescence there has often been open conflict with members of the opposite sex, but with the beginning of adolescence comes an attraction to and a desire to be accepted by some member of the opposite sex. Adolescents face the need for discovering ways of inviting the other sex to parties, to dances, to movies. These problems seem trivial to an adult, but to an early adolescent they are some of the biggest social problems he faces. Knowing what to wear, how to use make-up, being able to conduct an intelligent telephone conversation, whether or not to let a boy kiss her on a first date, how much money to spend on a girl, whether to send corsages, how to behave when you go to call on a girl and find you must talk with her parents are all concerns of adolescents. They need help in thinking them through. They constitute problems to which the child seeks answers. If he can get them at home, fine. But if he cannot and if he does not find answers to these problems and others that are similarly important to him at school, he comes to the conclusion that the high school is an abstract, unreal kind of experience that he has to go through in order to receive a diploma or to satisfy his parents.

The adolescent is concerned with whether or not he is normal. He begins to feel certain emotions that he has not known before. He would like to do things that heretofore he has not considered, or in some cases things that he has been told by his parents do not constitute socially acceptable behavior. Many adolescents, particularly those growing up in a religious home, begin to feel a sense of guilt about the feelings that they have. Unless there is opportunity for youngsters to talk over these concerns in a situation in which they can be frank and open with other adolescents and with an understanding adult, the feelings of guilt and uncertainty may persist.

Still another problem of the adolescent is to understand the world in which he lives. He sees all about him new ideas, new symbols, new ways of living, new values. All of these raise questions about things that he has come to believe as a result of his participation within his own family. New friends, television, books, radio, the life that is pictured in advertisements—all suggest that the things that he has known and experienced may not really constitute the core of living. How can he know what to do and what to believe? How can he know his place in the scheme of things? What is the universe? What are the forces that control the universe? What is his relation to it and those forces? How do other people gain the knowledge and understanding by which they guide their lives? How can he find the purpose by which to direct his own life?

Another concern of the adolescent is to be healthy. His body is undergoing greater change than at any previous period. He finds himself confronted by problems of how to care for his body. He wants to know what to do about the pimples on his face. He wants to know how to care for his hair. The boys want to know how to build strong muscles. Physical appearance and vigor are essential desires of adolescents.

In early adolescence there is a desire for securing enough money to be able to do the things that friends do, but in later adolescence the worry becomes focused more definitely on the necessary skills and the opportunities available for making a living. There is also a maturing of the concern about establishing a relationship with the opposite sex. In later adolescence the problem becomes one of selecting a mate. Students want to know the bases on which a choice should be made. They are in the process of establishing criteria to use in making their own selection.

The youth of minority groups have these concerns plus others that are even stronger. Will I always be kept out? Is there any use trying? Will my education make any difference in the type of job that is open to me? Is there any opportunity for me to achieve professional or managerial status if I excel and become thoroughly trained? Will people ever judge me as an individual and not as a member of a minority group? Should I reject the school and its activities because I am excluded from its social activities? Can I find an adult in the school who cares or who understands? Can I find an adult in the school who does not classify me as inferior to him? Can I find an adult in the school whom I can really trust?

These youths from minority groups find themselves confronted by a society in which the range of opportunities is limited and the social opportunities restricted, and by a school, which they are forced to attend, that is staffed by teachers whose purposes and values support the majority group, a school whose program is designed to deal with the problems of the already accepted.

What is the high school's responsibility for dealing with the concerns of youth? Should they be ignored? If they start to interfere with classwork should the school take steps? If so, what steps? Should an organized guidance program and guidance counselor be expected to handle the problem? Should course work be modified to permit inclusion of some topics related to adolescent concerns? Should courses or seminars designed to foster the exploration of concerns and conflicting values be established?

YOUTH WHO LEAVE THE HIGH SCHOOL

Two out of every five youngsters who start high school drop out. Why? All studies of reasons for dropping out have listed two as most frequently given: lack of interest in the program and lack of funds. But the problem is more complex than these answers seem to indicate. Researchers who have worked in this field have concluded that a student leaves school for a number of reasons. To try to give one cause for each drop-out oversimplifies the case. Evidence of this contention is found in the fact that it is possible to make a fairly accurate identification of persons who will drop out. After an intensive study of drop-outs in Grand Rapids, Michigan, schools, Douglas Blocksma listed twenty-two symptoms or conditions that constitute potential reasons for students dropping out of school before graduation:

1. Not being promoted or being passed on trial to the next grade.
2. Being two years older than one's grade group.
3. Having a poor attendance and tardiness record.
4. Aggressively resisting authority.
5. Having little or no interest in school.
6. Reading below one's mental age.
7. Having very little energy or being overly active (especially if a boy).
8. Attending a number of schools.
9. Being ignored or actively disliked by teachers.
10. Being ignored or actively disliked by fellow students.
11. Having playmates who are much older or much younger.
12. Having major interests and friends outside the school.
13. Being under psychiatric treatment.
14. Living in a broken home (especially if the family has no meals together).
15. Being seriously handicapped physically.
16. Having to receive books and supplies from the board of education.
17. Being different in size, physique, nationality, or dress.
18. Being financially unable to do what the rest of the group does.
19. Having an IQ of eighty or below.
20. Not participating in any extracurricular activities.
21. Refusing to participate in gym activities; refusing to get undressed in front of others; insisting on standing on the sidelines.
22. Feeling inferior educationally in comparison to a brother or sister, or being ashamed of a brother or sister's record.

An accumulation of these symptoms in one child increases his risk for leaving school. Apparently, lack of interest or lack of funds are only respectable statements which cover the real reasons for leaving school.

The U.S. Office of Education lists eleven characteristics of drop-outs. They often, if not usually:

1. Come from families whose members are engaged in unskilled and semiskilled occupations.
2. Come from families with low income.
3. Come from families with low cultural environment.
4. Are retarded in school.
5. Begin school later than other children.
6. Make considerably lower scores on intelligence tests.
7. Make considerably lower achievement test scores for their age' than the average.
8. Make somewhat lower achievement test scores for their grade than the average.
9. Make lower marks than other students.
10. Are less emotionally mature—nervous, feel less secure.
11. Lack interest in school.

These symptoms describe children whose needs are not being met at home or in school, children under tension. Studies in an eastern and a midwestern city showed that delinquency fell to its lowest level during the summer months. (See Kvaraceus, "Delinquency–A By-Product of the School," *School and Society,* May 13, 1944.) The school, instead of helping pupils solve their problems and thus decreasing delinquency, often seems to add to the existing tensions to such an extent that delinquency increases.

High school is for many adolescents a distasteful experience. They drop out of high school because they do not like it. They do not leave because of excellent job opportunities. Drop-outs, on the average, wait long months before obtaining their first job. During their first two years out of school they change jobs frequently. In interviews with students who leave school there is seldom one who has liked school or who has been accepted as a participating member of the school program. Most of them hate school and want to get away from it.

Some studies of drop-outs have revealed where the high school failed to meet their needs. The school did not help them feel that they belonged. Among hundreds of school leavers in Grand Rapids, Michigan, counselors did not find one who was an active, accepted member of a status clique in the school, a school club, or a team. The high school does not provide enough opportunity for all to exert leadership and participate in important activities.

The secondary school does not do enough to help emotionally disturbed children. They tend to drop out of school much more quickly. In a recent follow-up of emotionally disturbed grade school children in Grand Rapids, only two of the hundreds referred to the child guidance clinic were in the high school. Emotionally disturbed children and those from disturbed homes are a poor risk for high school graduation.

The secondary school does not provide a satisfying program for the less intelligent. The chances are good that a pupil with an IQ of less than ninety will not graduate from high school. However, all children with IQ's of less than ninety do not drop out of school. The ones who do graduate have athletic ability, talent, skill, brains, beauty, speaking ability, or other characteristics which help them to achieve status in the school.

The high school does not meet the needs of pupils from the lower social classes. Studies have found that teachers are generally from lower middle-class families and are mainly concerned with promoting acceptance of middle-class values. Teachers do not understand or meet the needs of the pupils from the lower class, and they support a peer society in the school which ostracizes the child who does not conform to middle-class standards of behavior. Verbal ability, quietness, cleanliness are things to be valued. But the lower-class child does not learn these things at home or in his gang. Reading and discussion are not stressed in his family life. People who amount to something have never come to his home. He learned early to conceive of himself as a follower or an outsider, and his slow progress in school has reinforced his acceptance of that role. By the time students reach the high school, most youngsters from lower-class homes have accepted an outsider role. Leadership roles, such as service clubs, honor societies, and class offices, are dominated by children from upper- and middle-class homes.

Delinquency, truancy, and disciplinary problems occur among children of all types of families, but especially among those from the impoverished and lower social status families. These types of behavior are symptoms of the school's failure to meet the needs of the youth involved. But if the secondary school does not meet the needs of the forty per cent who leave, what about those who graduate?

YOUTH EVALUATE THE HIGH SCHOOL

In 1950 the author, as consultant for the Connecticut Governor's Fact-Finding Committee on Education, made a study of fourteen hundred high school seniors in the state. More than one-tenth of all seniors were included in the study, and the population was a valid distribution of scholastic ability, economic strata, and various types of communities within the state. They were asked where the high school program had been helpful to them and where it had failed.

These Connecticut seniors felt that the high school had been helpful in answering their questions about *democracy, education, management,* and *labor.* It had helped them to answer their questions about *college choice, vocational choice, economics,* and *internal politics.* But in their opinion the high school had given them little aid in securing answers to their questions about *dating, marriage, child care, parent-child relations, religion,* and *personal problems.* This pattern of answers was consistent. It was the same for each of the quartiles based on scholastic achievement, and it was the same for boys and girls.

When these Connecticut seniors were asked to state what they liked best about the high school, they listed sports, student activities, and classmates. The pattern was uniform for boys and girls and for quartiles. The things these students liked least about the school were time schedule, some teachers, homework assignments, and poor cafeterias. When asked what course they would like most to add to their program, the seniors listed the following in the order given: sex education, driver training, Spanish, public speaking, chemistry, drafting, and auto mechanics. When considered separately, boys listed sex education at the top, followed by industrial arts, auto mechanics, Spanish, driver training, and advanced math. Girls wanted to add Spanish, sex education, driver training, typing, shorthand, and art appreciation.

To judge by the results in this one state, the secondary school in 1950 was not dealing satisfactorily with some of the most pressing problems of youth.

PROCEDURES TO MEET THE NEEDS OF YOUTH

No single program will meet the needs of all youth. Each individual has his own problems and his own purposes. But there are enough common needs and concerns to give direction to a staff seeking to design a program that will meet the needs of youth. Such a program will provide:

1. Opportunities for the adolescent to learn about himself through:

   (a) counseling interviews in which he can talk out his concerns;

(b) a testing program which gives him an estimate of his abilities and weaknesses;

(c) individual and group planning in which he becomes clear about his purposes in school and in life;

(d) materials which describe human growth and development.

2. Opportunities for the adolescent to develop a sense of belonging through:

(a) a homeroom group with which he can identify;

(b) a schoolwide tradition of friendliness which makes newcomers welcome;

(c) an orientation program that gets him acquainted with the school and the students in it;

(d) group work in classes which gives him an opportunity to work with others;

(e) activities which cut across social class lines;

(f) an emphasis on schoolwide social functions in which all can participate;

(g) rules based on a philosophy which prevents or minimizes exclusive social organizations.

3. Opportunities for the adolescent to develop self-direction through:

(a) pupil-teacher planning in classes;

(b) a student government organized in a manner which involves most of the student body in the decision-making process;

(c) use of evaluation procedures which include the pupil and help him to establish his goals and make judgments about his progress;

(d) a sufficiently large number of activities so that most students have the opportunity to exercise leadership;

(e) stress on creative activities which encourage individual judgment and expression of what one believes;

(f) disciplinary procedures which encourage self-discipline rather than adult enforcement of conformity;

(g) discussions with parents about problems which are causing conflicts;

(h) individual programs rather than one curriculum which all must follow.

4. Opportunities for the adolescent to develop skill in problem-solving through:

   (a) class activities which require seeking solutions rather than memorizing answers;

   (b) study of current controversial issues to which answers have not yet been found;

   (c) participation in community studies of community problems;

   (d) a testing program which measures skill in problem-solving and critical thinking;

   (e) individual work on individual problems as a part of regular class work;

   (f) group work which involves defining a problem, seeking sources of information, drawing conclusions, trying out proposed solutions, and developing criteria by which to judge authorities.

5. Opportunities for the adolescent to develop social skills through:

   (a) parties, dances, and teas which are a part of the regular program and open to all;

   (b) discussion of good manners in the planning of social events;

   (c) analysis of experiences at social events as a means of discovering errors and what to do about them;

   (d) stress on the value of knowing many types of people and increasing a person's range of friends;

   (e) excursions which include new social experiences;

   (f) intercultural and intergroup activities which give understanding of manners and customs that differ from those known to the individual;

   (g) attempts to build in the individual a sense of his own worth and of the worth of others;

   (h) many occasions for work and play with members of the opposite sex;

   (i) discussions of the qualities one wants in a mate.

6. Opportunities for the adolescent to examine the values he holds and to attempt to formulate a more consistent set of values through:

    (a) seminars where pupils talk freely with each other about their beliefs;

    (b) use of issues that arise between members of groups to examine and question the underlying values that each holds and the connection between values held and behavior;

    (c) the consideration of a number of solutions to problems that arise and the values related to each solution;

    (d) use of attitude scales as part of the testing program;

    (e) counseling interviews in which pupils talk about their concerns and conflicts.

7. Opportunities for the adolescent to discover a vocation through:

    (a) exploratory activities which acquaint him with a wider range of vocational activities;

    (b) guidance functions which make it possible for him to learn about the opportunities, restrictions, and disadvantages of various occupations;

    (c) a choice of curricular offerings which permits a person to select in terms of his vocational goals;

    (d) stress on getting along with others;

    (e) tryout experiences during vacations, weekends, or part-time work.

Society and the high school find themselves confronted by the following questions:

1. How to provide a role in which youth feel needed in an affluent society.
2. How to develop a sense of security without conformity.
3. How to preserve freedom of speech, thought, and press and still prevent misuse of the mass media.
4. How to provide the type of education in which diversity and many different contributions will be valued and fostered.
5. How to help children and youth live with conflicts in values and distance between present and ideal status without becoming cynical, cool, and uncommitted.

How much responsibility will the secondary school assume for meeting the needs of the adolescents who attend it? Are intellectual needs the only concern of the school? Is it safe to assume that intellectual needs can be satisfied if emotional ones are ignored? What must be the content and experiences provided by the secondary school if the law requires that all youth attend? These decisions must be made and reconsidered and revised year after year.

SELECTED READINGS

Abramovitz, Moses, "Growing Up in an Affluent Society" in *The Nation's Children* (Vol. I: *The Family and Social Change*), pp. 158-179. New York: Columbia University Press, 1960. Discusses the impact of the economy upon the lives of youth.

Association for Supervision and Curriculum Development, *Growing Up in an Anxious Age* (1952 Yearbook). Washington, D. C.: The Association, 1952. Analyzes the problems and anxieties of children in a complex and rapidly changing world.

Attwood, W. H., "The Age of Payola," *Look* 24:34-36, 41, March 29, 1960. Reports and interprets a survey of opinions held by American youth.

Barnes, Melvin W., "The Nature and Nurture of Early Adolescents," *Teachers College Record* 57: 513-521, May, 1956. Examines the adolescent in relation to culture, family, peers, and the school.

Bartlett, Claude J. and John E. Horrocks, "Study of the Needs Status of Adolescents from Broken Homes," *Journal of Genetic Psychology* 93: 153-159, September, 1958. Provides evidence that the loss of a parent does affect the psychological needs of the adolescent.

Bell, Howard M., *Youth Tell Their Story.* Washington, D. C.: American Council on Education, 1938. Reports the conditions and attitudes of young people in Maryland between the ages of sixteen and twenty-four.

Bernard, Harold W., *Adolescent Development in American Culture.* Tarrytown-on-Hudson, N. Y.: World Book Co., 1957. Considers the force of culture in shaping the lives of adolescents.

Bernert, Eleanor H., "Demographic Trends and Implications" in *The Nation's Children* (Vol. I, *op cit.*), pp. 26-49. Focuses on population trends and their influence on our society.

Blocksma, Douglas D., *Holding Power in the Grand Rapids, Michigan, Public Schools, K-14.* Grand Rapids, Mich., Public Schools (mimeographed), 1953. Reports data concerning reasons for pupils' leaving school.

Bossing, Nelson, *Principles of Secondary Education,* 2nd ed., Chapter 4. Englewood Cliffs, N. J.: Prentice-Hall, Inc., 1955. Presents the physiological changes, psychological developments, and social and economic problems of the adolescent.

Bowman, Paul H. and Maurine Pellman, "Socially Underprivileged Youth and the Schools," *High School Journal* 41: 331-335, May, 1958. Contends that the high school program should attend more to the needs of underprivileged youth.

Boy Scouts of America, *A Study of Adolescent Boys*. New Brunswick, N. J.: Boy Scouts of America, 1956. Provides a look at the concerns, activities, and interests of the fourteen- to sixteen-year-old male population.

Boyer, William H., "A Survey of the Attitudes, Opinions, and Objectives of High School Students in the Milwaukee Area," *Journal of Educational Sociology* 32: 344-348, March, 1959. Finds, through questioning a group of high school students, that they know little about the critical problems of the world.

Conant, James B., *The American High School Today*. New York: McGraw-Hill Book Co., Inc., 1959. Examines the curricula of American high schools and gives recommendations for improvement.

Coster, John K., "Some Characteristics of High School Pupils from Three Income Groups," *Journal of Educational Psychology* 50: 55-62, April, 1959. Finds real differences among the activities and achievements of pupils from different income groups.

Cowgill, Donald, "The Effect of Mobility" in *Children and Youth in the 1960's: Survey Papers,* pp. 33-42. Washington, D. C.: The White House Conference on Children and Youth, 1960. Focuses on the influence of changes of residence upon our society and especially upon our youth.

Dillon, Harold J., *Early School Leavers*. New York: National Child Labor Committee, 1949. Reports a statewide study of school drop-outs.

Dodson, Dan W., "The Effects of Suburban Living" in *Children and Youth in the 1960's: Survey Papers, op. cit.*, pp. 13-20. Discusses the impact of the suburb on the family, human relations, and community and personal values.

Dulles, Foster Rhea, "From Frontier to Suburbia" in *The Nation's Children* (Vol. I, *op. cit.*), pp. 1-23. Stresses the changing nature of our communities.

Friedenberg, Edgar, *The Vanishing Adolescent*. Boston, Mass.: Beacon Press, Inc., 1959. Presents a highly original interpretation of the changing role of the adolescent in American society.

Ginzberg, Eli, ed., *The Nation's Children* (Vol. I, *op. cit.*). Examines the family and other social institutions.

———, *Ibid.* (Vol. III: *Problems and Prospects*). Deals with the problems of specific youth groups: the rural minority and delinquent segments.

Girl Scouts of America, *Adolescent Girls*. New York: Girl Scouts of America, 1958. A companion report to *A Study of Adolescent Boys* (*op. cit.*).

Gottman, Jean, "The Impact of Urbanization" in *The Nation's Children* (Vol. I, *op. cit.*), pp. 180-208. Stresses the rising influence of urbanization on our society.

Gronlund, Norman E. and Loren Anderson, "Personality Characteristics of Socially Accepted, Socially Neglected, and Socially Rejected

Junior High School Pupils," *Educational Administration and Supervision* 43: 329-338, October, 1957. Provides insight for teachers in aiding rejected pupils to gain social acceptance.

Hollingshead, August B., *Elmtown's Youth*. New York: John Wiley and Sons, Inc., 1949. A study of adolescent life in a midwestern corn belt community.

Jersild, Arthur T., *Psychology of Adolescence*. New York: The Macmillan Co., 1957. Provides insight into the problems and behavior of the American teenager.

Jones, Lewis W., "Negro Youth in the South" in *The Nation's Children* (Vol. III, *op. cit.*), pp. 51-77. Devoted to a discussion of the problems of the Southern Negro youth.

Kolb, John H., "Rural Youth" in *Ibid.*, pp. 25-50. Examines the concerns and problems of rural youth.

Kuhlew, R. G., *The Psychology of Adolescent Development*. New York: Harper & Row, Publishers, 1952. Places less emphasis than most on adolescence as a period of stress.

Kvaraceus, W. C., "Delinquency—A By-Product of the School," *School and Society* 59: 350-351, May 13, 1944. Reports the relationship of delinquency to the school year.

McNassor, Donald, "The Changing Character of Adolescents," *California Journal of Secondary Education* 31: 128-133, March, 1956. Suggests ways in which the school can adjust to the changing character of adolescents.

Mead, Margaret, "Problems of the Late Adolescent and Young Adult" in *Children and Youth in the 1960's: Survey Papers, op. cit.*, pp. 3-12. Centers upon the results of the rapid changes that influence the lives and education of our young people.

Reeves, J. Maxson and Leo Goldman, "Social Class Perceptions and School Maladjustment," *Personnel and Guidance Journal* 35: 414-419, March, 1957. Supports the hypothesis that maladjustment is associated with discrepancies between internal and external measures of social class level.

Remmers, H. H. and D. H. Radler, *The American Teenager*. Indianapolis, Ind.: The Bobbs-Merrill Co., Inc., 1957. Reports the attitudes held by American youngsters.

Sando, Randolph, "This They Believe," *California Journal of Secondary Education* 31: 45-49, January, 1956. Reveals that the school is not adequately serving the needs of "nonacademic" pupils.

Wattenberg, William W., *The Adolescent Years*. New York: Harcourt, Brace and World, Inc., 1955. Emphasizes the broad patterns of teenage development.

Wayland, Sloan R., "The Social Context and the Adolescent" in *What Shall the High School Teach?* (1956 Yearbook of the Association for Supervision and Curriculum Development). Washington, D. C.: The Association, 1956. Presents the influence of the social scene upon both the school and the adolescent.

Witty, Paul, "The Effect of Mass Media" in *The Nation's Children* (Vol. I, *op. cit.*), pp. 1-23. Presents the influence on youth of the mass media of communication.

Wood, Robert C., *Suburbia: Its People and Their Politics*. Boston, Mass.: Houghton Mifflin Co., 1959. Gives insight into the political environment of suburban youth.

4

THE
CURRICULUM
NEEDED

Any realistic attempt to define the high school curriculum
needed in the American high school must be an outgrowth
of an analysis of the type of citizen who functions effectively
in the American society and of the problems and characteristics
of youth. Chapters 2 and 3 have described these
phenomena and provided the basis for the criteria proposed
in this chapter. Standards for six phases of the high school
program will be advanced: the growths sought, the atmosphere
of the school, classes, student activities, guidance, and
community relations.

GROWTHS SOUGHT

The basic test
that must be applied to a school is: "Do the growths sought in
pupils coincide with the function established for the school?"

A school for safecrackers is effective if it teaches its students to open safes. A school for Communists is effective if it produces dedicated and skillful Communists. Unless the pupil growths sought are consistent with the social function of the secondary school, it is not a good school even though it is housed in a beautiful building and supplied with all of the equipment the teachers want. The American public high school is good to the degree that it produces the types of growth in pupils which enable them to be successful in our society. Unless the growths sought are appropriate, the high school will be effective only by chance or error.

What are the types of growth the American high school should further? Although there seems to be violent disagreement concerning method and content, most sources agree that the school should produce students committed to democratic values and possessing the knowledge and skills necessary to implement them. Based upon this premise, an effective American high school seeks to promote the following types of growth in the students who attend.

Increasing acceptance of democratic values and growing understanding of the basic issues confronting the society in implementing these values. If the way faculty and pupils live together illustrates basic democratic values, pupils will acquire many of them from mere acceptance of the group's way of life. But living the values will not be enough. Time must be taken to verbalize the values that are implicit in the life of the school. Unstated values may not be recognized or accepted. In every school some democratic values will still be incompletely realized. These omissions should be faced honestly, and students and faculty should work together in devising ways in which these values can be more fully attained in the school. The process of working for greater attainment of democratic values will promote the realization that democracy is constantly emerging, that citizenship involves working with other people to achieve desirable goals.

Increasing skill in democratic group living. All students need to learn how to define problems, how to collect data, how to form conclusions, how to test these conclusions through actions, and how to revise the program in terms of the results obtained. Skill is needed, too, in learning to know and understand others and the contribution that they can make. Further, skill is needed in communicating ideas, in planning courses of action, in organizing to execute those plans, and in evaluating them with other members of the group.

> The seniors of a southern high school sought a return of senior privileges that had been gradually taken away by the faculty over

a period of years. The sponsors of the class informed them of the proper procedures to follow. The students did as suggested, taking the proposal through class meetings, the student government, and a joint committee of student government and faculty representatives. All five proposals were approved at these steps. In a faculty meeting which no students were permitted to attend, three of the proposals were turned down. The students had no means of appealing. No explanation of the faculty decision was given. Certain members of the senior class decided the only way to get reconsideration was to organize a strike against the school cafeteria. When the placards appeared and students began to boycott the food service, the administration brought the leaders to the office for a lecture and a warning that such behavior was not good citizenship and might affect their being admitted to the college of their choice. Although the school expressed verbal committment to teaching pupils how to take democratic action, it ignored, failed to recognize, or deliberately avoided this opportunity to demonstrate democratic methods.

Change is inevitable and new problems constantly arise, whether a person stays in the same community or moves from community to community. The new and the unexpected are not things to be feared when the individual has a technique for working out the problems with which the new and the unexpected confront him.

Opportunities should be provided for pupils to work on the social problems of the school and the community. They learn to solve social problems by having the opportunity to seek solutions. Skills are developed through action rather than mere "reading about." Projects in which students take action are essential.

Increasing proficiency in fundamental skills. To be an effective citizen an American must possess certain fundamental skills. These include reading, writing, spelling, speaking, and the basic arithmetic processes. But the skills needed go beyond this list. Another fundamental skill is how to get along with other people. Human living is group living, and unless the individual knows how to get along with other people he cannot become a successful human being. High schools cannot expect that all pupils who enter will have satisfactory human relations skills. Just as the high school must continue to teach communication skills, it must promote pupil growth in the ability to know and to understand others. To accomplish this task, teachers must stress the importance of each individual and the importance of each person helping the other person.

Many critics of the high school complain that graduates have not mastered the fundamental skills. But what are these skills? Ability to:

read seven hundred words per minute? spell five thousand words? diagram a sentence? swim one hundred yards? drive a car? What is expected of a high school graduate? Students don't know. Employers don't know. Teachers would not agree. It is time for high school faculties to attempt to state the minimum fundamental skills required for graduation.

Increasing skill in collecting information. Pupils need help in learning how to select and use facts from many sources. Adults today are deluged with facts from many groups who wish to influence public opinion. Not all information comes from books, although many school programs put the major emphasis on reading. Much of our information comes from the radio, television programs, or the comments of other people. An effective citizen must be able to tell what is true and what is inaccurate. He must be able to select the truth in oral statements, as well as from written statements.

No one today can become sufficiently informed about the issues in all areas in which he is required to make intelligent decisions. Each must rely on someone else for answers in many phases of modern living. In order to know on whom to rely, skill in choosing authorities is needed. Knowing how to select an authority who will make a valid judgment consistent with the values sought is as important a skill as individual problem-solving.

Increasing ability to form generalizations and draw conclusions. When students are required to memorize facts, a school is emphasizing the wrong thing. Research indicates that seventy per cent of isolated facts memorized will be forgotten in two years. But generalizations drawn are not forgotten, and skills acquired in interpreting data do not decrease but increase as the individual continues to interpret data in other areas. This evidence seems to imply that as far as class work is concerned students should use facts as the basis for drawing generalizations. Testing programs should not stress whether or not the student knows a certain group of facts, but rather what he can do with the facts that he has acquired.

Increasing clarification of values. Through his experiences in school, the pupil should become acquainted with a wide variety of ideas and select values for himself. Although these values change as the student progresses through school, the staff assists him to become more certain about their order, consistency, and inclusiveness. The school fulfills its function as it helps the student to test his values in day-to-day living and examine them in terms of their implications for society as well as for himself as an individual.

Increasing creativity. People learn to know as they try to express in their own way the conclusions that they have reached. They may do this through art, music, dramatics, speech, or writing. The important thing is for a person to have many opportunities to interpret the way he feels about his life and the activities around him.

Each pupil should have an opportunity to engage in creative activity in some medium. Not all can be creative in a given medium, but all do have some things they want to express. Reading and writing and speaking do not provide enough of an outlet for all people. Some communicate better through dramatics, through the dance, through song, through clay, through paint, and schools need to make other media available to boys and girls.

Greater emphasis on creativity is essential if the nation is to increase its productivity. As students make their own interpretation of their experience, they are engaging in creative activity. As they begin to convey to others the generalizations they have drawn, they are engaging in creative activity. As they attempt to organize their various generalizations into a pattern of beliefs, into a pattern of knowledge, they are engaging in creative activity.

Creativity may be expressed in the production of plays that students write. It may be in the landscaping of the school grounds. It may be in the art that students produce. It may be in the music that they compose or play. It may be in the dance as interpreted in the physical education classes. But a school out of which creative citizens will come is one in which there is a constant stress on creativity and on the recognition of the creative genius of the school population through displaying its products.

> In a junior high school in lower Manhattan, the entrance hall is large and dark. The floor is soiled. The side walls have dingy paint. But at the back of this entrance hall is a beautiful mural depicting life in that school. This mural is there because an art teacher in that school saw the importance of the creativity of youngsters. He brought volunteers from his art class together and they laid out a mural which depicted, as they saw it, and as other students told them, the activities of that school. After they had worked and reworked their ideas, they transferred their mural to the wall in the back of this hall. Not only was the mural an expression of creativity which gave the youngsters who participated in it a sense of importance and a sense that the school was theirs, but it gave every other student in the school an increased sense of dignity and worth. In addition, it increased the extent to which creativity was fostered in other classes. Other students began to say: "What

is the contribution that we can make to this school?" As pupils see the school as a place where their ideas and products are valued, it becomes an enterprise into which they can and will pour their energy and effort.

Increasing growth in mental and physical fitness. A healthy body contributes to good citizenship. Recognizing this fact, the school should provide experiences in which students have the opportunity to develop their physical power and to learn ways of caring for their bodies. Each individual should have the opportunity to participate in appropriate physical activities. Not everyone should play basketball or football or baseball. Some youngsters should rest during the physical education period or take corrective drills. The total program should be examined to see whether any practices are detrimental to eyesight, mental health, or nutrition.

Increasing social skills. Not all persons believe that the secondary school should accept responsibility for pupil growth in the social graces. Those who object to the school being concerned with social development do not belittle this phase of human growth. They merely proclaim that the school has enough to do if it stresses intellectual development, and that other agencies should care for the social growth.

Manners, social dancing, how to be a host or a guest are important skills. To say that the teaching of such skills is the responsibility of the home does not solve the problem. Some pupils need more help than the home is able to give if they are to feel adequate and able to participate without handicap in present-day society.

Increasing knowledge of the cultural and intellectual heritage of the society. Growth in intellectual ability involves increased ability to locate and use information and to acquire and organize knowledge in the process. The primary goal of the school in fostering the intellectual growth of pupils is to develop skill in self-education. But a supplementary product is the collection of a body of information. These facts, although many of them will be forgotten, constitute an acquaintance with the cultural heritage and enable the student to discover the field of endeavor he wishes to pursue.

High schools may establish growths other than those included in this list as ones that they wish to promote. But clarity of purpose with regard to the types of growth sought is essential. A basic difference between high schools that are effective and those that are not is the degree of agreement among the faculty members of a school concerning the pupil growths sought.

ENVIRONMENT

The types of growth that occur in a high school are determined by the atmosphere provided. A pupil does his own learning. He selects from his environment the things with which he will interact, and his interaction determines his growth. The qualities of the environment will limit the range of possible growths and will encourage some growths and discourage others. Without question, the atmosphere of the school is a basic element of the curriculum structure.

Intellectual

The environment should be intellectually stimulating. If pupil discussion in the school cafeteria relates to outside activities, to parties, to beach activities, to radio programs, television, magazines that are read on the outside, and no reference is made to what occurs in classes, it is evidence that the school is an intellectual wilderness. If a school is rich in intellectual stimulation, students talk about the ideas that they are encountering in their reading and their class work.

Emotional

Another important aspect of the environment is the emotional climate. Sometimes school staffs fail to realize that how a pupil feels about a situation and his place in it determines how worthwhile the situation is for him. A pupil who does not feel accepted does not learn the content that the teacher hopes that he will acquire in the situation. His concern about his lack of acceptance will keep him from focusing his attention on the class activities in progress. Emotions screen out some learnings and reinforce others. If a child is seriously unhappy or deeply troubled he is not able to think about anything else, and his unhappiness becomes associated with the activity in progress. He rejects the activity and the learnings associated with it as unsatisfactory. If he does learn what the teacher hopes he will learn, he learns it in such an emotional context that he will seek ways of avoiding further contact with that knowledge in the future, or he may learn it as a perverted kind of truth. For example, the teacher may be attempting to teach that democracy is the best way of life but do it in such a way that he insults students of certain national backgrounds. He teaches youngsters to be able to repeat the generalizations, but with a negative emotional reaction which leads certain youngsters to believe that this point of view is the one to express to get along, but that people of their nationality really do not find it the best way to live. Each generalization or fact learned is in an emotional matrix that determines a student's interpretation of the fact or generalization and the use that he makes of it.

The emotional climate of the school has even deeper implications. It helps a student form the two most important generalizations that he makes during his life. What am I like? What are other people like? The emotional climate helps him determine whether or not he has worth, whether he is respected and accepted, whether he can contribute or achieve, whether he feels superior or inferior. All of these feelings determine his course of action and what he does with all of the other knowledge that he acquires. The emotional content of the situation determines whether he concludes that other people want to be friends, whether they can be trusted, whether they are out to defeat him, or whether they are there to help him.

Knowing these things, faculty members must be as much concerned about the emotional atmosphere and the human relations in the school as they are about the course outlines. They need to examine the extent to which pupils accept each other. Are there small social cliques that refuse to associate with other students? Are there exclusive organizations which exclude students from certain socioeconomic levels and social groups? Are there regular fights between members of the student body? Are the athletic teams being disrupted by social discrimination? Does only a small portion of the student body feel welcome to come to school social activities? Do community conditions set one group against another? Are the teacher-administrator relations the kind that hinder teachers from being at ease with children? All of these are important questions in looking at the curriculum of the school. The answers determine how students see their academic learnings and what they do with them.

Another indication of the need for a satisfactory emotional climate is the percentage of the national population who need treatment for mental and emotional disorders. At the present time in one state, one out of every ten persons spends some portion of his life in a hospital for treatment of a mental or emotional disorder. In the nation as a whole, the figure is one out of every twelve. A school cannot avoid a responsibility for contributing to the emotional development of people. The experiences that a pupil has in school contribute to the sound development of his mental health or constitute a detriment to it. In many schools not enough stress has been placed on making the school a place that contributes to good mental health. If the emotional climate is right, people learn to accept themselves and believe that they have a contribution to make. If it is unsatisfactory, they learn that they are not important and that they do not make the kind of contribution that can be accepted. If the emotional climate is right, they learn to believe that the other person is a person whom they can trust, is a person who is concerned about them, is a person who will make his contribution to the group. If the emotional climate is not right, they learn that the other person is trying to take advantage of them, is trying to win from them, is not to be trusted, and will take every advantage he can get. These two concepts, belief about self and belief about others, are the very foundation stones of life. Unless the school does the job of helping pupils see themselves and others in true perspective, mental health is impaired.

If the emotional climate is satisfactory, the teacher feels secure in his relationships with the administration and knows that he will have help in developing the kind of program that is important. If teachers are insecure, that insecurity is passed along to children. If they are afraid of the administration, they will be unable to be themselves with pupils; they will have to judge each action by what they believe the administrator will think rather than what they deem best for youth. They will be unable to be open and honest with pupils, for fear their comments will be wrong or misinterpreted. When teachers are uncertain, pupils must protect themselves and be less willing to explore problems fully.

What teachers feel about their pupils makes a difference. Robert Fleming's study of pupils with psychosomatic symptoms in elementary school in Dobbs Ferry, New York, indicated that teacher acceptance of pupils affects the pupils' physical health. The results of Ann Burrell's study of elementary school pupils in New York City suggest that teacher acceptance of pupils influences the subject matter achievement of boys and girls. On the basis of available research, it seems that if a faculty wants a situation in which boys and girls are healthy and in which they mature and learn most effectively, it should be one in which the emotional climate is good.

If the climate is satisfactory, pupils feel wanted. The teacher lets them know that they are wanted and that they are missed when they are absent. Boys and girls accept each other and help each other. Each pupil feels that he belongs. When the reasons pupils leave school are examined, it is found that very few children who have any friends in the school leave. The Grand Rapids, Michigan, report that not a single pupil who was an active, accepted member of a status clique or a school club or team or activity left the school is evidence of the importance of having a school where people feel that they are wanted.

A good school atmosphere is one that teachers and pupils enjoy. Learning occurs most effectively in an environment in which people are secure and happy. If the situation in which learning occurs is one in which pupils are having fun, the chances are greater that they are more nearly learning what the teacher hopes they will learn. If the situation is an unhappy one, the students may only be learning either ways to avoid the teacher or else the reverse of the ideas the teacher hopes they are gaining.

If American mass media are examined, it is evident that the teaching-learning situation is not ordinarily regarded as one in which people have fun. Teachers are stereotyped in the cartoons as rigid, harsh, unattractive persons who force pupils to do unpleasant tasks. Schools are pictured as something to be avoided, not something to be rushed to and enjoyed. Such manifestations of the adult's beliefs about school indicate the need for teachers to exert greater effort in making school an enjoyable situation.

A school with a desirable atmosphere has a fine school spirit. Youngsters believe in their school. They take pride in the program, the building, and the accepted pattern of behavior. They pass the traditions of the school along to new students. They are proud of the school and its ideals and want new students to be also.

Physical

Physical environment limits or facilitates the program. If rooms are small and crowded, teachers will find it necessary to be more rigid and directive; movement must be restricted. If rooms contain plenty of work space, a teacher is free to work in a variety of ways with his students. If the building does not contain adequate laboratories, special rooms, and facilities which permit effective work in a variety of fields, the staff is handicapped in developing a program and a pleasant working atmosphere.

It helps if the building is one in which each pupil lives in a classroom where there is color, light, and ventilation. Not only is much taught about art and color harmony by the environment, but the emotions of the inhabitants are affected by the choice and use of color. Many high school programs are less effective because they are housed in unattractive buildings.

The cafeteria and the way it is operated affect the atmosphere of the school. Does it have the appearance and the background music of a good eating establishment? Is it a place where adults would choose to eat if they were not required to do so? Does it suggest regimentation, with people waiting in long lines and having little choice in food? Or is it arranged in a manner to keep noise and crowding at a minimum, with food selections offered to tempt an array of tastes? Is the cafeteria a place where good manners are the norm and self-control usually evident? Or are throwing and loud talking customary, and patrolling by faculty necessary? Students learn what they live in the cafeteria.

The high school library helps to set the atmosphere. Is it a place where all the chairs are straight and hard? Or is it a place where there is at least one reading nook where people can sit in soft chairs as they read? Are there books that people read for fun? Is there a place where people can work together in committee without disturbing everybody? Libraries reflect the philosophy and work pattern of the school. Their content and organization reveal the breadth of the curriculum and the way of life that is approved and valued.

If recreation and lounge areas for students are located at strategic points throughout the building, they promote friendliness in the student body and add to the attractiveness of the building. If there are places where students can relax and talk informally, the desired social atmosphere is suggested.

Classrooms that are flexible permit pupils and teachers to arrange the furniture to facilitate the activity in process. Decrease in the difficulties faced results in less frustration and more satisfaction with the situation. Adequate work space in the classroom improves the emotional climate. When people are crowded together they are forced to infringe on each others' rights and freedom, and irritations increase and become grievances unless time and effort are expended in developing understanding and cooperation. Further, adequate space makes possible moving the furniture into the structural arrangement needed to carry out the particular function the class is undertaking. Flexible furniture without space to move it when necessary has little value.

Some classrooms appeal to a visitor as soon as he sees them. It is apparent that someone cares about them. Steps have been taken to make them attractive. Colors harmonize. Pictures and displays are unique and appropriate to the activities conducted. The room is inviting—the type of place the visitor would like to spend the day. Other classrooms, however, repel because of barrenness, drabness, lack of positive stimuli; they are like prison cells to which students are confined. A walk down the halls of a high school, with a brief examination of the rooms opening into them, will tell much about the atmosphere of a school.

The atmosphere, a basic part of the curriculum, from which a pupil learns many things about himself, others, and a way of living, consists of intellectual, emotional, and physical factors. The high school we need must be intellectually stimulating, emotionally satisfying, and physically attractive and functional.

COURSES

The courses offered should be of a sufficient number and variety to enable each student to find meaning, purpose, and satisfaction in his work. With the exception of a basic general education core, each pupil's selection of courses should be individually made in terms of his purposes, needs, and level of achievement. The teaching in the courses should make possible each pupil working at maximum efficiency.

General Education

The curriculum needed will provide a general education that gives an understanding of family living, economic concepts, democratic values, and a respect for work. These are essentials for everyone in our society. Although the general education phase of the curriculum may take many forms and may have different names applied to it, somewhere in a good high school program boys and girls must have the experiences which develop the concepts and competencies essential to being effective family members and citizens. The courses in which these concepts and competencies are developed should be the ones all students are required to take, and the number should be kept as small as possible. General education courses constitute the basic citizenship education which promotes as far as possible the mental health, the commitment to democratic values, and the es-

sential skills of a citizen. The courses which serve this purpose should
be identified, labeled, and operated in a unique manner.

*In some of the required courses, pupils should have an opportunity
to work with persons from all segments of the population.* Each boy
or girl in a democracy needs an opportunity for at least a portion of the
school day to live and think with people who are different from himself. He needs the chance to get to know the kinds of economic, social, religious, and political thinking that other people in the population do. He needs to develop the skills necessary to make democracy
work. He needs skill in working with groups with a wide range of
intellectual abilities and cultural backgrounds. If the more intelligent
youngsters do not learn ways of communicating with less intelligent
people they are going to be less effective as citizens. The high school
is, for most youth, the last formal experience designed to help develop
the common values, the feelings of unity, the skill in working together
that is needed to allow the nation to provide for individual and minority uniqueness while maintaining cooperation without coercion.

Within the required general education courses students should be
grouped heterogeneously, should have a part in establishing purposes
and evaluating progress, and should be passed if they are exerting
effort. In a program where the task is to take the student to the highest
competency possible for him, the school's role is to provide experiences and counsel, not to classify or eliminate. The extent to which a
staff is willing to operate courses in this manner should determine
which courses are classified as general education and required of all
students.

Individual Programs

*The major portion of each student's program should be indi-
vidualized elective education.* Within this phase of each student's
curriculum should be the courses he chooses to further his vocational
goals and those he selects to satisfy avocational interests. Apart from
the general education classes, each student should be free to select
from the total course offering of the school in terms of his purposes
and his level of ability. The only curricula offered in a high school
should be individual programs. Organization of types of curricula
within a school unnecessarily limits the choice of students and makes
it less possible for the school to meet the needs of individuals.

Each school should offer a wide variety of courses, and a student,
with the agreement of parents and counselor, should select those which

further his purposes. Moreover, he should be able to revise the program each year in the light of new achievements and new goals—and without loss of credit. As he plans his individual program the student should be counseled to select some courses, probably a third of his program, that are vocational courses. Note that the courses will be *vocational for him*. For a pupil intending to enter an engineering college, advanced mathematics is vocational. Another course, typing for example, might be vocational for a girl intending to become a secretary and avocational for a boy who wants to learn to type his class notes.

The remaining courses a student selects should be in terms of his interests. These courses will broaden his background or give him depth and an abiding interest in one phase of human knowledge. Classes in the elective portion of the curriculum can, to a much greater degree, be planned in advance and teacher-directed. Pupils enroll in certain courses because they want to acquire a particular knowledge or competency. The teacher is more able, therefore, to assume that students will want to explore his organization of the content and pursue the activities which in his opinion develop the needed competencies.

Quality Teaching

Classes, whether in the general education or the elective portion of the curriculum, should be intellectually stimulating. Rooms should be filled with exhibits, displays, and items that indicate the range of interests students may pursue. The materials available should include items that are within the reading range of all the students enrolled, and the activities should be varied enough to permit each to find a way in which he can contribute.

Teachers of each class should believe in what they are doing and the way they are teaching. If they do not, they cannot give their wholehearted effort and the learning situation suffers. It is better for a teacher to be doing something that is less satisfactory, as judged in terms of theory and research evidence concerning the learning process, than it is for him to be doing what research supports and not believe that it is the way for him to teach. Each person does well what he believes is best.

If the school program is good, teachers base choices concerning method on their beliefs. Teaching is a continuous process of making choices, and each teacher is confronted each hour by the need to make a number of choices. What shall he do when the student has not prepared his work? What kind of question shall he ask when a student states a generalization that he cannot support? What shall he do when a disagreement occurs between two students? What shall he do when students become disgusted with the activity being conducted? In each of the decisions a teacher must make he needs his own set of values if he is to have any security or if his behavior is to have any consistency that gives youngsters security. He needs to know what he believes and have the professional freedom to make the choice his beliefs indicate. If a teacher must consider a school policy concerning method which is contrary to his values and decide what compromises he must make between the two, he cannot but be indecisive and therefore less effective.

The standards in classes must be realistic. If a situation is one in which the pupil cannot possibly reach the standards that are established, he becomes frustrated and loses faith in self or rejects and resents those who have established the standards. To be realistic, standards must be established for the individual. Grade standards rigidly interpreted and enforced violate what is known about growth and development. By the time students get to the seventh grade, some students, working at their top level, will be only at the fifth or sixth grade level of achievement while others will be at the ninth or tenth grade level. To require all work in terms of the same standard prevents the school from being a rich experience for the advanced student and insures that it will be a frustrating experience for the least advanced student. If high levels of performance are to be maintained, standards must be individual standards established in terms of a student's present status and his goals.

Standards of performance are many times confused with marking practices. As a class works, the same marking standards must be applied if students are to feel they are being treated fairly. But the range of excellence associated with each mark should be wide, and each pupil should be assisted in establishing his own standards within the range.

Every pupil should have a chance to see his own progress. The record of his progress should not be kept confidential in a teacher's grade book. Each student should keep a record of his own work and samples of his effort so that he can judge at any time how well he is doing and what he needs to do in order to move more rapidly in the direction of the goals he has established.

A teacher should be free to adapt the program to the group with which he works. If a teacher who is working with a group of youngsters who have an average IQ of eighty is told: "We must bring this seventh grade up to seventh grade norm," he is asked to do the impossible. If these youngsters are working at their seventh year in school and have an average IQ of eighty, they are at about the fifth grade level of achievement. To say to a teacher: "You must have these youngsters at the seventh grade level," is to say to that teacher: "You are going to be a failure all year long." The task is an impossible one. To say to youngsters: "Because you are now classified as seventh grade you must produce at the seventh grade level or you must read at the seventh grade level" is saying to them: "You must do the impossible." When people are faced with the impossible, they fail to perform even at the level of which they are capable.

The instructional material for each class should provide for at least a five grade spread in reading ability. With social promotion, which takes into account emotional and social, as well as intellectual, development, each group beyond the seventh grade has a reading span of at least five years, possibly seven. To meet that range of individual differences, reading material suitable for a span of no less than five grade levels is essential.

Intellectually stimulating classes make use of the out-of-school experiences of children. Less than half of the student's waking hours are spent in the school. To be effective, the teacher utilizes the experience that the student has during the other portion of his day. Instead of assuming that his function is to provide the experiences, he conceives of his job as one of analyzing with the student his experiences and helping him interpret his life both in school and out.

Teachers of classes for adolescents need special skill. In addition to knowing their field and methods of teaching, they _should have the ability to move from dominant to supporting roles as necessary_. Adolescents want to be self-directing and independent at times, but at other moments they want someone else to assume the responsibility and give direction. Teachers of adolescents want to assist boys and girls to increase their skill in self-direction. They must be sensitive to adolescents' feelings and supply the leadership appropriate to the moment. Developing the ability to be self-directing calls for skill in encouraging students to challenge and question, to form their own generalizations and values, and to take action to apply their conclusions. To perform this role requires that the teacher have a high degree of poise and self-confidence, that he be more concerned with helping pupils grow than with demonstrating his own competence.

STUDENT ACTIVITIES

Student activities should be judged by whether they contribute to the growths sought by the school faculty. Unless an activity can be justified by results produced by student participation, it has no place in the school program.

Activities exist to provide a wider range of experiences for students. Through them more students find phases of the school program that are important and vital. Not all students are interested in class work or find it important. Some students want experiences in which they can be more creative and less directed by adults. Properly organized activities serve this role and must be as available as classes. They should be held during regular school hours, with students free to enroll in them on the same basis on which they choose classes. No student should be excluded from an activity because he has low marks in other classes, unless those marks indicate a quality of scholarship which will make him incapable of participating effectively in the activity he chooses.

The breadth of activities provided should be much broader than the class offering and should be freer structurally. If an attempt is made to divide an activity into a number of sessions paralleling the classes of a semester, many of the benefits will be lost. Activities offer the opportunity to be creative, and participating in the planning by those who will execute the project is the basic contribution of most activities.

Some activities, such as interscholastic sports, are under the direction of staff members and involve presentations for spectators. Sometimes educational values are sacrificed to secure excellent performance. Under no circumstances should the educational welfare of participants be second to entertainment goals, and each activity should be evaluated each year to see if modification should be made to increase the emphasis given to seeking desirable pupil growth.

Student activities are a major portion of the curriculum of a good secondary school, and adequate provision must be made to keep them responsive to student needs and under competent supervision. Both students and faculty have a deep interest in the way student activities are conducted, and both should be adequately represented on the body that organizes, regulates, and evaluates the activities program. To serve its function the program should be broad enough and challenging enough to insure the participation of each student in at least one important activity outside of his class work.

GUIDANCE

Each boy and girl should have one adult on the faculty who knows him well and who can plan his program with him. Guidance is provided through this close working relationship with a teacher rather than through assigning hundreds of students to counselors who may not know them as persons and who do not have their confidence.

Where possible, the school should organize its schedule so that one teacher stays with each student for more than one period per day. The arrangement may be for a homeroom and a class period with one teacher, or it may be a double period with a teacher who is able to teach more than one subject. This teacher serves as the focal contact between the school and the pupil and his parents.

Each pupil should have some adult in the school whom he trusts well enough to talk with about any personal problems. Adolescents, like other people, choose their own counselors. They decide which person they trust and respect and turn to him to talk through the personal problems that confront them. Labels and titles make no difference. Simply because a person is called a counselor does not mean students will use him as their counselor. Sometimes a school nurse, a coach, or even a custodian is used by many students to assist in facing the real problems of adolescence. In the truly good secondary school most of the faculty members have empathy, skill in communication, and a willingness to listen.

In addition, the school needs specialists who can advise students with regard to job opportunities, choice of college, and college entrance requirements. They aid teachers by talking through with them problems on which help is requested and by making referrals when needed. These specialists help get the program of guidance organized, collect information and materials, conduct needed tests and maintain records, and serve as counselors to teachers, referral cases, and students who choose them as the person they trust.

The guidance in the school should be judged by the extent to which all pupils have been able to get individualized programs and by the percentage of pupils who have at least one faculty member whom they trust and in whom they will confide.

COMMUNITY RELATIONS

For the most part, high schools are not close enough to the community. In a study in Tampa, Florida, it was found that no high school had as good a relationship with the community as the average elementary school. Parents did not think the program was as good. Relatively few parents had been at school to talk to the principal and teachers unless their children had been in trouble. Advisory committees and use of parents as resource people were exceedingly rare.

Two factors may explain the relative lack of closeness between the high school and the community. High school students live further from the school, and, in many cases, they do not want their parents to come to the school. Both distance and pupil desire for independence make the development of good school-community relations more difficult for the high school.

But the total community educates adolescents, and the high school needs a close working relationship with the other educational forces in the community. Youth today feel much isolated from the community, without real responsibility or a significant role. To educate them for effective citizenship, the high school needs to work with other agencies to discover opportunities for youth to assume a more responsible role.

In addition, the school needs the help of persons in the community who can aid in the development of special phases of the program. Advisory committees of parents in the fields of music, art, science, and various aspects of vocational education are examples. These advisory committees keep the school program closer to the needs of the community and give assistance in acquiring more support from the community. An advisory committee for the principal is a method of securing consultation before action and serves as a channel of communication to many members of the community.

One of the ways in which a high school can help make the transition to adult status easier is to give adolescents opportunities to work with adults. The high school needs to bring many adults into the school as resource people. They add certain competencies that the staff does not possess and make working shoulder-to-shoulder with adults who are not paid teachers a common experience for the pupils. School seems more vital and earnest when adults bring real problems and experiences into the classroom.

Adults will be present through adult education programs, too. Use of the building by adult groups not only gives the community added return on its money invested in school buildings, but it also helps high school pupils to see that education is a continuous process and is used for a purpose. They will have evidence that school is not "to get through" but to use for personal growth.

SUMMARY

The high school needed is not in the far distant future. Many present-day schools approach the program described, and all of the features presented in this chapter are to be found in varying degrees in schools throughout the country. But a program with these features and benefits is needed for *all* youth in *all* high schools—today!

SELECTED READINGS

Association for Supervision and Curriculum Development, *Balance in the Curriculum* (1961 Yearbook). Washington, D. C.: The Association, 1961. Offers some guiding principles on achieving and maintaining a well-rounded curriculum.

Burrell, Ann Porter, "Facilitating Learning Through Emphasis on Meeting Children's Basic Emotional Needs: An In-Service Program," *Journal of Educational Sociology* 24: 381-393, March, 1951. Reports the effect on achievement of teachers' attempts to meet basic emotional needs.

Conant, James B., *The American High School Today.* New York: McGraw-Hill Book Co., Inc., 1959. Examines the curricula of American high schools and gives recommendations for improvement.

——, *Recommendations for Education in the Junior High School Years.* Princeton, N. J.: Educational Testing Service, 1960. Serves as a companion report to *The American High School Today.*

Fleming, Robert, "Psychosomatic Illness and Emotional Needs," *Educational Leadership* 9: 119-123, November, 1951. Shows how teachers' attitudes toward students can affect students' physical health.

Grambs, Jean, et al. for the Commission on Secondary Curriculum of the Association for Supervision and Curriculum Development, *The Junior High School We Need.* Washington, D. C.: The Association, 1961. Discusses the functions, problems, and needs of the junior high school of today and of the future.

Hovet, Kenneth, "What Are the High Schools Teaching?" in *What Shall the High Schools Teach?* (1956 Yearbook of the Association for

Supervision and Curriculum Development), pp. 69-96. Washington, D. C.: The Association, 1956. Presents a broad overview of the range and scope of courses being taught in secondary schools.

Wiles, Kimball and Franklin Patterson for the Commission on the Education of Adolescents of the Association for Supervision and Curriculum Development, *The High School We Need*. Washington, D. C.: The Association, 1959. Outlines the curriculum that should be offered by the American high school.

5

A LOOK
AT A HIGH SCHOOL
CURRICULUM

To attempt to describe a high school program in terms
of national averages and United States Office of Education
statistics would be misleading. If the data concerning the
great number of small high schools and the relatively
few very large high schools are combined, the results does not
give an accurate picture of any high school.
In this chapter attention will be directed to a single
high school with a common program. Deviations from
its program by other high schools will be indicated.

ONE HIGH SCHOOL'S CURRICULUM

Although no
high school is exactly like another, the offering of Centerville
High School is typical. This school, with an enrollment of
thirteen hundred, is located in a community of thirty thousand.
The courses from which a student may select are:

89

Acc. English	Creative Writing	Latin III
Acc. Math	Drivers Ed. I	Math Essentials
Ag. I	Drivers Ed. II	Office Mach
Ag. II	Economics	Phy. Sci.
Algebra I	Engl. 10	Phys. Ed. II
Algebra II	Engl. 11	Physics
Algebra III	Engl. 12	Psychology
Am. Govt.	Engl. Essentials	PSSC Physics
Am. History	French I	Plane Geometry
Am. Inst.	French II	Shorthand I
Arch. Drafting	French III	Shop
Art	Girls P. E.	Speech
Biology	Graphics	Solid Geometry
Bookkeeping I	Home Ec II	Sr. Grammar
Bookkeeping II	Home Ec III	Spanish I
Boys P. E.	Home Ec IV	Spanish II
Bus. Engl.	Inter. Typing	Spanish III
Bus. Law	Journalism	Typing I
Bus. Math	Latin I	Typing Advanced
Crafts	Latin II	World History

But a student's choice of courses is limited by the curriculum in which he is enrolled. Each student, upon entering the high school, must select the academic, commercial, vocational, or general curriculum. If he is in the academic curriculum he has seven electives. The commercial curriculum permits seven electives, the vocational seven, and the general seven. If he has a B average he may have eleven electives in any curriculum and is permitted to carry six classes a year.

If eligible, each student may participate in the following activities:

Anchor	Future Farmers of America
Hi Y	Future Homemakers of America
Civinette	Future Secretaries of America
Jr. Civitans	Future Teachers of America
Key	Dramatics
Keyette	Jr. Academy of Science
Wheel	Latin
Chess	Paramedical
French	Spanish
Orchestra	Scribblers
Band	Newspaper
Majorettes	Glee Club

Cheer Leaders   Distributive Education Club
               Technical Education Club

This high school offers sixty courses and requires twenty units of credit for graduation. A unit or a partial unit of credit is awarded for the successful completion of each course. The typical unit of credit is given for attending a class for forty-five minutes a day five days a week for thirty-six weeks. But there are variations of this pattern. Some courses offered by high schools do not entitle the student to a full unit of credit, and in other courses the student must spend more than forty-five minutes a day to receive a unit of credit.

The unit-of-credit system used in high schools today is inherited. As accrediting agencies were established, they were faced with the necessity of determining some way of judging the quality of school programs. A plan for accreditation had to be established. The counting of minutes and the accumulation of units were accepted as the most logical method. It became the accepted pattern, and the high school curriculum design is governed by it. As a result of decisions made years ago when the accrediting plans were being established the amount of time spent at work in some courses is not worth, in units of credit, as much time as work in others. If a student is in a laboratory course, he must spend double the amount of time in order to receive the same credit. This practice applies to home economics and agriculture, as well as to the sciences. If a student spends time in music or art or another of the so-called minor subjects, he receives less credit toward graduation for being in the course and receiving instruction for the same number of minutes. The difference in the credit value assigned to the different courses was due to the assumption that there are certain courses where students learn best by outside preparation and in-class recitation or explanation. The courses not requiring outside preparation are given less credit.

Many accrediting associations and state departments of education are beginning to question variable credit. Newer teaching practices have decreased the amount of outside preparation and increased in-class problem-solving. It has become increasingly difficult to tell a laboratory period from a class period. Further, the assumption that certain courses have more inherent value for all than other courses and should thus receive greater credit is being seriously questioned.

This school does not offer all of the courses that its faculty believes should be provided. The size of the student body, the ability of the community to pay, the special interests of the faculty, and the need of the community all influence the number and kinds of courses offered. Centerville is not different in this respect from other high schools.

The school administration designates certain courses that must be passed by all students who receive diplomas. The decision to require a certain course may be based on accrediting association standards, state department of education regulations, or local board of education decisions, but the program for every student in the school must include that course. The required courses constitute thirty-five per cent of the total number of courses that a student takes.

The courses offered in a high school are drastically influenced by college entrance requirements and by the accrediting associations. When the secondary school served a small portion of the population, chiefly the group going to college, it was necessary to provide the kind of program that would enable graduates to secure admission to college. State education department and accrediting association regulations, formulated for the most part after the college entrance requirements had been established, adopted the pattern that had already been laid down by the colleges. The courses established as required courses in the curriculum have been, in a large percentage of the cases, the ones required for college entrance.

The courses offered in the school are grouped in several curricula: college preparatory, commercial, general, and vocational. This order is the commonly accepted ranking according to respectability. Students of the highest intellectual ability are encouraged to go into the academic curriculum. The commercial curriculum is designed to prepare the second level of students for white-collar positions. The trade and vocational program is a preparation for those who work best with their hands, the artisans. The general curriculum is for what is left of the school population, which has little ability or has as yet to decide upon vocational or long-term life goals. Although the correlation is not perfect, the student's choice of curriculum reflects roughly his social class status. Each curriculum contains the courses required by the state department for graduation from high school, other courses established as required by the local board for graduation from high school, still other courses established as required for students who select that curriculum, and a few elective courses that the student may choose from the total high school offering.

In addition to enrolling for the courses, the student may also include some nonclass activities in his curriculum. These usually are not given a definite place in the curriculum, and the state department of education does not require that any be offered. Neither is a student compelled to include them in his program. A school may offer as many or as few as it chooses. Its faculty may attach importance to student activities or consider them evils to be endured or dispelled as soon as possible. If activities have an important place and function in the program of a given school, it is because staff members sincerely support them and contribute their creativeness toward developing an activities program.

GROWTHS SOUGHT

Although the pupil growth sought varies from teacher to teacher in Centerville High School, the only goal that all faculty members would agree to work for is knowledge of subject matter. No attempt has been made to identify and list desired pupil growths, even though the school has a general philosophy that would support the growths listed in Chapter Four. The formal testing program of the school is designed to obtain information about pupil intelligence, reading ability, and vocational interests and to measure knowledge gained in sciences, mathematics, languages, and social science.

This high school is not unusual. Few faculties have much agreement on growths sought, and fewer still have devised ways of collecting evidence of success or failure in any area except knowledge acquired. In many high schools emphasis on the fundamental skills is neglected. Teachers simply assume that their job is to teach the subject matter of a specific field. If the student does not know basic spelling, writing, arithmetic, and reading skills, the elementary school has failed. It is bad for the pupil, but he must get by as best he can without the fundamental skills. Such a point of view prevents the school from meeting students' needs. Unless someone takes the time to teach the basic skills that the student lacks, he will be hindered in his progress through school and in life. If a high school fails to increase pupil skill in presenting ideas orally, listening to what other people say, planning, organizing, taking action, and evaluating, it has an inadequate curriculum.

Failure to help students develop a philosophy of life or commitment to a set of values which will guide their behavior is a major weakness of many schools. Some teachers are so concerned with having students learn certain facts that they neglect to take the time to talk through

with them the values which will determine how they use the facts
they have. As James Bushong, executive vice president of Kamehameha
schools, says: "What good does it do to teach a pupil to speak five
languages if he can't tell the truth in any?" Teachers in some schools
have the impression that it is a waste of time to discuss how people
feel and what they believe. These teachers are so indoctrinated with
the necessity of being objective and basing judgments on facts that
they do not realize that judgments are not based on facts alone, that
facts are many times only data that people use in deciding how to
carry out the basic judgments that they have already made. A school
that teaches a youngster many facts without helping him acquire a
philosophy of life is inadequate.

Some schools have recognized the situation and taken steps to improve it. In these schools teachers place great emphasis on teaching
democratic skills and loyalty to democratic values. Out of conflicts that
have arisen in the communities has come a recognition of the need
for increasing people's skill in working together. Group work has been
used to develop the skills of cooperative planning and evaluation.
Intergroup education has been introduced. The schools attempt to
help boys and girls understand and value the differences that exist in
the community and among members of the student body. Festivals are
held in which different national groups within the school contribute
from the dancing and music of their own culture. Students have the
opportunity to study the background and history of other groups within
the school. But knowledge has not been enough. Teachers have to
work with student government on developing school spirit and a sense
of unity within the student body. Big brother and big sister organizations are formed to increase the students' feeling of responsibility for
one another.

In all of these efforts, the attempt is made to increase the communication and cooperative effort among those who are in the favored
groups and those who are on the outside. More and more schools are
initiating activities which give students greater opportunity for knowing each other and expressing friendliness toward each other. Within
the classroom they are using motion pictures such as *The High Wall*
to help students understand each other and the frictions that occur
among themselves.

These schools recognize, however, that their efforts cannot be successful unless they are supported by similar efforts within the community. In many situations the schools have instituted adult programs
in which parents from different social and racial groups have oppor-

tunities to work together on joint projects and to share the knowledges and skills that they have.

Many high schools do not have an adequate health program. Health instruction is left to the elementary school. The high school lunch program is haphazard. A high percentage of pupils spend their lunch money in fly-by-night eating establishments located around the school campus, with the result that for many lunch lacks balance or sufficient nutrition. The physical education program places major emphasis on providing body development experiences for those students who are most developed physically, because the interscholastic sports program gives the major portion of the physical education staff's time to those few who compete in varsity sports. Health examinations and available medical care are almost unknown. Physical development for the average student is largely left to chance. Neither boys nor girls have people available to whom they can go to talk about the physical changes that occur during the adolescent period.

Other schools place a major emphasis on the health program. They have nurses as a part of their regular staff, have access to school psychologists who aid with the testing program, and provide special counseling service to youngsters who need it most. Nutrition and the school food service are recognized as major contributions of the school to the development of future citizens. Government subsidy of the school lunch program is an accepted part of the cost of secondary education. Development of physical and mental health is recognized by verbal commitment plus action.

In many high schools emphasis is placed on a social program and the development of social skills. Parties and dances are a part of the program. Class time and effort are devoted to planning parties, thinking through acceptable behavior, and evaluating the experiences at the party after the group reconvenes. One of the difficulties that many of the schools experience is that the majority of the students who attend the parties and dances are those who have already acquired the necessary social skills. The students who are least adequate in social situations do not come because of their feelings of inadequacy. To overcome this difficulty, fewer schoolwide functions and more class group functions have been instituted in some schools. By this procedure, all students have a part in the planning, feel freer to tell of the kind of assistance that they want, feel more welcome (and even that they would be missed if they did not come), and can evaluate their own participation.

In the senior high school particularly, one cause of students' withdrawing from social activities has been lack of dancing skill. To develop this skill, some schools have introduced dancing instruction into the physical education program, and noon-hour social dancing has been provided in which members of the student body who are skillful dancers teach the students who desire assistance.

In schools that emphasize social development youngsters acquire the information and skill necessary to improve their appearance. Classes discuss what boys and girls like about each other's dress. Opportunity is provided for students to consult with teachers about make-up and dress.

The teaching of manners is added. High schools have always taught proper behavior in class, but many of the students entering want to know about proper out-of-school behavior. In homemaking courses and core classes, boys and girls are given the opportunity to learn how to set a table, how to eat properly, how to behave on a date, how to entertain, and various social customs for many special occasions.

These schools recognize the need for a student to feel socially accepted if he is to do his best work. They realize that a pupil who does not feel that he belongs in a social situation will put the major portion of his attention to developing techniques for achieving acceptance rather than to the content which many deem the important part of the curriculum.

Since Sputnik, high schools have received pressure to neglect types of growth other than acquisition of knowledge. Critics and pressure groups in the nation and local community have attempted to persuade or even force high school faculties to eliminate or decrease the fostering of social skills, value analysis, and democratic participation skills.

ENVIRONMENT

The environment of Centerville High School consists of course of intellectual, emotional, and physical elements.

Intellectual

All members of the faculty give verbal allegience to the importance of a stimulating intellectual climate. A number of teachers provide it. Their classes promote questioning, thinking, and creativity. Other teachers put major emphasis on memory and recall. A minority are not themselves interested in intellectual pursuits, and pupils in their classes are not challenged or stimulated.

Thirty per cent of the student body achieve great intellectual growth. Fifteen per cent find school so unrewarding that they drop out before graduation. Thirty per cent keep trying to carry out assigned tasks because it is the socially approved thing to do. Twenty-five per cent more are the "psychological drop-outs," who are physically present but emotionally absent because they find the activities of the classroom so meaningless. They find themselves forced to take classes in which they cannot possibly succeed. They find themselves confronted with a decision: they must reject themselves as inadequate, or they must reject school work as unimportant. To remain emotionally healthy, they reject the school and become the despair of teachers because they must be driven to perform the assigned tasks.

The pattern of Centerville's intellectual environment is typical. The percentage of challenged, psychological drop-outs and of actual withdrawals varies in terms of the nature of the community in which the school exists and the extent to which a faculty attempts to adapt the program to the population served.

Emotional

The principal of the school knows each of the thirteen hundred boys and girls who attend. He can describe the family, and he is seen by pupils as a friend—even though he does not hesitate to administer punishment when he thinks it is needed. The teachers respect the principal, like him, and want to work with him. They believe he supports them. Because of this relationship with pupils and teachers, the principal does much to set the emotional climate of the school. A similar conclusion concerning the role of the principal was reached in the Kellogg Leadership Study at the University of Florida, where the researchers found that the way a principal behaved influenced human relations in the teaching staff and the student body.

But all is not perfect in the emotional climate of Centerville. Portions of the student body are isolated, and little is done to help them feel a sense of belonging or to help others accept them. A high proportion of the student body is forced to feel more and more inadequate, and some withdraw. Some teachers do not accept or tolerate pupils who are not successful in their classes.

This school differs from many high schools because most pupils feel they have someone who knows them and is concerned about them. A major problem of many large high schools is the great number of pupils who feel unknown and psychologically unsupported as they pass through the program without a relationship of sufficient duration or intensity with any staff member to come to believe that anyone cares what happens to them.

Physical

Centerville is housed in a modern plant on twenty acres of land. The grounds are beautifully landscaped and each classroom has light and air and is isolated from the noise of other classes. The library, cafeteria, auditorium, and gymnasium are excellent. Classrooms are large and adequately supplied for the activities to be conducted in them. But all are relatively the same size, and modification is difficult.

Most secondary schools are similarly housed. Although some school plants are overcrowded and others dilapidated, the buildings are usually good. Innovation is being started in developing flexible structures and different sized work areas.

COURSES

As indicated, Centerville offers sixty courses divided into four curricula. Programs are not tailor-made for individuals. After the choice of a curriculum, the student has only seven elective choices.

Few new courses have been added. A distributive education program has been started within the past ten years. Advanced courses in mathematics and science have been provided. The content of the required courses has been modified, usually by adding to the academic curriculum classes and by "watering down" the general curriculum classes.

The problems of this school in its content offering are like those of other secondary schools. The offering is too restricted. Similarly, many large high schools delimit the offerings for their students by establishing separate curricula that are so rigid that the individual has little choice except to decide which curriculum he will enter. Small high schools with only a few teachers have even greater problems and concentrate on offering the courses that will make it possible for students to be admitted to college.

A major weakness of this school and many other secondary schools lies in the type of instruction provided by a portion of the teachers. Using a single textbook, focusing teaching on the average pupil, making the same assignment for all, teaching for memorization and recall, talking about rather than doing, leaving pupils out of the planning and evaluating, ignoring the role of emotions in learning, and lack of creativity in class organization and operation all interfere with the school's developing the full potential of its students.

Some high schools have put more effort into curriculum change. They have added courses, modified schedules, and provided greater flexibility in individual programs. Work programs have been instituted. Some schools have attempted to provide work experience for all youngsters through various functions performed on the school campus and through summer work activities. Other schools have used the federal government-sponsored programs of distributive education and trade and industrial training which give part-time work experiences during the regular school day to the small percentage of the student body who are enrolled.

Since Sputnik, federal government-financed experimentation is being conducted in mathematics and science. An attempt is being made to determine the structure and meaning of the disciplines and to develop courses that will present the structure and meaning rather than the application. The University of Illinois Committee on School Mathematics (UICSM), the School Mathematics Study Group (SMSG), the University of Maryland junior high school mathematics project, and the Ball State Teachers College Experimental Program are typical of the innovations being fostered in mathematics. In science the Physical Science Study Committee (PSSC), the Biological Science Curriculum Study (BSCS), the Chemical Education Materials Study (CEMS), and the Bond Approach to Teaching Chemistry are the major experimental efforts. Many high schools throughout the country are trying these courses on an experimental basis. Recognition of the responsibility to modify continually the content of existing curricula is increasing.

Some schools have added family life education to their curriculum. Seeing that one out of three marriages ends in the divorce courts, certain schools have begun to institute units in family relationships and choosing a mate. Home economics classes put more attention on budgeting, child rearing, and other kinds of problems which cause families difficulty. More high school students are provided with opportunities to work with younger children, so that they may develop insight into the growth pattern of children and, concurrently, insight into their own relationships with their siblings. Social studies and core courses are used to provide for the study of problems of courtship and the selection of a mate. Schools have recognized that for many students the high school is the last formal education situation that will be available for them to discuss these universal problems.

Other schools are conducting similar experiments with economic education. New York City, concerned with the number of pupils rejecting the present program, organized the Higher Horizons project to help youngsters living in the slums have experiences that would enable them to have greater opportunity and to establish higher goals for themselves. Students were provided with experiences they could not otherwise have obtained, such as trips to operas, plays, colleges. The results reported indicate sensational success (see *High Points* 40: 5-23) and make clear the necessity of considering the relationship between the courses offered and the psychological environment of the student.

Not all people agree with the changes that are being undertaken. Different schools are experimenting with different courses, and the direction is not consistent. But change is occurring, and the indications are that the rate and range will increase.

During the forties and fifties there was a movement toward organizing the secondary school schedule into larger blocks of time. The typical daily schedule in a secondary school has been six or seven forty-five- to fifty-minute periods, with each student taking a different class each period. Students were supposed to enter a class, become interested in that subject in the first five or ten minutes, think and study about it for thirty minutes, and then take five to ten minutes getting the assignment of homework to be done before coming back the next day. At the end of the period, students changed classes in five minutes and started the same process all over again. The procedure continued all day long. During the day the student was supposed to pursue a study of at least four major fields and then to carry the pattern of work of all four home with him to guide his thinking during study at night.

A number of educators became convinced that, with this constant shifting from one field to another, students really did not have the opportunity to study and move ahead as they should. They believed that it was impossible to turn interest on and off as quickly as the schedule demanded. As a result, they established larger blocks of time with one teacher and reduced the number of different courses per day.

An additional factor motivated the establishing of a larger block of time with one teacher. It was a way of decreasing the teacher's pupil load. When a teacher was expected to meet one hundred fifty to two hundred students a day and to know the problems and progress of each one and how to help him, the task was impossible. By increasing the length of periods and thereby reducing the number of students that a single teacher meets during the day, it became possible for a teacher to teach more in terms of individual needs and purposes.

The larger block of time in the school day has been achieved in several ways. One method is to schedule the same teacher to teach two separate subject-matter courses to the same group of students. For example, the same teacher might teach the same students English and social studies or mathematics and science. Even though the teacher keeps the organization of the two content fields separate, the same group of students stays with him, and there is opportunity for transition from one topic to another if the teacher and the class plan it. If a teacher becomes more accustomed to working in longer blocks of time, he can turn to what has been called an integrated course, in which he does not try to keep English and social studies as separate as he has before. When he finds occasions where the two fields parallel each other, he has the class work both periods on activities that involve using content from both fields.

Another type of large block scheduling is the organization of core curriculum classes utilizing two or more periods of the school day. In the core the students and the teacher study topics that call for use of content from many organized fields of subject matter. Emphasis is placed on teacher-pupil planning, teacher-pupil execution of plans, and teacher-pupil evaluation.

Another approach to the problem of providing for more satisfactory teaching-learning situations has been attempted by team-teaching. Some schools have assigned three teachers of different fields to work in consecutive periods with the same three classes. These teachers, assigned the same planning period in their daily schedule, have been given responsibility for knowing well the seventy-five to ninety pupils in the three sections and guiding their total program.

During the early sixties, another effort at team-teaching has been to provide a master teacher and some assistants who provide a program for a large group of students in a single period. Individual teachers make presentation to the total group, and the members of the total teaching team work with small segments of the block of students in discussion and work periods. The purpose is to provide quality presentations and to create more flexibility in providing for individual needs.

Preliminary efforts are underway, too, in developing flexible schedules. Some periods are eighty to ninety minutes in length; others are as short as thirty. No widely accepted technique has emerged, but experimentation is being done.

Teaching by television is being tried. It is assumed that presentation of subject matter by master teachers to large groups is more effective than teaching-learning situations with a low pupil-teacher ratio where the teacher is not as well prepared. Results indicate that as many facts can be taught by a television teacher to a large group as by a teacher in a typical classroom, but no evidence is yet available concerning the relative effectiveness of television teaching in promoting other types of growth that may be considered important.

Some schools have attempted to provide for greater individualization of programs. They have reduced the number of courses that are required of all students. It has been common practice to require approximately three-fourths of the courses that a student takes. In some states the state department has specified that certain units of credit must be in every student's program in order to receive a high school certificate. In other cases the local board of education or the local school faculty have made certain required courses in designated fields a prerequisite for graduation. With the past few years there has been a growing concern about too much regimentation and an increasing recognition that too much requiring of all students to take the same courses has resulted in a high school curriculum that has not been good for all students. Because of the variety of student needs, it was felt by the ASCD Commission on Education of Adolescents that the most suitable curriculum is one in which a student, his parents, and his counselor can tailor-make the program for an individual by selecting from the total offering of the school (see *The High School We Need*).

The Advanced Placement Program was initiated in 1953 to enable the exceptionally able, college-bound high school student to pursue courses of college-level difficulty in his high school under his regular teachers. A student in a cooperating high school may take any one of eleven subjects (English, Mathematics, French, German, Spanish, Latin, American History, European History, Biology, Chemistry, and Physics) and take an examination administered by the College Entrance Board. If he is successful on the examination and his high school recommends it, the student is eligible for college credit in the field. The high school is free under the program to handle the Advanced Placement work in any manner it deems desirable. The plan has spread since its inception and is one way in which schools are trying to provide for individual differences in student ability (see Copley, *The American High School and the Talented Student*).

STUDENT ACTIVITIES

Centerville places a heavy emphasis on exhibition activities. It has a strong interscholastic athletic program; its teams are winners. It has a marching band, a chorus, special ensembles, an orchestra. Its productions include class plays, concerts, and speech contests.

The club and intramural programs are weak. Less than half of the student body engages in intramural activities, and the club participation follows the social class system of the school, with pupils from the lower social groups abstaining. The physical education staff is insufficient to staff both interscholastic and intramural, and the intramural suffers. Wherever possible teachers avoid club sponsorship unless it is a club that supplements their class work.

The student government is excellent. Students who are elected are given leadership training, and government activities are included in their schedules. A large number of high schools are placing more emphasis on student government. They serve as channels through which the student body can assume greater responsibility for life within the school. In schools where student government has worked well, the areas in which students may make decisions have been clearly defined, and they know they must live with their own decisions. Faculty sponsorship for the student government has restricted itself to ways of attacking problems instead of telling students what should be done.

Many schools recognize that the development of democratic skills comes through practicing them, and that student activities constitute an area in which democratic skills can be exercised. Activities also have been seen as possible situations in which more pupils can have success experiences. The greater the range of available activities, the more opportunity there is for a wider variety of students to exert leadership. As the activities program has developed, it has spread in some schools beyond clubs, publications, sports, and social activities to community improvement projects and cooperation with community enterprises.

SUMMARY

The school described in this chapter was selected because it is representative of accredited high schools throughout the United States. The examination of its strengths and weaknesses has been an attempt to clarify the task confronting those who wish to improve secondary education.

SELECTED READINGS

Alexander, William M. and Galen Saylor, *Modern Secondary Education,* Chapter 9. New York: Holt, Rinehart & Winston, Inc., 1959. Outlines the curricula most commonly found in high schools today.

Association for Supervision and Curriculum Development, *What Shall the High Schools Teach?* (1956 Yearbook), Chapter 3. Washington, D. C.: The Association, 1956. Outlines, in general terms, the courses of study found in the "typical" high school.

Bossing, Nelson, *Principles of Secondary Education,* 2nd ed., Chapter 9. Englewood Cliffs, N. J.: Prentice-Hall, Inc., 1955. Describes the present status of the secondary school.

Brink, William G., "Patterns of Curriculum Organization in Large Secondary Schools," *School Review* 63: 372-377, October, 1955. Outlines the basic types of curriculum organization, requirements for graduation, and courses offered.

——, "Secondary Education—Programs" in *Encyclopedia of Educational Research,* Chester W. Harris, ed., 3rd ed., pp. 1259-1272. New York: The Macmillan Co., 1960. Describes the range of present programs offered by secondary schools.

Conant, James B., *The American High School Today.* New York: McGraw-Hill Book Co., Inc., 1959. Examines the curricula of American high schools, with recommendations for improvement.

——, *Slums and Suburbs.* New York: McGraw-Hill Book Co., Inc., 1961. Reports on the status of selected secondary schools in both impoverished and wealthy metropolitan areas.

Copley, Frank, *The American High School and the Talented Student,* Ann Arbor, Mich.: University of Michigan Press, 1961. Presents the Advanced Placement Program.

Hovet, Kenneth, "What Are the High Schools Teaching?" in *What Shall the High Schools Teach?, op. cit.,* pp. 69-96. Presents a broad overview of the range and scope of courses being taught in secondary schools.

Keller, Robert J., "Secondary Education—Organization and Administration" in *Encyclopedia of Educational Research, op. cit.,* pp. 1241-1259. Reviews the organizational and administrative aspects of secondary education.

Krug, Edward A., Clifford S. Liddle, and Quentin Schenk, *Multiple-Period Curricular Organization in Wisconsin Secondary Schools.* Madison, Wis.: School of Education, University of Wisconsin, 1952. Reports a survey study of multiple-period classes, grades seven through twelve, in Wisconsin schools in 1950-1951.

McWilliams, Earl M., *A Survey of the Opinions of Pittsburgh Senior High School Teachers on the Aims and Objectives of Secondary Education.* Doctor's thesis. Pittsburgh, Pa.: University of Pittsburgh, 1955. Abstract: *Dissertation Abstracts* 15: 755-756, No. 5, 1955. Reveals that teacher opinions are often at variance with both educational theory and research.

Morris, J. R., "Contemporary Secondary-School Curricular Patterns," *National Association of Secondary School Principals Bulletin* 44: 74-78, October, 1960. Describes and discusses briefly the types and kinds of curricular organization found in American secondary schools.

National Society of the Study of Education, *Integration of Educational Experiences* (Fifty-seventh Yearbook), Part III, Chapter 10. Chicago, Ill.: The Society, 1958. Presents an outline of various courses and programs of selected secondary schools.

Schreiber, D., "Identifying and Developing Able Students from Less Privileged Groups," *High Points* 40: 5-23, December, 1958. Reports results of experiments in relating courses and opportunities offered to students' psychological and economic environment.

Sturges, A. W., "The High School Schedule in Midwestern Secondary Schools," *Journal of Educational Research* 55: 64-70, October, 1961. Describes the daily and weekly schedule of secondary schools in Illinois, Iowa, Minnesota, Missouri, and Wisconsin.

Thomas, Harrison C., "The High School as a Common School," *School Review* 63: 214-219, April, 1955. Discusses the role of the school as it serves "all the children of all the people."

Umstattd, J. G. and Robert D. Thornton, "Secondary Education—Student Population" in *Encyclopedia of Educational Research, op. cit.,* pp. 1272-1282. Describes the student population of the secondary schools.

Van Til, William, G. F. Vars, and John H. Founsbury, *Modern Education for the Junior High School Years,* Chapter 3. Indianapolis, Ind.: Bobbs-Merrill Co., Inc., 1961. Describes various programs, policies, and practices of junior high schools in the 1950's.

Wiles, Kimball and Franklin Patterson, *The High School We Need.* Washington, D. C.: The Association for Supervision and Curriculum Development, 1959. Reports the conclusions of the Association's Commission on the Education of Adolescents.

Wright, Grace S., *Block-Time Classes and the Core Program in the Junior High School*, U. S. Department of Health, Education, and Welfare, Office of Education, Bulletin No. 6, 1958. Washington, D. C.: Superintendent of Documents, U. S. Government Printing Office, 1958. Outlines the extent and characteristics of block-time classes and their relationship to core programs.

———, *Requirements for High School Graduation in States and Large Cities*, U. S. Department of Health, Education and Welfare, Office of Education, Bulletin No. 12, 1961. Washington, D. C.; Superintendent of Documents, U. S. Government Printing Office, 1961. Reports the subjects and units required for graduation in the fifty states and selected large cities.

———, "Trends in High-School Graduation Requirements at the State Level," *School Review* 64: 178-180, April, 1956. Outlines the elective and subject requirements commonly found among the states.

II
ELEMENTS OF
THE CURRICULUM

From an image of the desired, it is necessary to develop the specifics of implementation. This step consists of pulling together from many schools practices that seem to coincide with this image and of integrating them into a coordinated plan of operation. The model produced may not be satisfying to all. It should be tested against the experience and insight of the evaluator and modifications made on the basis of a wider range of alternatives or evidence of greater effectiveness of other procedures.

6

THE COURSES
IN THE CURRICULUM

The courses offered constitute the skeleton around which
the rest of the curriculum is organized. Community environment,
buildings and grounds, administration, nonclass facilities and
activities, guidance, and methods are all integral parts of the
curriculum. But the most essential element of a secondary
school is an offering of courses suitable for the students who
attend the school and organized to make it possible for each
student to select from the total number of classes those that
will best develop his abilities, promote his purposes, and make
him the most effective citizen possible.

WIDE RANGE OF COURSES

The secondary school
should offer a wide range of classes from which the
students may choose. As the student body attending secondary
schools has become more representative of the total population
(over eighty per cent of all youth in the age group), it has

109

become necessary to provide a diversity of offering if each student is to find courses that will benefit him and his society. No one who has worked with the range of abilities and purposes of students attending secondary school or has made a realistic study of the situation can assume that all youth will profit by the same program of mathematics, foreign language, science, social studies, and English. If the capacities of all youth are to be developed, the course offerings of the secondary school should be as comprehensive as are the educational needs of the society which supports it. Although financial limitations and population distribution may make this goal unobtainable for a given school, the direction of possible change should be determined by this guidepost.

The courses of the secondary school should be divided into two categories: general education courses and specialized courses. The general education courses should be those designed to provide the knowledge and skills essential for effective citizenship and family membership. The specialized courses should be much more numerous and include all those that any student may choose to further a vocational goal or to develop an avocational interest.

GENERAL EDUCATION REQUIRED FOR ALL

The secondary school in America is confronted with two fundamental tasks: to develop contributing members of the social group and to assist the individual to cultivate his unique potentialities. Sometimes the two purposes may seem to be in conflict. The emphasis is always subject to debate. But most people will agree that schools maintained by a society must produce citizens who will preserve and improve the society. The segment of education designed to help the individual become an effective participant in the social organization is called general education.

Although many definitions have been advanced, the most useful classifies as general education the elements of the school program that are of such importance that all youth growing up in the United States should become acquainted with them. Agreement that the secondary school should help each boy and girl become acquainted with the essential features of the culture is easy to reach, but the execution of the task is not. What is that central core of the culture that all pupils should acquire? Who decides?

Determining the Content of General Education

One approach that has been made to this problem is legislation stating that certain information must be taught. Sometimes state legislatures have passed laws which required the teaching of certain areas of content, such as conservation, safety education, and alcohol education, and in other states the state department of education has passed regulations which require all schools to teach certain content. In either case, the governmental bodies decided what was essential for all to study.

A second way in which the core of the culture has been determined has been by the decisions of scholars or organizations of scholars in a particular field. Needless to say, complete agreement has not been reached by the scholars on the basic body of content. Representatives of a particular scholastic field are prone to choose the knowledge that they know as the most essential core of the culture. A musician and an historian, for example, differ in their choice of items to be identified as the essence of our culture.

A third method that has been used in selecting the core content is to have representatives of different subject-matter fields work together as a team to try to reach agreement on the essence of the culture. Under this procedure the special prejudices and knowledges of representatives of a particular field are counterbalanced against those from other disciplines, and the content from a particular field is subjected to a more critical test.

Any attempt to identify the content that all students should have by any of the three preceding processes is not representative of the total population of the nation or of the community. The group that participates in the selection of content is a special segment of the population, either the scholars or the politicians. In either case they view the culture from a particular point of view that may not be held by other members of the society.

A fourth procedure that is being used increasingly in schools throughout America is a community approach. Representatives from the various community groups work together to decide upon the core of the culture essential for that community. An attempt is made to secure representatives of all social, racial, religious, economic, and political groups whose children attend the school to serve as members of the team that makes decisions concerning what should be included. Usually the lay group has been called an advisory committee on curriculum and in most cases restricts its decisions to selecting courses rather than specific content in a course. Many believe that this procedure will result in a more valid interpretation of the culture, because a variety of people who live and experience the culture from different positions and with different biases have a part in saying what is important. By providing an opportunity for persons from different segments of the culture to state what to them seems essential, a wider sampling is secured. By broadening the sample it is hoped that the validity of the selection will be increased.

All of the above approaches to deciding what shall be the content of general education put the teacher in the situation in which he has a body of content to communicate to students. The assumption is made in each case that it is possible to organize knowledge and insights for someone else, that because the teacher presents generalizations and facts in a certain way the student will perceive that information in the same way.

Research indicates that each individual perceives and interprets new facts and experiences in light of his purposes and his past experiences. If this be true, it is impossible for a teacher to communicate to someone what any individual or group has selected as general education content. It is necessary for the individual to experience by reading, hearing, seeing, or acting, and then interpreting for himself. The knowledge with which a student emerges from a class experience is his own interpretation and organization.

Persons who espouse this point of view propose for general education a class group identifying what to it seems to be important and then creatively formulating its own interpretation of the culture. As proponents of this approach to general education see it, the teacher works with a class in such a way that it shares purposes, concerns, experiences, and actions. Each pupil has his horizons broadened, and through class analysis of experiences many common perceptions are achieved. These common understandings and increased skill in investigation are seen as general education for the individual.

Many times when a group of teachers, supervisors, administrators, and parents begin to discuss how the content of general education shall be determined, all of these approaches underlie the statements of individuals in the group without being identified or recognized. Confusion results, and the discussion becomes unfruitful.

Cultural Unity Sought

One point is accepted by all who discuss curriculum: the general education portion of the curriculum must build cultural unity. The American people are a combination of many nationalities and cultures. The early settlers came from several Western European countries, and to this population during the years have come people from most of the countries of the earth. To the basic ideas around which the government was formed have been added a myriad of philosophical, religious, social, economic, and political ideas. Diversity has been valued and encouraged.

Although many benefits have come from this heterogeneity, a major problem has ensued. How can the best of the existing structure be maintained, while the treasure of the new is added? How can a people with such a variety of backgrounds acquire and maintain the unity that is necessary for a strong nation?

The schools have been assigned the task of developing the bonds of agreement that will keep the people together while the society profits from their differences. To perform this function for the nation the schools must develop a sense of belonging, commitment to some common values, and skill in living cooperatively in spite of difference. The task of general education is to fulfill these objectives and to develop both communication skills and an understanding of the basic concepts that an effective citizen must know.

METHODS OF PROVIDING GENERAL EDUCATION

Little agreement has existed as to how general education should be conducted. Some schools have required that all students take certain courses and call the required courses general education. Other schools have established courses called common learnings, core, broad fields, and integrated courses.

Required Courses

Most schools have referred to their required courses as general education, but in many cases little thought has been given to the content or organization to see whether they are appropriate. After the profession became concerned with the problem of general education, the easiest solution without serious study was to label the courses that had traditionally been required of all students "general education." Usually these courses have been English (three units), social studies (three units), science (two units), mathematics (one unit), and physical education (one unit). Neither the courses nor the content have been examined to see if they contain the elements of the culture which should be included in the experiences provided for all.

A hard, cutting definition of general education would eliminate at least a portion of the content of these courses. The subject matter thus deleted is worthwhile and important for many citizens but not essential for the effective functioning of all. If the required course approach to general education is to continue to be used, and it probably will be, the content should be carefully screened by the most competent and impartial members of the staff, the number of required units decreased to the minimum needed to cover the necessary material and experiences, and the remainder of the offering placed in the specialized portion of the curriculum.

Broad Field Courses

Some secondary schools have attempted to provide general education in broad field or integrated courses. In these courses, content has been selected from an area such as social studies, science, or humanities rather than from one separate discipline such as history or physics. Teachers have taken a topic such as family relationships and have gone to the fields of economics, history, sociology, home economics, and psychology, collecting information that they believe has a bearing upon the way in which families should live together. This knowledge was then organized into a unit in family living. By this collation of information from a number of fields it was hoped that students would gain a clearer understanding of family relationships, a concern of most individuals. As they studied the topic, students were not limited to the confines of a single field. It was believed that freedom to select information and research from several disciplines contributed to greater understanding of the problem or subject.

Some broad field courses in social studies, science, and humanities have used a different approach. The content has been organized around generalizations or principles that the persons preparing the course outline believed were supported by the content of the fields. The generalizations were agreed upon, and the content that supported them was incorporated into the course.

Under either broad field approach the pupil typically has played the role of examining and learning a body of preorganized information without having a part in its selection or organization. If he has not had previous experience with courses restricted to one discipline within a broad field, such as history in social studies, he has not seen the broad field courses as much different from his other school work.

Correlation of Content in Courses

Other schools have felt the need for an interdisciplinary approach to general education but have hesitated to leave the traditional course organization. They have attempted to correlate courses. They have taught their courses in such a way that recognition was given to the relationship between the information in one course and the information in other courses. For example, a person teaching the history of the Elizabethan period would describe to students the relationship of the historical facts to the writings of Shakespeare and Jonson. The literature teacher would have her work parallel the chronological development of English history and would be teaching about the works of Shakespeare and Jonson and pointing out the influence of historical events of the time upon their writing. It was hoped that students would make a greater integration of the information by this procedure than many had done in the past.

The attempts to produce broad field, correlated, and integrated courses have been thoughtful. Much planning and curriculum study have gone into the preparation of syllabi and materials. But the validity of their contribution to the general education of a citizen has not been ascertained.

Core

A more drastic approach to this problem of general education has been that taken by the advocates of the core curriculum. In some core courses, subject-matter lines were completely abandoned. The class activities centered around problems that were important in the lives of the members of the class. These problems may have been selected by the teacher, the teacher and the children, or the children themselves, depending upon the philosophy of the school. The method of studying these problems varied. The entire class might study a single problem, or each individual might be studying a different problem. That, too, depended upon the method and philosophy of the school. When a problem was selected, the class or the individual determined the information that would be necessary to solve it and then went to available sources, completely disregarding subject-matter lines, and collected the data needed.

The basic purpose of core work was to prepare the pupil to solve the problems of life. The most important aims were:

> to teach democratic ideals;
> to develop individuality;
> to teach the scientific method as the approach to the solution of problems;
> to help the pupil set up his own goals and work out a way to achieve them;
> to help the pupil use the factors of his environment to attain his purposes;
> to teach an effective method of using sources of recorded knowledge;
> to develop an individual whose behavior was consistent with his ideals;
> to teach the pupil to work independently;
> to teach the pupil to work in groups and to cooperate with others;
> to develop in the pupil the ability to establish purposes sufficiently strong to govern his actions over a long period of time;
> to help the pupil recognize his own needs.

Under the core approach, general education content has been viewed differently. Specific items of information were not important in themselves. Facts and principles were acquired and used in the solving of problems. Major emphasis was placed by the teacher on the development of the types of growth listed above. The general education that a citizen needs was conceived to be the acquisition and refinement of these qualities and skills.

Little evidence is available concerning the effectiveness of core in providing general education. Some studies have found that students who went through core acquired as much information as pupils who took the typical high school courses. But no follow-up studies, which would provide evidence of the citizenship contribution of those who have gone through core courses, have been reported.

THE BASIC CONFLICT IN PLANNING A PROGRAM OF GENERAL EDUCATION

In order to answer the problem of general education, it is necessary to look at what is known about the learning process. If the human being can be brought into contact with a certain set of facts and values and accept the interpretation given him by an instructor, the task of providing a common culture will not be too difficult. If, however, the individual selects and interprets for himself, the task requires a different approach. The Dartmouth Studies reported by Earl Kelley in *Education for What Is Real* offer evidence that human beings interpret symbols in terms of their past experiences. The same objects, the same words, the same actions on the part of a teacher may be interpreted in twenty-five different ways by twenty-five different pupils in the room. According to this evidence, it would seem to be impossible to give pupils something that they would all accept. It is only possible to create a situation in which an individual learns.

Learning comes from the inside out. Learning is a process of interaction between the individual and his environment and involves all of the individual's past experiences with similar symbols and all of the uses of the symbols which the individual projects into the future. The learner's interpretation of his experience with the symbol is colored by his past experience, the total environment in which his experience with the symbol occurs, and the future uses he sees for the symbol.

From the point of view of organismic or phenomenological psychologists, the old stimulus-response (S-R) bond theory was too simple. The illustration of the dog that began to drool every time he heard the bell ring (after he had become accustomed to receiving food when the bell was rung) left out many factors. For example, if another dog in the same room had received a beating every time he heard the bell ring, he would have begun to whimper and cringe as the bell rang. If a third dog had been beaten and had food provided each time the bell rang, what would he do? The same symbol would have led to a different reaction on the part of each dog to his total environment—past, present, and projected future. Learning occurs through interaction with the environment and results in establishing new, different ways of interacting with that environment.

But the stimuli for the human are complex. If the learner cannot be given a fact or formula or a way of interacting with his environment, it is impossible to integrate subject matter for him. Each individual conducts his own integration of new experiences with his previous ones.

As described earlier, many schools and teachers have attempted to achieve a more functional organization of knowledge for the learner by predigesting facts and formulas into some type of arrangement which seems to be logical for the person making the organization. They have felt that by this process of correlating facts from several of the organized fields of knowledge and giving their combinations to the learner it was possible to provide a more desirable learning experience. In the opinion of some psychologists, the experience was most beneficial for the person making the reorganization of the subject matter. In the process of interacting with the facts that he was attempting to organize, he developed a new structure of knowledge for his own use. He began to see relationships that he had not seen before. From the phenomenological interpretation of learning, the facts appeared as unrelated to the student as though the scholar had not played around with them. Organization of new knowledge into the previously known can come only from within. It cannot be provided by someone on the outside.

In an attempt to provide better general education, some schools have moved to a longer period of time that teachers spend with a given group of students. This method is certainly open to question if the phenomenological point of view about learning is accepted. If the teacher is attempting to give certain preorganized facts, the experience is no more valid as a learning situation than if students had taken up separate subject-matter fields in separate periods. Longer blocks of time with the same teacher result in more effective learning situations only if the teacher operates the class in such a way that students have a chance to play a greater part in organizing and directing the learning situation or through the teacher knowing a student better and becoming better able to guide him.

Individuals learn as they develop more effective ways of interacting with the environment. Learning is an active process. It consists of facing something in our environment that creates a tension and of seeking ways to resolve that tension. In school a learning situation is created as the teacher develops a situation in which students come to feel tensions in the environment and seek ways of resolving them.

Some teachers have conceived of teaching as telling youngsters a series of facts which the youngsters did not want to know. The facts did not fill a felt need of the youngster or resolve a tension. The only way that teachers in such a situation were able to create a tension that the youngster wanted to resolve was by artifically establishing marks which created a disturbance in the youngster's environment. As the youngster sought to achieve the type of mark that would satisfactorily relieve the tension in his environment, he incidentally acquired certain facts and formulas. In the course of such an experience some youngsters acquired a purpose, such as graduation from school or from college, which created enough of a tension so that there was a drive to learn the necessary facts and figures to achieve the diploma desired. Such learning of facts as occurred incidentally was in most cases artificial and inefficient. It is not to be wondered at that cheating and getting by as easily as possible became the primary modes of behavior in such a situation.

From the point of view that learning consists of developing more effective ways of interacting with the environment, the common learning question becomes quite simple. The common learnings that a person in our society needs are the ways of effectively interacting within a democratic environment. They boil down to such simple things as being able to define problems; being able to collect data; being able to interpret data and to draw conclusions; being able to take action to implement the conclusions; being able to work cooperatively with others in organizing, planning, and executing a course of action; being able to evaluate the effectiveness of the procedures used and to formulate revisions for more efficient ways of working; being able to abstract from the experiences one has the values that promote the welfare of the individual and the group; being able to act consistently with the values that one holds and to reformulate values as necessary. All of these are essential for more effective interaction with an environment of constant change and conflict. They are essential for a youngster regardless of whether he is going to be a ditch-digger or a college professor. These skills, together with reading, writing, and arithmetic, constitute the common learnings that a member of our society must have.

It does not matter whether the curriculum is organized so that one subject is merged with another. The important feature is the way in which the experiences that a student has in school are conducted. If school is conducted in such a way that students have an opportunity to identify their problems, to collect data to solve them, to formulate hypotheses, to check the hypotheses in action, to evaluate the success of the procedures used, and to reformulate hypotheses and test again, the student will develop these common learnings. He can be carrying on this course of action in a class in home economics or a class in business ethics. The success of the general education program will be judged by how well these common learnings are achieved. As for subject matter, such facts and formulas as are picked up incidentally will be regarded as incidental learning. They are valuable, but they are not essential. They are individualized information whose nature is determined by the type of interaction that the student has had with these facts and formulas while he has been developing the common learnings.

But the issue is not settled. Agreement concerning the most desirable procedure has not been reached. Advocates of a more behavioristic approach to learning point to a different method of selection and organization of subject matter for general education. They believe that any subject can be taught effectively in some intellectual form to any child at any stage of development; that the individual at each stage of development has a characteristic way of viewing the world and explaining it to himself; that the teacher for any age child can present the structure of a subject in terms of the child's way of viewing things; that learning is a process of acquisition, transformation, and evaluation, and that pupils of all ages can be taken through these steps by adequate external motivation; that the curriculum should be built around the great issues and values that a society deems worthy of the continual concern of its members; that massive transfer of training can and does occur if the learner has acquired the structure and method of a discipline. (Based on statements in Bruner's *The Process of Education*.)

If those planning general education accept this viewpoint, they make an analysis of the cultural heritage to determine the basic principles that they deem it important for all to know and then proceed to develop a program that will present their organization of mankind's accumulation of basic knowledge. The emphasis is upon devising and sharing a functional structure of knowledge rather than upon the student's perceptions and concerns. It should be noted that the groups working on mathematics and science programs with the support of the National Science Foundation seem to follow this approach. They are attempting to decide upon the basic principles, concepts, and ways of investigation in a discipline (mathematics, biology, chemistry, physics) and to prepare in each field a course of study that will present the structure of knowledge and the methods of inquiry that are used to increase the known in that field.

The general education program provided will be determined by the belief of the faculty concerning the learning process. If it is thought that students can be taught a certain interpretation of the culture, the approach will be through an analysis of our society, its past, its institutions, its aspirations, and its processes. If it is accepted that pupils make their own interpretations and organization, the planning will deal with ways of helping a pupil study some phase of the culture as a means of acquiring skill in problem-solving and social action.

VOCATIONAL EDUCATION FOR ALL

Every pupil's program should contain certain courses that are designated as vocational courses for him. Since 1918 the responsibility of the secondary school to provide this vocational education has been recognized. In that year the Seven Cardinal Principles, as listed by the Committee on the Reorganization of Secondary Education, included vocational efficiency, and the Smith-Hughes Act (1917) provided federal support for vocational education in high schools. But there has been lack of preciseness in the definition of vocational education. The national government has underwritten home economics, agriculture, trade, and industrial and distributive education but has not provided funds for business education or industrial arts. Before any decision can be made concerning ways to provide vocational education, it is necessary to examine the meaning of the term.

Vocational education has a variety of meanings to educators in the American secondary schools. Some teachers are classified as vocational education teachers, operate under special regulations, and are very certain that their courses constitute vocational training. Other teachers operate courses which are designed to prepare students for specific occupations, but they are not classified as vocational education teachers. Many teachers offer courses which students choose because they wish to develop a competency that will be of use in a particular profession, but the teachers resent and resist being considered vocational education teachers. Some schools offer a vocational curriculum but prepare more students for post-high school jobs in a commercial curriculum. The vocational preparation that the majority of American citizens obtain is in the regular high schools. A number of school systems have established vocational high schools, but only a small segment of the youth attend them. It is time for those planning secondary school curricula to cut to the heart of the problem and redefine vocational education, even though in the process many current beliefs and prejudices will be challenged.

The definition should be very simple. *Courses used by a student to prepare for an occupation should be considered vocational education.* The difficulty has arisen when attempts have been made to classify courses on the basis of jobs rather than student goals. Training programs for a few occupations in agriculture, business, and industry have been prepared, and these have been designated as vocational. What about the thousands of other jobs that American youth will enter? They, too, are vocations. The courses in which youth develop competencies to use in these positions are vocational also. It is obviously impossible to start with the jobs and prepare and present training programs leading to each without endless duplication. The only feasible way to start classification of courses as vocational is in terms of the purposes of the pupil and to so classify them on the individual's program rather than in the curricular organization of the school.

A number of high school faculties have created difficulties for themselves and their students by confusing general with vocational education. They have made the mistake of assuming that a course required for college entrance has a general education value and, operating on this false assumption, have required that all students consider the college entrance prerequisites as general education. By recognizing that certain courses required for college entrance are primarily vocational courses, a faculty is free to develop a general education program that is suitable for all students (a program designed to prepare for citizenship, cultural insight, and family membership) and to plan vocational courses on an individual basis (with courses selected by the student with the guidance of his parents and his counselor).

Much is done to clarify the meaning of vocational education when general education is defined as courses required for all students, designed to develop the skills, attitudes, and knowledge needed for citizenship or family membership. For example, courses dealing with local, state, national, and international affairs, communication, health, human growth and development, and family living would fall within the general education category. All other courses would be vocational or avocational and not required of any student.

Vocational education for a given student consists of the courses that a student chooses to further his vocational objectives. For some boys the courses may be plumbing, woodwork, or salesmanship. For some girls, typing, homemaking, or shorthand may be preparation for life work. In these examples the classification is easy. But the distinction has not been widely recognized when advanced algebra or second-year French are considered. Although most pupils who enroll in these courses are planning to go to college and take these offerings to meet college entrance requirements or because of counselor advice that such courses constitute good preparation for college work, the courses have not been labeled vocational. They should be for those students.

Under this approach, *vocational education should be a required part of each pupil's program but planned individually to meet his purposes.* The only basis for decision as to whether a given course is vocational education would be the way in which a student uses it. Some students choose French as a college prerequisite, while other pupils in the same class are taking the course as an elective for personal satisfaction. The same art course may be taken as preparation for a career as a cartoonist by one boy and for fun by another because he likes to paint. A student not heading for a career as a secretary may select typing as an elective; a student not planning to farm may select agriculture as an elective. Under this concept of vocational education, the curriculum is divided into two major sections—general education and specialization. Specialization consists of vocational and elective courses.

If this concept of vocational education were accepted much of the bickering and argument that have developed between vocational and general education people would be eliminated. Teachers of required general education courses would become clearer in their purposes and could concentrate on developing citizenship and home membership skills without feeling guilty about not covering certain academic work. Teachers of specialized courses, vocational or avocational, could put primary emphasis on developing competency in that particular area.

Each faculty needs to think through this issue. It must accept its responsibility for providing vocational education for each student. If the definition of vocational education proposed above is not accepted, a functional substitute must be developed and a method for implementing it established. Secondary schools will continue to fail in one of their major functions if their faculties continue to think of vocational education as the experiences provided for the ten per cent who elect the vocational curriculum.

THE OFFERING IN VOCATIONAL EDUCATION

Since the range of vocational choices is so great, it is impossible for any high school to offer specific vocational education in every field. The basic plan must be to offer a wide variety of courses from which selections can be made by the individual to form a pattern of competencies usable for entrance into the vocational field chosen.

Although at first glance this plan seems inadequate, it is supported by the position taken by many industries that have their own training programs. They prefer to develop the specific skills needed for a particular job, training the employee to use the company's methods and techniques. They want the schools to provide the basic skills and understandings necessary for work in the field but not to concentrate on details of technical operation.

To insure an adequate vocational education the faculty should examine its offerings and students' programs. Are they broad enough? Do the courses sample many fields? Do students make a variety of choices? Do the patterns of students' programs vary, or do most follow three or four typical plans? A wide offering is meaningless unless student choice is free enough so that many program patterns are possible—and used.

For the major portion of the student body the vocational education will consist of individual choices made from a wide range of offerings. To facilitate the practice, the student should not be restricted by being forced to choose a specific curriculum (academic, vocational, commercial, general). Except for a small number, not more than one-third, of required general education courses, he should be able to form an individual curriculum.

For a small portion of the student body special prevocational training should be made available. The national vocational education programs (Trade and Industrial Education, Distributive Education, Vocational Agriculture, and Vocational Homemaking), should be continued and expanded. But they should not be expected to care for the needs of the total student body. They should be available for the students who have made definite vocational choices in these fields. They should not be considered dumping grounds for students who cannot be successful in other programs. Neither should they be privileged fields, draining all the support and funds for vocational education from other segments of the curriculum. They should be seen in proper perspective as one of the types of vocational education the school supplies.

The students enrolling in the special vocational education programs should not be segregated from the remainder of the students. At least the general education courses should be taken with students following other types of programs. Unless the special vocational students receive a portion of their high school program with the other students, there is a danger of their not feeling a part of the total social group. If educators provide a separate program, usually for those with less social status, the youth in special vocational education program will not learn to work with, to understand, and to communicate with other population groups.

Experience has also shown that the special vocational education group should not be put in separate schools. If the total program is kept within one school, the individual student has a wider range of classes and activities from which to choose. Separation of this type denies students the opportunity to learn to live socially with a wide range of population groups. Usually the separated vocational group has a less adequate social and activities program—even though these youth may need it most.

In 1950 the State of Connecticut had ten regional vocational high schools. Only one out of ten staffs listed worthy use of leisure time as a major objective. Only three out of ten named social competency. In the ten schools:

Ten offered interscholastic athletics;
Ten offered intramural athletics;
Eight had student councils;
Seven had school dances;
Six had clubs;
Four had yearbooks;
Four had glee clubs or choruses;
Three had a school paper;
Two had a band or orchestra;
One had dramatics.

In the schools with the activities, pupil participation was low:

Thirty-three per cent participated in school clubs;
Thirty-one per cent attended school dances;
Twenty-eight per cent engaged in intramural athletics;
Twenty-two per cent participated in interscholastic athletics;

Fifteen per cent served on student councils;
Four per cent were in dramatics;
Three per cent sang in glee clubs;
Three per cent played in bands or orchestras;
Two per cent worked on yearbooks.

Both the opportunity and the participation were much less than in comprehensive high schools in the same state in the same year.

The drop-out rate in the vocational schools was much higher than in other high schools. Only three out of ten entering freshmen graduated, as compared with seven out of ten in the comprehensive high schools. Obviously, if these conditions are typical, and they seem to be, separate vocational high schools are not the way to provide the best vocational education.

Vocational education should be considered an integral part of the secondary education curriculum and of the program of each student. Planning for vocational education should be a curriculum problem of every faculty and the concern of each student in making his individual course selection.

RELATIONSHIP OF VOCATIONAL EDUCATION TO THE COMMUNITY

Vocational education can no longer be planned solely in terms of the community in which a high school exists. Over half of the average school's graduates will migrate to another community, and many will go to another state. Seemingly the wisest step for curriculum planners to take, then, is to study industrial and commercial operations and plan in terms of clusters of competencies. When a student has developed a particular set of abilities he may enter a variety of related occupations.

Few industries expect or want the schools to provide training for their specific occupations. Most industries take the position that they want the school to provide a worker with a background of cultural and citizenship education and with the attitudes which lead him to be industrious and willing to give value returned for salaries paid. They believe that each industry itself should do the specific type of training that is necessary for the operation of the machines and the specific work techniques that the individual will need.

An example of one of the fundamental competencies schools should attempt to provide is ability to get along with people. When studies of causes of employee terminations are examined it is evident that vocational success depends upon this. In one study involving ten thousand cases, over eighty per cent of the dismissals were due to inability to work harmoniously with others. Thus it would seem appropriate to recognize that work in human relations, communications, leadership, and group living constitute fundamental vocational education, once again illustrating the difficulty of distinguishing between general and vocational education.

Community Planning

Any approach to planning vocational education must be communitywide. Sometimes in the past, educators have felt that industry is the major community group with an interest in vocational education. But this point of view is not true in most communities. Labor, too, is concerned with the secondary school program. They state that the school should do more than it has done to date to acquaint students with the labor movement and the place of the worker in the labor market. They feel that a high percentage of the high school teaching staff does not fully understand labor's point of view and fails to give labor's economic interpretation of the current scene.

Both industry and labor want the school to give the student a fair objective analysis of labor-management relationships. Social studies teachers in particular recognize the difficulty of obtaining an analysis that both groups would agree is fair. The difference in the viewpoints held by management and labor makes this ideal hard to fulfill. Only with joint planning and evaluation is it likely to be reached.

The task of developing cooperative planning with the two groups has been made easier by the activities of such national agencies as the Joint Council for Economic Education. This and other groups have demonstrated a way of thinking and planning together to produce a better secondary school program in economic education that can be adapted to local communities.

High schools should give serious consideration to the formation of lay vocational education advisory committees comprised of management, labor, and other groups in the community with a special interest in economic and vocational education. Administrations and faculties will find it profitable to have these groups assist with the evaluation of the present program and the projection of needed improvements. If the community has a concentration of certain types of occupations, the secondary school will have a special responsibility for vocational education designed to prepare workers for the field. When this condition is present, it is advisable to form special curriculum advisory committees for each field, which will contain representatives of management, labor, and craftsmen who can define the kind of competencies needed and assist in planning the type of vocational experiences the school should provide for persons hoping to enter that occupation.

The in-service program should also be oriented to improve the adequacy of teachers to conduct the vocational education program. Many communities have inaugurated Business-Education Days. One day a year the teachers spend a day in a cooperating business or industry of their choice. On another day representatives of the cooperating concerns spend a day in the schools. By the process each gains more understanding of the operation and problems of the other. Institutions of higher learning are providing graduate courses designed to give teachers more experience in the vocations for which they prepare workers. For example, one university offers a laboratory course for Business Education teachers in which they spend the summer working in business firms and hold biweekly seminars where they examine the implications of their experience for the curriculum of the schools in which they work.

Vocational education is a community enterprise, and the secondary school staff must take the lead in bringing about cooperative planning of it.

Work Experience

A recent development in vocational education has been the provision of work experience for high school youth. The ideal sought is to provide work experience for every student, but few high schools have yet reached this goal. Most schools with special vocational education programs have actual work experiences for some students enrolled in the program. For example, students in most Distributive Education programs spend half of their time on the job. Their work program is designed to do three things: to help them gain an understanding of the value and necessity of work, to develop a sense of responsibility to the group, and to provide an opportunity for vocational tryouts.

In some schools work experience is sought as a part of the program of all youth and is not confined to those who are using the high school as a prevocational experience. Perhaps its greatest value is for

129

the children of families who do not have any compulsion to work or who regard manual work as beneath their dignity. It is hoped that through participating in a work experience as a part of the high school program the student will gain a greater appreciation of those who contribute manual effort.

Work experience may occur in the camp program, in the summer activities planned by the school, or in projects in the community or on the campus. It may be as a part of a school work day, or it may be through voluntary work to beautify the school grounds. In any case it should be a situation in which the teacher works with the student. Attitudes toward work will be taught by the teacher's participation. If the teacher avoids the work situation students, too, will seek ways of avoiding it. If the teacher works with the students in carrying out the project the work activities will be looked upon as important and worth the effort of all members of the group, regardless of the status they feel they have.

In schools in which the work program is being tried it is considered a fundamental part of the vocational education of the student body. Its promise has been greater than its fulfillment to date, but it deserves further experimentation.

A DIFFERENT PROGRAM FOR EACH STUDENT

The program of courses taken by each student should be one planned for him. It should be uniquely his as a tailored suit. The only element of the curriculum suitable for every student's program is general education, and it should be less than half of the total class load taken by the student. The remainder of the classes programed for a student should be chosen in terms of his purposes, his achievements, his needs, and his abilities, and should be specialization designed to promote his uniqueness and his special competencies. This part of his program should contain vocational and avocational courses. Courses that enable the student to move toward his vocational goal will be classified as vocational; those chosen because of his interests will be listed as avocational. The way a given course should be classified on a student's program depends upon the way he proposes to use it. Thus the same course might be listed on one student's program as vocational and on another's as avocational.

Individualization of program also requires that grade placement of courses other than general education courses be modified. Any specialization course should be available to a student for any year of his program if he is ready for it in terms of achievement and purpose. For example, a boy with a strong background in mathematics and science might take physics or chemistry as a ninth-grader, or a girl with advanced reading ability and a deep interest in literature would be permitted to take a twelfth-grade course in American literature as a tenth-grader. The selection of courses would be made by the student, his parents, and his counselor in terms of his purposes, his level of achievement, and the intensity of his purposes.

It is obvious that the purpose of such program planning is to increase the differences in levels of achievement of each chronological age group. It is a procedure designed to provide more adequately for the gifted and the slow learner. It moves away from the assumption that some magic exists in keeping pupils of the same age together. If any assumption has interfered more with developing the potential of all pupils than the assumption that certain material should be studied by all fifth grade students, or tenth grade students, it would be hard to identify. Why is biology better for tenth grade students than for eleventh grade students? Why should algebra be considered a ninth grade course?

Students grow and develop at different rates. By the time some enter high school they are reading at college level. Others, through travel, home background, or other experiences, have acquired information and competency in special fields. Some have already built their own television sets and rockets. Some are in the theatre. To develop the potential of each requires that the school make the selection of courses as flexible as possible. Any elective course should be available to any qualified student, regardless of his grade level.

The program for each student should be planned for him. No two students are alike. The youth in secondary schools do not fall into four categories that can be labeled academic, vocational, commercial, and general. Establishing four curricula, given these or other names, and placing each student in one classification or the other is not the answer.

At the end of the eighth grade each pupil, with his parents and counselor, should plan a four-year program from the offerings of the school. The courses for each year should be listed. With the exception of the courses required of all students, the program should be established in terms of the purposes, achievements, and abilities of the student. But the choices made at the end of the eighth grade should not be binding for more than one year. Each pupil, with the advice and consent of his parents and counselor, should be able to change his program each year without penalty. One of the difficulties that has been encountered in establishing four separate curricula in the high school and requiring students to follow one of them is that a student started in one is penalized if he transfers to another. If his vocational goals change and he tries to shift to another, he is forced to take additional units in order to meet graduation requirements. The difficulty of transfer to a different curriculum increases as the student progresses through school. If, however, each student has an individual program planned in terms of his needs and purposes, he can change it as his needs and purposes change. At the end of his first semester in the ninth grade and at the end of each year as he progresses through the school his program should be revised through the joint planning of the pupil, his parents, and a teacher. If he has changed his goals or he has not attained the level of achievement that will enable him to be successful in the courses previously planned for the following year, his program should be modified. Thus each student not only has a program that is planned for him, but one that is revised, at least annually, in terms of his changing needs. No decision is capricious; each is based on the best judgment of pupil, parents, and teacher.

The administrative routine involved in planning individual programs is no greater than the typical practice of classifying by curriculum (general, academic, commercial, or vocational) and seeing that each student follows the appropriate curriculum. The preparation of an individual program calls for a planning conference with a teacher or counselor at the end of the eighth grade, first semester of the ninth grade, and the end of the ninth, tenth, and eleventh grades. All of these interviews would be necessary under a pattern of programing by curriculum.

The form used in the P. K. Yonge High School in Gainesville, Florida, for cooperative planning is shown on page 132. Note the provision for total program planning and for yearly revision with the approval of the parents and counselor. A few days prior to the student-counselor interview at the end of the ninth grade, the pupil takes his program home. In light of his progress, his changed goals, his new interests, and his chances of success under the existing program, the program is revised for the next three years or continued in its original form. The parent-student revision is taken back to school and the student-counselor interview occurs. The counselor approves the revision, or a three-way parent-pupil-counselor conference is held to decide what is best. The process is repeated at the end of the tenth and eleventh years. As vocational goals shift, the courses necessary for entrance to a job or advanced education change, and the student's program is revised accordingly. Even under this plan continued unwise choices would mean that a student would be forced to extend his high school career to obtain courses required for admission to advanced training, but the cause of the delay is the continued indecision of the students and parents rather than the rigidity of the high school organization.

PLANNED PROGRAM IN P.K. YONGE LABORATORY SCHOOL FOR _____

GRADE 9	GRADE 10	GRADE 11	GRADE 12
DID TAKE IN 9th GRADE ( )( )( )( )( )( )( )	( )( )( )( )( )( )( )	( )( )( )( )( )( )( )	
	DID TAKE IN 10th GRADE ( )( )( )( )( )( )( )	( )( )( )( )( )( )( )	
		DID TAKE IN 11th GRADE ( )( )( )( )( )( )( )	
			DID TAKE IN 12th GRADE

Approval by parent or school of this selection of courses is with the understanding that it may be changed if the necessity arises.

SPRING REGISTRATION

FOR GRADE   Parent   Core Teacher   Date
9)_____ _____ _____
10)_____ _____ _____
11)_____ _____ _____
12)_____ _____ _____

Individual programing does demand two things. Each student needs one staff member who guides him throughout his high school career. This person will need to know the student and his parents and to have access to all of the information about the student. Secondly, the school must have a testing program that helps each pupil, his parents, and his counselor secure a reliable estimate of his ability and his achievement level. Wise choices concerning the individual's program cannot be made without sufficient information. Parent expectations and pupil aspirations may be unrealistic. Unless information is collected about each pupil by intelligence, achievement, and aptitude tests and the results interpreted to pupils and parents, program planning may be based on aspirations and estimates of potential that are either too high or too low.

EVALUATION OF THE COURSES

The evaluation of the courses offered should be based primarily on their effectiveness in producing the pupil growth desired. Do the general education courses provide the basic understandings and skills needed by a citizen? Do the specialized courses enable most students to find courses that contribute to their purposes? Do the specialized courses increase the difference in achievement among the members of the student body?

Faculty and parents will also need to judge the offering by whether it permits necessary adjustment of program for students. Schools may have the range of courses that permits above average students to make desirable changes but provides very little for the lower quartile. In an individual program that is constantly being revised in terms of a pupil's achievement and a more realistic appraisal of his abilities, some students will need less difficult courses and courses without prerequisites in their junior and senior years. For such students to utilize these years well, the specialized offering must have one-semester courses that sample such fields as family finance, sociology, psychology, and world affairs.

A third criterion should be whether the typical programs selected give the breadth and depth desired. Do the citizenship and avocational courses provide a world picture and principles for personal living? Do students achieve the depth of scholarship in their vocational choices to succeed in college or on the job?

Decisions based on these criteria should lead to a continuous changing of the courses offered and a revision of content within courses. In the future, the pattern of courses offered by the secondary school should become more varied rather than more uniform.

SELECTED READINGS

Association for Supervision and Curriculum Development, *What Shall the High Schools Teach?* (1956 Yearbook), Chapters 4-6. Washington, D. C.: The Association, 1956. Deals with the organization and scope of the curriculum.

Bruner, Jerome S., *The Process of Education*. Cambridge, Mass.: Harvard University Press, 1960. Emphasizes the importance of students' acquiring the structure and method of a discipline.

Dimond, Stanley E., *Schools and the Development of Good Citizens*. Detroit, Mich.: Wayne University Press, 1953. Reports the findings of the Detroit Citizenship Education Study.

Educational Policies Commission of the National Education Association, *Education for All American Youth—A Further Look*. Washington, D. C.: The Association, 1952. Outlines ways and means of improving secondary education for all American youth.

French, Will and associates, *Behavioral Goals of General Education in High School*. New York: Russell Sage Foundation, 1957. Report of a survey made to develop a comprehensive statement of the goals of general education in terms of observable behavior.

Harvard Committee on the Objectives of General Education in a Free Society, *General Education in a Free Society*. Cambridge, Mass.: Harvard University Press, 1945. Report of the Committee.

"High Schools for Tomorrow," *Teachers College Record* 56: 355-420, April, 1955. Entire issue devoted to the theme "Secondary Schools of Tomorrow."

Kelley, Earl, *Education for What Is Real*. New York: Harper & Row, Publishers, 1947. Reports studies in perception and suggests their implications for school programs.

National Society for the Study of Education, *Adapting the Secondary School Program to the Needs of Youth* (Fifty-second Yearbook), Part I. Chicago, Ill.: University of Chicago Press, 1953. Focuses upon the possible improvement of secondary education by having the program better designed to meet the needs of the students.

Stiles, Dan, *High Schools for Tomorrow*. New York: Harper & Row, Publishers, 1946. Outlines a plan for the over-all improvement of the high school program as it existed in 1945.

Wiles, Kimball and Franklin Patterson for the Commission on the Education of Adolescents of the Association for Supervision and Curriculum Development, *The High School We Need*. Washington, D. C.: The Association, 1959. Outlines the curriculum that should be offered by the American high school.

7
THE IN-CLASS
EXPERIENCES

The development of a school philosophy, an administrative
organization, a curriculum framework and course syllabi,
the collection of instructional materials, the schedule, all are
provided in the school structure to make possible the meeting
of the teacher and his class for an exploration of some facet
of human knowledge. What happens in the classroom
is of crucial importance.

The in-class experiences of a pupil consist of his working
relationship with the teacher and the other pupils, the physical
setting in which he works, the content he explores, and the
instructional materials made available to him. A student's
curriculum includes all of these features of his classroom living.

THE LEARNING PROCESS

The way the teach-
er works with pupils in the classroom constitutes a major portion
of the curriculum for pupils. Not only do youth learn certain

subject matter, but they also learn how to feel about themselves and others and how to seek truth. To know how to work most effectively with pupils, it is necessary to take a look at how learning takes place and how one person can relate himself to the learning of another.

Teachers in the present decade can be guided by such generalizations as the following:

Learning is going on all the time. Learning is not something that a teacher turns on and off in his pupils. In fact, some sketchy research indicates that if a person while asleep hears some unknown facts from a phonograph record he will acquire a portion of the information; when he awakes he will be able to answer questions based on the content that he could not have answered before he went to sleep.

Learning is personal. The learner does his own learning. He selects from his environment the things with which he will interact and he interprets in terms of his past experiences, his needs, and his purposes. In research projects at Dartmouth and Princeton, displays were set up which are designed to create the wrong impression by restricting the cues that the observer received. Viewers were asked to identify an object and then were shown what it really was. Most were not correct. People did not see the object accurately. They perceived and interpreted in terms of their past experiences (see Kelley, *Education for What Is Real*). At the University of Chicago, McClelland and others have done research on perception which indicates that need affects perception. A picture of light and shadows was cast upon a screen. Persons who had been given a test that they could not possibly pass, a test that made them feel inadequate, were brought in to see the "picture" and asked to tell what they saw. Most of the subjects saw people having success experiences. Another group was kept from having food for eighteen hours. When they were brought in to see the "picture," they saw people eating. Thus people also perceive in terms of their needs (see *Journal of Psychology* 25:205-222; 27:311-330).

The knowledge that people perceive in terms of their past experiences and their needs means that when a teacher tells pupils something he can never be sure that they hear what he has said in the way he meant it. *Telling and teaching are not synonymous.* People learn in all situations, but they learn in terms of their own needs, perceptions, and background, and it is important for a person who hopes to serve in the role of a teacher to know how people perceive what is being said or read or done.

People want to learn things that are significant to them. When difficulty arises in getting pupils to learn what the teacher desires, it is not because the pupil does not want to learn but because the things that the teacher is presenting seem insignificant to the pupil. Pupils are learning continuously through their perception of the features of their environment with which they choose to interact.

Learning is affected by the emotional climate. Pupils' emotions either interfere with or facilitate the learnings that teachers desire them to make. Burrell found that learning was facilitated when the teacher became concerned about meeting the emotional needs of youngsters (see *Journal of Educational Sociology* 24: 381-393). Bills discovered that if, in addition to studying reading, youngsters are given an opportunity to talk out their emotional concerns, they make greater gains in the development of reading skill (see *Journal of Consulting Psychology* 14: 140-149).

In any learning situation there are certain limitations on the learning that pupils can do. Persistent emotional problems limit the range of information that the learner considers significant. A child with a serious emotional problem may find his school environment less stimulating, and the amount of his learning of school subjects may decrease. A pupil is further limited in what he can learn in a given situation by his previous experiences and by the values determining the range of information that he considers significant. Organic maturity limits the amount of learning of any given individual in any situation. Although all people follow the same growth patterns, they mature at different rates. For example, some pupils enter puberty at nine, while others—in rare cases—are eighteen. At the age of thirteen and a half, girls are two years ahead of boys in their maturity level, and girls typically find school work easier. The level of maturity limits the amount of learning that a pupil can do at a given time. The operational intelligence of the pupil, usually called the IQ, determines the rate at which a person is able to learn at the time. The amount and type of learning of each member of a class is limited by these factors.

If learning is going on all the time, if it is unique and each pupil learns at his own rate in terms of his perceptions and what he considers significant, it is evident that effective teaching cannot consist of telling and directing and judging. Instead, teaching is a process of relating to youngsters in such a way as to facilitate their learning. It consists of creating the kind of emotional climate in which pupils will feel secure enough to venture and the type of intellectual climate that provides a range of stimuli sufficiently wide to seem significant to youngsters with different backgrounds, needs, and purposes.

ENVIRONMENT

Emotional

The teacher can create an emotional climate which facilitates desirable learning by accepting pupils, helping pupils accept themselves, and encouraging pupils to accept each other.

Accepting pupils means that the teacher looks for the strengths in them rather than concentrating his attention on the things he dislikes about them or the weaknesses he feels that they have.

A new teacher in a Kentucky high school found a six-foot, two twenty-pound boy in her class. During the first month of school he was many times a disciplinary problem to her. She discovered that he had been troublesome to the older teachers in the school and began to resent the fact that he had been assigned to her, a beginning teacher. After the first month, she faced herself with the realization that she did not want this kind of a relationship with a pupil. She resolved that she would go back to school the next day and look for just one good quality in this big, overgrown boy. She concludes her story of her experiences by saying that a remarkable change took place in the boy in the following two weeks. Actually, she knows and we know that no change took place in the boy, because human personality does not change that fast; the change took place in her perception of the boy when she began to concentrate on the positive potential she saw in him rather than on the things she disliked about him.

If a teacher accepts pupils he accentuates the positive in his thinking about them.

Accepting pupils means learning about them. If the teacher is to interpret pupil behavior accurately and relate to a pupil in a way that will promote his growth, it is necessary that he understand the student's background and goals.

In a California junior high school a fourteen-year-old girl was wearing a skirt that was so tight that the boys began to whistle at her and to make remarks that the teachers considered improper. Some of the teachers on the staff drew the conclusion that this girl needed some advice on relationships with boys. The Dean of Girls called her into the office and began to talk about proper behavior for adolescent girls. The girl began to cry and ran out of the office. The Dean of Girls followed her and discovered that the girl's father and mother had been divorced two years before. The girl had loved her father and wanted to go with him, but the court had assigned her to her mother. The only thing she had left that her father had given her was the skirt.

It is so easy to misinterpret behavior if the teacher does not know the background and the needs of the students with whom he works. Taking the steps to learn and know about them not only helps the teacher to understand and relate to pupils, but is also an indication to them of the teacher's valuing of them.

If a teacher accepts pupils, he gives them support when they need it. If a pupil is having difficulty or is experiencing failure the teacher encourages, instead of censuring, and offers to give as much help as possible. Acceptance of pupils on the part of the teacher does much to create the kind of situation in which they can put their full attention to learning the things the curriculum planners deemed desirable.

Another quality of a good emotional climate is that the pupil is able to accept himself. Psychiatrists claim that the difference between people who are mentally healthy and those who are not is that the mentally healthy person loves himself; that normal people are those who feel that they are worthy, wanted, and adequate; that the abnormal, those who have to be institutionalized, are those who feel unworthy, unwanted, and inadequate. Teachers create a better learning situation when they work in a way that helps a pupil accept himself and realize his worth.

Teachers help pupils feel worthy if they make it possible for individuals to know their own progress. In too many classes a student who starts out with a C or D and is unable to do much better throughout the rest of the year gains no sense of making progress. If, however, he is brought into the record-keeping, where he keeps samples of his work so that he can compare work done in January with that done in September, he will have a way of seeing for himself that he is making progress.

Another way that a teacher can help people accept themselves is to recognize many types of leadership. In some classrooms the honor roll listed on the board is the only outward recognition given of leadership. In adjoining rooms it is possible to see various committees listed on the board in which almost every member of the class is recognized for some responsibility in leadership. In the P. K. Yonge School at the University of Florida, it was found that over two hundred of the two hundred and forty pupils in the high school were recognized by their fellows as leaders. Too many times teachers are prone to see leadership as restricted to a few members of the student body. Too often they fail to recognize that leadership is widely diffused and manifest in many different ways.

The third factor in a good emotional climate is pupil acceptance of each other. It is not enough for a pupil to be accepted by the teacher and to accept himself. Unless other pupils make him feel that he belongs and has value he will be devoting much of his energy and learning to the problem of how to become accepted by his peers.

A study by Lippett and White of the role of the adult leader in a group of adolescents indicates some of the things teachers can do to help pupils accept each other. Lippett and White found that when the adult leader planned and evaluated with the members of the group rather than telling them what to do and making solely personal judgments about their work, there were thirty times less aggression from member to member of the group and twice as many "we" comments (*Readings in Social Psychology*, pp. 315-330).

Pupils are helped to accept each other by the teacher encouraging them to assist each other. In some classes it is looked upon as undesirable for one student to aid another student. Penalties are established for any attempts at cooperative work. In schools where staffs are concerned about pupils' accepting each other, provision is made for students to assist each other in their work. One Michigan high school has an English workshop. Members of the senior class who have scholastic ability and leadership in the student body relinquish their study period each day to serve as counselors in the workshop. Other students who have the same study period and need help with themes or poems, other English responsibilities, or even personal problems can secure it from these student leaders.

Where students feel that they belong, the condition is more favorable to learning the content of the courses than if the opposite is true. If teachers want students to feel that much of the school's content is significant, they seek to decrease the number and intensity of the emotional problems of students and to help a greater percentage of the student body feel wanted, worthy, and adequate.

Intellectual

From research in the field of learning, it is evident that not all youngsters react to the same stimuli. *If a teacher wants to have a stimulating intellectual climate in his classroom, many stimuli must be present.*

As a person walks down the hallway in a school, he may see a classroom so barren that it would be impossible to tell what kind of class is usually conducted in it. Next door is a classroom filled with displays, reports, pictures, plants, and other objects that reveal, without anyone's saying, the kind of living and learning that go on there. The second room has many stimuli for youngsters that are present without the teacher taking any action whatsoever. If a teacher is trying to create a stimulating intellectual climate, he will recognize that the physical environment contains objects which illustrate many facets of a field.

A teacher who is concerned about the intellectual development of youngsters looks for different ways of providing stimuli.

> For example, a typing teacher, feeling that typing of routine textbook exercises was not giving the youngsters as much as could be provided by another procedure, had the class type pages from the American history book. She discovered that the class was learning many facts about American history, as well as making normal progress in developing typing skill.

Another way in which a teacher provides a stimulating intellectual climate is by expecting and valuing difference. Whenever a teacher attempts to get youngsters to become more alike and to do the same level of work he makes the situation less stimulating to two types of pupils. The students who are below the level of performance the teacher expects become frustrated and do less adequate work than they are capable of doing. The students who are superior to the level of work the teacher has set become bored and cease to be challenged. In a normal ninth grade class, if the teaching has been good and the learners have tried, the reading range will be seven to nine years. Some youngsters will be reading at the fifth grade level, and some will be reading at the twelfth grade level. No teacher has failed. Each person has learned as rapidly as he could. Any teacher should hope and expect that the longer he works with a class the greater will be the differences among the individuals within it. Since the rate of learning is different among children, to expect youngsters to move forward at the same pace is to create a sterile intellectual climate for many. A stimulating intellectual climate is one in which the teacher attempts to provide a variety of activities and have youngsters work at tasks of different levels of difficulty.

The teacher who hopes to have a stimulating intellectual climate maintains high standards. If there is one quality that causes students to fail to respect a teacher, it is that of the teacher who does not insist upon a high level of work. However, there has been much loose think-ing about what constitutes high standards.

> When he was in the fifth grade, a boy was reading at the eighth grade level and was able to do arithmetic at the third grade level. If the teacher had insisted that he do fifth grade arithmetic he would have found it impossible and would have become con-vinced that he was one of the millions of Americans who cannot understand arithmetic.

Some teachers and parents have assumed that maintaining high standards of work requires *one* standard that the entire class must attain. It is a false assumption. Maintaining high standards means that the teacher gets to know each youngster well enough to know what he is capable of doing and then insists that he work on projects and tasks just a little above what he is capable of doing at present. If the teacher establishes a group standard too far in advance of a given pupil's level he creates frustration, which results in discouragement and evasiveness. If the group standard is below the pupil's level of ability, the teacher convinces him that school is a waste of time.

The fourth thing that the teacher does to provide a stimulating intellectual climate is to stress creative activity. The learning that lasts is the learning that has been creative. This creative activity may be the drawing of a generalization or the interpretation of a poem through a dance, but it is the learner's because he has had a part in creating it. There are many ways that teachers can promote creativity.

> In an eleventh grade English class in western New York, the book reports were of an unusual variety. They were spread on the table. They were many sizes, shapes, and colors. One that I remember particularly was a report on *The Egg and I*. It was an eggshell colored sky-blue. Into one end had been stuck two matches. When I pulled the matches out of the shell and pulled them apart, I found a scroll one inch wide and twenty-four inches long. On this strip of paper the student had written his impression of *The Egg and I*. Other books were reported in a similarly creative way.

> In Hilo, Hawaii, one hundred and twenty water colors and pastels were displayed on the walls of an eleventh grade English classroom. They represented the efforts of one hundred and twenty students to share their feelings and interpretation. Each picture was different, and most were of good quality. The teacher described their production as follows: "We had finished reading *The Chambered Nautilus*. I asked each pupil to pick the line that had the most meaning for him and to share his interpreta-tion with others through water colors or pastel."

How different from classes in which teachers tell pupils what lines are important and what they mean! In this teacher's class each student had been free to express himself not only in terms of his feelings about what he had read, but also with a visual representation of the material on which he was reporting. An alert teacher plans assignments and class activities in which a pupil uses information to formulate his own organization or product.

The classroom climate is intellectually stimulating when pupils know that it is possible to talk through their values. The teacher takes away the challenge when he says to youngsters: "These are areas that we are not free to discuss"—whether he makes this kind of a statement as he talks about labor and management, or segregation, or diplomatic relations with Russia. When answers are already in, the challenge is gone. The areas a pupil is really interested in exploring intellectually are the phases of his culture or his personal life in which he has not yet reached an answer. If the teacher attempts to supply the answer in the areas in which the pupil is uncertain, he withdraws or accepts without question. In either case the intellectual challenge is gone.

> An eleventh grade girls' health class in a New York high school was discussing the bone structure of the body. Suddenly one girl spoke up and said: "The thing that really bothers me is whether or not I daydream too much." Then she proceeded to describe how much she daydreamed. Other girls chimed in, and the majority of the class stated that this was one of their problems, too. Instead of insisting that the class return to a discussion of the bone structure, the teacher accepted this teachable moment. She operated on the judgment that the most important thing she could do at this time was to help these students think through the normality of daydreaming among teenage girls.

Most teaching of values will come this way. A teacher cannot plan to help youngsters explore their value conflicts. He can only be ready to work with them as they discover value conflicts in the course of conducting other activities. He makes it possible for them to examine their value conflicts insofar as he is permissive in his reaction to what they say. If he makes value judgments and tells them they are wrong or tries to give them his answers, they cease to explore their questions with him.

The teacher who is concerned with the intellectual climate puts an emphasis on drawing generalizations and developing techniques of problem-solving rather than on memory and recall of specific facts. In 1933 Ralph Tyler did some research on retention (see *Journal of*

Higher Education 4: 203-205). Ohio State University students were checked fifteen months later on the knowledge that they had possessed at the end of a zoology course. It was found that these students had forgotten over seventy per cent of the specific facts that they had known but only twenty-five per cent of the principles and generalizations that they had drawn, and they had not decreased at all in their problem-solving techniques and procedures. When a teacher stresses names and dates he is spending his time teaching the kinds of things that are soon forgotten. The type of intellectual achievement that will stay with students is the creative activity in which they engage, such as drawing generalizations and solving problems.

The teacher brings pupils into the evaluation if he hopes to keep the classroom intellectually stimulating. When he leaves them out he ignores important data that should be included in decisions about purposes, procedures, and products, and risks failing to achieve common goals which make the learning situation more efficient. As pupils are brought into the process of deciding what is important, intellectual tasks become their responsibility as well as the teacher's.

One of the most important aspects of the intellectual climate is the kind of person the teacher is. *If he hopes to stimulate youngsters to follow intellectual pursuits they need to see in him a person who is continuing to grow intellectually.* It is not chance that the English teachers who have difficulty getting students to read outside of class are the teachers whom the pupils do not see reading, or that the science teachers who are successful in developing young scientists willing and ready to experiment are themselves persons who work in the laboratory on scientific problems. Teachers teach more by what they do than what they say.

Sometimes poets have insights and are able to phrase succinctly the ideas that are basic. Kahlil Gibran has done this for teaching when in *The Prophet* he describes the teacher's role:

> No man can reveal to you aught but that which already lies half asleep in the dawning of your knowledge.
>
> The teacher who walks in the shadow of the temple, among his followers, gives not of his wisdom but rather of his faith and his lovingness.
>
> If he is indeed wise he does not bid you enter the house of his wisdom, but rather leads you to the threshold of your own mind.

The basic element of desirable in-class experiences in a high school is a teacher who accentuates intellectual curiosity and creativeness and who is concerned with building the kind of work group where each pupil feels worthy and wanted.

Physical

At the turn of the century classrooms were almost all alike. Most were rectangular. The furniture consisted of rows of desks, all facing the teacher's desk. If the school was modern, windows were on the left of the pupils. In the front of the room, directly in front of the teacher's desk, was the recitation bench. Behind the teacher and on the right side of the room were blackboards. The floor was bare and oiled. The walls were unpainted plaster, turning dingy gray or painted a light tan with dark woodwork.

Since 1900, largely during the last three decades, educational thinking regarding classroom architecture and organization has changed. Gone is the recitation bench. No longer is a single classroom pattern considered appropriate. Classroom structure depends upon the function it must fulfill. A speech classroom does not resemble a physics laboratory, nor a woodworking shop an English room.

A visitor should be able to identify the type of work that occurs in a room as soon as he enters it. It is easy to tell whether the work follows the recitation plan or whether the teacher "rules with an iron hand." But the atmosphere of a room should reveal even more. A desirable classroom, even without pupils, presents a picture that shouts in a thousand ways: "This is a social studies room, and the teacher who teaches here works with children rather than gives them orders." Or: "Pupils conduct individual research projects in their work with the science teacher in this room." Numerous clues inform the observer: the type and arrangement of furniture, the position of the teacher's desk, the amount of display space, the wall coverings, the classroom library, the files and cupboards.

The type of room used affects the in-class experiences of pupils. Rooms that are overcrowded limit the activities that can be conducted in them and decrease the creativity of teachers. Functionality, flexibility, and space for display, storage, and instructional materials all facilitate good instruction.

A classroom must be functional. Does it permit the teacher to work in the way he thinks best? A room with seats fastened in rows hinders effective discussion groups. A room with chairs and tables may not encourage quiet, individual study. A teacher must decide upon the way he wants to work before he can arrange classroom furniture intelligently, and the room structure and furniture should assist him in his purposes.

A room needs to be flexible. If the teacher plans to vary methods, and most teachers do, the furniture should be movable so that new arrangements can be found to care for different-sized groups of students. Work techniques may vary from one unit to another, and ability to change study and work accommodations may spell the difference between failure or success in the work. No one organization of furniture can be satisfactory for all methods. The curriculum can be improved by securing more appropriate and more flexible furniture.

To meet the needs of creative teachers, a classroom must contain certain elements. Display surface must be available for announcements, motivating posters, exhibits of pupil work, commercial collections loaned to the school, and other material that the entire class may want or need to see. Storage space is equally essential. Teaching aids or supplies that clutter up the room interfere with quality teaching. A kindred need is a filing cabinet for the storage of paper material and pupil records. As greater use has been made of pamphlets and paperbound bulletins, the problem of storage has become pressing. As the types of records teachers keep have changed, the demand for space has increased. A filing cabinet is as much a necessity as a teacher's desk.

A class that uses more than one text must have a classroom library. If the class is ever to work by the laboratory or workshop method, students should have valuable references within easy access. Division of the class to send some to the library during the class period will deprive some students of the constant teacher guidance they need. If possible, a corner of each classroom should be made into a reading or study nook, where individuals can work undisturbed by the committee and group work of the rest of the class. One feature of the classroom library should be a supply of magazines in the field suited to the maturity level of the class. Certainly the classroom library will contain references on several reading levels if the teacher is to provide for individual differences in reading ability.

A must on the list of many teachers will be room decorations: window boxes for flowers, wall hangings illustrating some phase of the field, pictures related to the field, specimens, or models. All of these give the room distinction and express the personality of the teacher and the class. All of these elements are in addition to the texts, specific reference books, dictionaries, magazines, and specialized equipment that are needed in every field. Interesting, challenging teachers make their rooms breathe their subject.

Showmen and industrialists have recognized that light and color condition the emotional response, and they use them to promote the desired effect. In a New Jersey school a class and a teacher were assigned to a room that had been a storeroom. It was dingy and not very light. The paint was dark. The walls were repainted a light pastel shade, but the room still had a cold feeling. The teacher and the art instructor planned with the class how to use one small portion of a dark corner. They painted it a bright red, and that corner became the focus of the room. It was warm, alive, and vibrant. The use of color affects the emotional tone and the receptiveness of students. School personnel, too, should utilize these forces to produce classrooms that are conducive to the kind of behavior sought.

SELECTION OF CONTENT

Man has accumulated a vast store of information. No scholar, even though he devotes his entire life to study, can hope to master the knowledge of mankind. Obviously, the secondary school cannot hope to present all the accumulated knowledge. A choice must be made. *Upon what bases should the selection of the content of a class be made?*

Many teachers never raise this question. They accept the present curriculum as the most desirable selection of information and teach the facts contained in their textbook and course outlines. When asked how they justify attempting to teach a certain fact, the length of the Great Wall of China, for example, they respond: "It is in the textbook, and I feel the author is more capable of determining the important facts than I am."

Such a viewpoint may be correct if the teacher assumes that the body of knowledge that an educated man should possess has already been determined. A scholar who has devoted his life to the exploration and organization of a particular field is undoubtedly able to organize the facts, laws, and principles of his field more logically than the average teacher. But can teachers assume that the present curriculum is composed of the most important knowledge for every child? Can they believe that the subject-matter fields that attained representation in the secondary school curriculum, by fate or political pressure, are the most necessary for effective living in the present? Quite possibly it is more essential to know how to buy intelligently than it is to be able to name the characters in *The Merchant of Venice*. Not all teachers or pupils will agree with the preceding suggestion. And the dissenters may be correct. If they are professors of English or majoring in English literature in college, a speaking acquaintance with Portia and her colleagues may well be more important. But must the same answer be true for the average high school student? The question of what material to use becomes a matter of deciding whose needs the curriculum should meet.

From the late twenties until the mid-fifties many teachers and professors argued about the selection of content from two theoretical positions called the "subject-matter approach" and the "experience approach."

The starting place, if the teacher chose the subject-matter approach, was with a logically organized body of subject matter. The material had been organized by scholars in the field to promote learning the basic information first and gradually leading the boys and girls to the finer points of the organized bodies of subject matter. The organization of the subject-matter field determined where a particular teacher or class would start in their study.

In contrast, the experience approach started with the child. The teacher examined the child's environment and way of life to determine his needs. He then selected the knowledge that had been acquired by civilization which he felt could be turned into worthwhile experiences designed to assist the child in meeting those needs. The teacher contended that information which did not have a bearing upon the needs of the child would be meaningless and unimportant to him. He believed that teaching information not bearing upon the immediate needs and desires of children built up the attitude in the child that the school was foolish and unimportant, and that the child learned because he wanted to learn, because he felt that the material being studied would help him.

The teacher who followed the subject-matter approach made the assumption that certain subject matter was good because it had been tested by time and represented the culture of our civilization. Since in his opinion it was the basis on which all future development must take place, pupils would benefit by knowing it.

The teacher who made the experience approach argued that it was impossible to learn all of the information that has been acquired through the ages. Since there must be some criteria established to

determine exclusion or inclusion of subject matter, these criteria should
be the needs of the child and of the community in which he lives.

Under the subject-matter approach, the major portion of planning
was done by the teacher. He was an expert in the field and he knew
best the sequence in which the material should be studied and the
ways of acquiring the information most easily. An inexperienced child
could not be expected to select the type of subject matter that would
produce proper development in himself. He could not be expected to
organize his work in such a way that the field would be covered thoroughly. He could not be expected to know the sources of material that
would provide him with the most adequate information. The teacher
had training in all of these areas, and he had an understanding of the
body of material that was to be studied. Thus it was quite natural that
he should do the planning for the class.

In the experience approach, much more planning was done by
teacher and pupils together. The pupil alone knows the problems that
are important to him. The teacher's task consists of helping the child
to plan an attack upon them. It was assumed that developing the ability to plan and to establish goals was an important educative process.
Therefore, the school should give the child opportunities to develop
these abilities. Also, teachers who followed the experience theory felt
that this procedure was more in harmony with present-day psychology.
The pupil was active—not passively doing what he was told. Motivation was obtained by assisting the child to set up his own goal, and
the teacher's task ceased to be forcing boys and girls to acquire the
material. The goals established by joint planning were teacher-pupil
goals. True, the teacher had objectives in mind and he guided boys
and girls in terms of them, but he allowed the children to establish
their problems and to work them through.

Under the subject-matter approach, the content was something to
be acquired. The task of the school and the teacher was to have boys
and girls acquire a certain body of factual information. Under the
experience approach, the subject matter was considered a means to
an end. Knowledge of certain facts by themselves was considered
unimportant. Facts were used as tools to solve problems or to conduct
a project; many would become a part of the student's fund of knowledge, but that was a secondary benefit.

A very fundamental distinction existed between the two approaches.
The subject-matter approach conceived of school *as preparation for
life*. It was recognized that the culture of the past might not constitute
real problems for modern children, but it was hoped and assumed that

by learning this information the child would become an effective participant in twentieth-century life. The experience people, on the other hand, thought of *school as life*. They contended that pupils learn to live effectively in society by living intelligently and not by studying how others have lived and thought. They feel that if children met and solved problems in the simplified environment of the school, they developed the ability to solve their personal and social problems in the more complex environment of out-of-school life.

Under the subject-matter approach, much of the learning came through drill. If a certain portion of subject matter could not be learned easily, the child repeated the task over and over until it was learned. The teacher did not worry whether the pupil saw purpose in what he was doing; he operated on an assumption that learning comes by effort, and that hard tasks, even though dull, are effective in developing the mind. Under the experience program, habits and skills were developed when necessary to accomplish a purpose. Drill was used when the child saw that it would help him achieve some goal that he considered important. In the opinion of the teacher, drill was an inefficient learning method unless the pupil saw purpose in the exercises.

If the teacher assumed that the acquisition of a certain body of subject matter was the key to the development of an effective citizen, it was clear that all students must seek to acquire the same subject matter. If the teacher did not require the same material for everyone, then he was denying those who did not acquire all of the material the opportunity to become as effective as they might be. Under the experience approach, the subject matter varied from individual to individual in terms of the particular needs that each had. The teacher recognized not only that all students cannot be expected to reach the same level of attainment, but also that they do not need to do so.

Since the mid-fifties the conflict has not been as pronounced. The profession, for the most part, has sought functional answers to the question of the choice of subject matter. Scholars, particularly in mathematics and the sciences, have been re-examining the content presented in high school textbooks and courses. Much that was nonfunctional is being discarded. Teachers have been subjecting their procedures and class activities to careful scrutiny. A significant portion of public opinion has demanded greater effectiveness. In the interaction among the three groups—teachers, scholars, public—the differences have decreased in the face of common purposes. *Agreement obtains that a developed intellect, commitment to a set of values, and mental health are desired. Content for a given class must be judged by its contribution to these goals.*

If teachers are candid in their evaluation of the worth of the information included in the classes in many secondary schools, they are forced to admit that much of it can only be justified on the basis of preparing for college. High school curricula have been designed for the most part to meet the needs of the precollege group. At the present time only one out of two high school graduates—and three out of ten enrollees—ever goes to college. Thus much of the high school curricular material meets the needs of only thirty per cent of the high school enrollment. How then can teachers know what to teach if they do not follow a textbook or prepared course of study?

First, teachers must become very clear concerning their teaching goals; they must know what types of changes they want to produce in students. The first step in deciding upon goals consists of gaining an understanding of the purpose of the secondary school. The objectives of any class should contribute to general attainment of the school's purposes. If the *raison d'être* of the secondary school is to prepare students for college (as it once certainly was), the teacher's objective is to give the children sufficient facts to enable them to pass the entrance examinations. If the purposes are improving the immediate life of the child and community, the objectives must be related to some phase of that improvement. For example, if one of the purposes of the school is to improve living conditions in the community, one of the objectives of the home economics teacher might well be to teach how to plan balanced diets from available food supplies, without covering information and principles selected from the total field of home economics. Clarity with regard to the role and function of the school is essential.

After the teacher determines the contribution his class can make to the school purposes, the second step consists of stating his objectives clearly. The most satisfactory way of stating objectives is in terms of the observable changes in behavior. Much haziness concerning objectives is removed if teachers are definite enough to say: "My students should type sixty words per minute at the end of two semesters of typing." Or: "A student should be able to plan a balanced diet for a family of five on a weekly allowance of fifty dollars when she finishes my course." Each of these objectives is stated clearly enough to give the teacher guidance in selecting the material to be taught and the examination to be given.

The more specific the definition of behavior, the greater the direction obtained from the statement of the objective. To illustrate: If a teacher has the objective to develop appreciation of good music, the only guidance that he has is the term "good music." What is it? What does a person do who appreciates it? However, if he defines appreciation in terms of what boys and girls do when they appreciate good music, he can know whether his teaching produces the results sought. If he says he wants pupils to choose Beethoven's music instead of Goodman, to attend symphony concerts without compulsion, to ask to hear the Moonlight Sonata, to be able to point out the differences between the music of Gershwin and Strauss, he has certain definite types of behavior that he wants to see. Appreciation is no longer an abstract conception. It has been defined in terms of types of behavior for which the teacher can watch.

When these two steps are taken, the teacher chooses from the content assigned to his course and the materials made available those activities which in his opinion will further the types of growth he seeks to promote in pupils with the abilities and backgrounds of his class members. Since his judgments may be wrong, he collects evidence of the effectiveness of his selection, organization, and procedures and evaluates his choices and revises his selection as needed. The final judgment of the validity of a given choice must be made in terms of its effectiveness in producing the desired growth. The quality teacher brings pupils, parents, supervisors, college representatives, and others who have pertinent evidence into the judgment-making.

THE TEXTBOOK

A few years ago teaching was associated primarily with textbooks. Teachers used textbooks to determine what they should teach and estimated the results of their teaching by the extent to which they had been able to make the pupils read, memorize, and report on the content of the text. Many teachers were not satisfied to have their pupils study a single text. They felt that following the outline of material as presented by one author might not give their pupils the body of information best suited to improving living in the community in which the school was located and so began to use a variety of sources of information.

> The dangers of one-text teaching were demonstrated in the work of a civics teacher in a depressed rural area. She was assigning the material in the book in the order in which the author wrote

it. No study material other than the text was used by the pupils. One of the chapters treated the part that government plays in the health of its citizens. A look at the pinched, sallow faces of the forty pupils in the class, at least half of whom were suffering from hookworm and malnutrition, was sufficient to convince any observer that a study of health was not amiss. But the chapter on health in the text described the organization and services of the health department in New York City, and the teacher and class read and recited on the chapter as it was presented in the text. Then the teacher wondered why the pupils were not interested in the lesson!

Despite the movement away from dependence on a single text, textbooks continue to be a major source of information in the classroom, and teachers concerned with improving the curriculum see a better choice of textbooks as one step.

Whether a teacher and a class buy a text should be determined by the nature of available texts, the availability of additional study material, the purposes of the teacher, and his competence in the field he is teaching. If a text is suited to the community in which the school is located, if it is written and prepared in a desirable manner, it may be satisfactory for a portion of the class. No text will suit all reading levels in the class.

Even if the available texts do not measure up to the desired quality, the selection of a text may be necessary. If the school lacks a good library, if there are insufficient funds to purchase reference books or to subscribe to magazines, a teacher would need to be a genius to provide worthwhile educational experiences for forty boys and girls. Neither should a teacher inadequately prepared in a subject-matter field attempt to guide children through the field without the aid of the map provided by a good text. Even with a text, the teacher who lacks knowledge and skill in the field he is teaching will do an inferior job; without a text, the task is hopeless. If the school possesses a wealth of teaching materal and aids, and the teacher is sufficiently specialized in training to enable him to select his path through the intricacies of a particular body of subject matter, the decision concerning a text should rest on the purposes that a teacher has. If a teacher wants to give his pupils a body of information and a text contains it, the text might well be chosen. If, on the other hand, a teacher feels that learning to collect and organize data is as important as the facts learned, a decision to buy a text would be unwise.

If the teacher does feel that a text is necessary for effective work in his class there are certain standards he can use to make a choice that will improve the learning situation.

First, the text should be attractive. A bright text with colored pictures will stimulate the pupils more than a dark cover and a printed page with small black and white pictures. Eye appeal is important; it sets the tone. Color, the kind of print, the way the material is laid out on the page, the headings, and the organization of content around the concerns of students at the age level for which the material is being prepared are all important.

The most important criterion a text must meet is that of *relevancy*. *It must contain information suited to the needs of the locality and of the pupils.* If the content of a text bears on the problems of another region or includes only illustrations foreign to the past experience of the student, it is obviously unsuited. Too many textbooks in the past have been directed to an urban audience because the largest sale for the book was in city systems and because the experience of the writer did not include country life. One solution, in some fields at least, lies in the writing of regional texts by authors from that region. But when regional books are produced, care must be exercised to prevent local bias and prejudice from coloring the presentation. Regionalism should be manifest in the choice of problems presented, not in point of view or selection of the evidence.

Closely akin to the relevancy of the content is the *accuracy* of information. If on glancing through the book an error or two is discovered, future examination will probably prove unprofitable. If no obvious mistakes are apparent, it is well to compare the information given with that in other standard references to see if there are any discrepancies. If a difference is found a check should be made to find out which source is more accurate.

"How current is the information contained?" is another important question the teacher must ask. A book that is outdated, particularly in such areas as science and social studies, will be relatively useless. Some high schools are using science textbooks that were written before atomic power was developed. These students are being supplied with information that is false in light of present insight into the nature of matter and energy. The copyright date is not always an adequate clue. It is necessary to sample thoroughly in order to discover how recent the research is upon which the writing is based.

The text should cover the phases of the field that the teacher considers important. A title can be misleading. On the shelf is a text whose title and cover indicate that the geography deals with the countries of the Far East. But when one looks through the book one discovers that it contains only a little about the Far East and much that is usually included in the typical world geography.

The book should be free of bias. Bias is displayed in many ways. It may be leaving out certain facts; it may be playing up certain facts and playing down others so that a false impression is given; it may be the amount of space or the place on the page given one viewpoint; it may be the type of picture that is used. All books have some bias. The task of the teacher in text selection is to determine which is most free of bias. One of the best ways to find a book that is relatively free of bias is to seek one that puts the emphasis on students' drawing their own conclusions rather than on telling youngsters what they should believe.

The text should be an honest presentation. It should not omit facts because certain vested interests will be offended if they are included. A textbook writer, more than any other author, has the responsibility for presenting a factual record, and divergence from the total truth as it is known is evidence of a poorly written text.

The text should be written in an interesting, easily understood style. For some reason certain educators have assumed that a text does not have to be as well written as a novel. As a result, many texts have been full of cumbersome sentences. Few people turn to a text if they want to read for pleasure. This avoidance of texts is not because the topics treated are not interesting but because the writing makes the reading of a text a task instead of a pleasure. Much of the failure of teachers to motivate their classes may correctly be attributed to the choice of a poorly written text. Pupils want simple, direct writing. The more abstract the writing or the more complicated the sentences, the more difficult it is for students to understand it. Making understanding as easy as possible is good teaching.

Print is important. Some of the newer styles of print are much more attractive and easier on the eyes than the old styles. Format attracts or repels. Most people find long blocks of uninterrupted print hard to read. They like a format that leaves blocks of white scattered among the print. A desirable textbook is well illustrated. If there is a choice between books that are of equal merit as far as content is concerned, the one that has the greatest number and the best quality of illustrations is the one that is most helpful.

The text book should suggest a variety of class activities. No class will follow all of the activities. In fact, a class may not follow any of them. But the better the list of suggested activities, the greater the chance that the student or teacher, at a time when they are not sure what the important thing is for them to do, will get an idea as to something they should undertake.

A good textbook contains an index, a glossary, and a bibliography. The index should consist of the topics that students at that particular age level will be seeking in their research. The glossary should list the technical terms that will be new to most of the students. The bibliography must be adequate. Not all of the information on any subject can be put into a single book. The author, if he has done a good job, has suggested supplementary references that deal with other phases of the topics studied and has indicated types of materials to which classroom committees may go to get further information. The bibliography is better if it has been annotated so that it indicates the kind of help a student may expect from a particular reference.

No one text is satisfactory for a total class. In the average class, where the reading range is seven to nine years, no one text meets the reading requirements of every student. To expect the ninth grade student with fifth grade reading ability to read the ninth grade text is almost like compelling him to study a Latin edition, and for the student with the college freshman ability the average ninth grade text is as boring as a Mother Goose book would be. To meet the abilities of the students of an average class and to keep them doing challenging work it is necessary to have texts in the field prepared for readers at different levels.

If textbooks are used, a second difficulty should be considered. By following a single text, students get the idea that knowledge is already organized and that it is their job to learn and accept someone else's organization. If it is recognized that pupils select and organize information in terms of their own purposes, the danger of a single text is apparent. When students are placed in the position of acquiring someone else's organization, their purpose becomes the attainment of a satisfactory mark in the course. For those students who are not motivated by marks, the experience is insignificant and a waste of valuable time. Schools enrich their curriculum by adopting multiple texts for a single course or by putting money into developing school and class libraries which make it possible for students to collect information from a variety of sources and to organize it in terms of what they consider to be the important problems in the various fields. Few secondary classes should rely on one text.

OTHER INSTRUCTIONAL MATERIALS

Multiple texts do not comprise the total answer. Texts are expensive and in some fields are rapidly outdated. Pamphlet material fills this need. It is cheap and it is up-to-date. Since it is inexpensive, it is expendable. By the time the pamphlet is worn out, it is usually out-of-date. Use of pamphlets enables a teacher to supplement the text with up-to-date material suitable to the needs of the community in which he works and to provide materials on a variety of reading levels.

Motion pictures and film strips are valuable in many fields. They present material in a form which less able readers can comprehend. They provide more concrete presentation of ideas and procedures than most lectures and discussions. If films are to be used, the teacher should have a part in planning the film schedule to insure that the most helpful films will be available when needed. A teaching film should be scheduled for a class when it is needed there, not when it arrives on a schedule determined the year before. It may be used to supply data, to explore an area or motivate further exploration on the part of the students, or to summarize. But films not related to the immediate needs of a class should not be shown.

If it seems that the content of a film is appropriate, there are certain minimum criteria that should be applied before it is used: the sound should be clear; the photography should be adequate; the information should be accurate; it should not present stereotypes that overgeneralize about people and processes. A film is a powerful piece of instructional material and should be as carefully examined as a text before a class is asked to spend time viewing it.

Among the audio-visual materials, the tape recorder has become very important in many classrooms. It is versatile, and it is inexpensive. It has proved to be a medium through which the class can be creative, and the information collected and organized is available to group after group. Tapes also enable a teacher to enrich the learning environment by keeping records of resource people who visited his classes. Each new class has all previous resource people available to them, too.

In preparing his work for the term, the creative teacher forms a file of materials for the units he thinks he will teach. Although he cannot predict exactly the materials he will need as he works with pupils, he can make some guesses as to the types of units that he will use.

He collects materials that bear on these topics. The greater the range in reading level of materials secured, the greater the chances that the teacher will have materials suited to the needs of the various youngsters within his class.

In addition to the teacher's forming a file of materials, the school librarian should collect and maintain a vertical file of materials that correspond with the units taught in the school. To do this efficiently the librarian should work closely with the curriculum planning committee and have a record of the kinds and types of units that are ordinarily taught. These materials should be organized for loan to individual classes as they are needed.

An important method of providing a class with instructional material is a traveling library. Collections of materials related to the units taught in the school are prepared in the school library. They contain reference books, pamphlets, and related fiction. These collections are loaned to classes as they study the units. Such traveling shelves of materials increase the topics that can be explored within a unit and bring the thinking of more authorities to a classroom.

A wider concept of materials of instruction has led to the conclusion that many classes have placed too much emphasis on learning from materials that are written and printed. The curriculum is improved for many students by providing a greater variety of ways of collecting information. Experience is being recognized more widely as learning material. Camp life is one example. As boys and girls have experiences in camp, the living together, the contact with nature, the necessity for preparing food and cleaning up, serving, making beds, all provide facts and ideas that can be used. Class activities are being extended beyond the walls of the classroom in many schools. Community resources are being used as learning materials; speakers from the community, projects in community improvement, excursions to factories, museums, and the like are all recognized as learning materials. Through the use of nonprinted instructional materials, class work is being made meaningful for a high percentage of the students.

A recent development in the instructional aids field has been the teaching machine. Although at the time of this writing few high schools are using teaching machines, much experimental work is being done. Attempts are being made to program courses and portions of courses. The results give room for hope that much of the basic factual material of some courses can be programed. Certainly it can be expected that programs to teach fundamental skills will be produced.

High school staffs should proceed immediately to define the basic skills required for graduation and to seek programs that will teach them. After the skills have been defined and the programs secured, pupils will be able to work at their own speed in a laboratory associated with the library. Teachers guiding in-class activities could eliminate most of the drill and use class time for more creative activities.

The method of class operation that is desirable depends upon the outcomes sought, the background and maturity of the pupils, the facilities available, and the ability of the teacher. It is unwise to make judgments about the activities of a class unless these factors are known. Not all competencies and understandings are developed by the same procedure; not all teachers find the same methods effective.

If activities are desirable they are conducted in an atmosphere where the pupil feels accepted and believes he has some real possibility of success. The activities provide for individual differences. The more gifted pupils can move ahead at a faster rate, and the slower ones have more time and can secure help when needed. Such conditions cannot be obtained in a large class where all have the same assignments and all must keep together. *Desirable class activities provide for choice, for variation in rate of progress, and for individualized assignments.* More than one project to choose from for homework, reading lists dealing with the topic or problem under consideration with references of varying degrees of difficulty, opportunity to get an evaluation of quality of assignments done and reports prepared, all contribute to the possibility that the class activities are desirable. Teaching machines or other devices that enable a teacher to individualize instruction increase the possibility that activities will be worthwhile for all.

The activity that is desirable for one student is not necessarily so for another. One student may need drill on pronouns; for another it is a waste of time. If the classroom is a desirable teaching-learning situation, the teacher knows each pupil well enough to recognize his present level of ability and to provide or plan with the pupil the next steps that are appropriate for him.

Some efforts are underway in high schools to provide for individualized instruction by team teaching. A number of teachers, two to seven, work with a number of pupils, fifty to one hundred seventy-five. Class activities consist of large group presentations and small group or individual investigations. Proponents of the plan proclaim that the large group presentations can be better prepared than is typical now in regular classes; that students can be provided with assignments more suited to their needs and abilities in the small groups; and that greater flexibility for meeting individual needs and abilities exists because students can be shifted from one small group to another without disrupting their schedule or disturbing classes.

Television teaching is being tried in many classrooms. The results obtained vary and are being studied. It has been proved that pupils can learn facts by television teaching. So can they learn facts by reading a book. Few claim that teaching should be by television alone, and the extent to which enrollment in college elective courses taught by television lags behind enrollment in sections of the same courses taught "live" challenges those who do claim so. Television is but one more instructional material, and its future depends upon its contribution to providing more stimulation without decreasing the possibility of individualizing instruction.

SUMMARY

The high school curriculum is satisfactory when the student works in a class where: he is accepted, supported, challenged, and stimulated; the physical setting is functional, flexible, and pleasing; the content studied is selected because it effectively promotes the student growth that the teacher hopes will result; and the instructional materials available are suitable and varied enough to accommodate a wide range of individual purposes and abilities.

SELECTED READINGS

Alexander, William M. and Paul M. Halverson, *Effective Teaching in Secondary Schools*. New York: Holt, Rinehart & Winston, Inc., 1956. Presents the theory and describes the practices of modern secondary school teaching.

Association for Supervision and Curriculum Development, *Toward Better Teaching* (1949 Yearbook). Washington, D. C.: The Association, 1949. Identifies and describes seven key characteristics of better teaching.

Bills, Robert E., "Non-Directive Therapy with Retarded Readers," *Journal of Consulting Psychology* 14: 140-149, April, 1950. Describes the results of attempting to improve reading ability by play therapy.

————, "Personality Changes During Student-Centered Teaching," *Journal of Educational Research* 50: 121-126, October, 1956. Reports a study indicating that student-centered teaching may bring about personality changes in students.

Boeck, Clarence H., "Teaching Chemistry for Scientific Method and Attitude Development," *Science Education* 37: 81-84, March, 1953. Provides evidence that attitudes can be changed as a result of the teaching-learning situation.

Burrell, Ann Porter, "Facilitating Learning Through Emphasis on Meeting Children's Basic Emotional Needs: An In-Service Program," *Journal of Educational Sociology* 24: 381-393, March, 1951. Reports the effect on achievement of teachers' attempts to meet basic emotional needs.

Bush, Robert N., *The Teacher-Pupil Relationship*. Englewood Cliffs, N. J.: Prentice-Hall, Inc., 1954. Offers evidence concerning effective teacher-pupil relationships.

Grambs, Jean, William Iverson, and Franklin Patterson, *Modern Methods in Secondary Education,* rev. ed. New York: The Dryden Press, 1958. Outlines in practical details some of the modern methods used in today's schools.

Harrah, Delvin D., *A Study of the Effectiveness of Five Kinds of Grouping in the Classroom*. Doctor's thesis. Charlottesville, Va.: University of Virginia, 1955. Abstract: *Dissertation Abstracts* 16: 715, No. 4, 1956. Finds that friendship grouping provides better achievement and social behavior than either interest or ability grouping.

Hoover, Kenneth, "An Experiment on Grouping Within the Classroom," *California Journal of Secondary Education* 30: 326-331, October, 1955. Demonstrates the results that can be accomplished by within-the-class grouping.

Keislar, Evan R., "Peer Group Ratings of High School Pupils with High and Low School Marks." *Journal of Experimental Education* 23: 375-378, June, 1955. For both sexes, pupils having high marks were rated high on liking school work, putting studies first, and being persistent.

Kelley, Earl, *Education for What Is Real*. New York: Harper & Row, Publishers, 1947. Stresses the importance of perception in learning.

Labrant, Lou, "Mental-Health Practices in the High School Grades" in *Mental Health in Modern Education* (Fifty-fourth Yearbook of the National Society for the Study of Education), Part II, Chapter 10, pp. 216-235. Chicago, Ill.: University of Chicago Press, 1955. Relates the mental health problems of adolescence directly to the school curriculum.

Lane, Howard and Mary Beauchamp, *Human Relations in Teaching: The Dynamics of Helping Children Grow*. Englewood Cliffs, N. J.: Prentice-Hall, Inc., 1955. Stresses the importance of human relations in the teaching-learning process.

Lippitt, Ronald and Ralph K. White, "An Experimental Study of Leadership and Group Life" in *Readings in Social Psychology*, Newcomb and Hartley, eds., pp. 315-330. New York: Holt, Rinehart & Winston, Inc., 1947. Reports results produced by three different types of adult leadership in youth groups.

McClelland, David C. and John W. Atkinson, "The Projective Expression of Needs: Part I, The Effect of Different Intensities of the Hunger Drive on Perception," *Journal of Psychology* 25: 205-222, January-April, 1948.

———, and Russell Clark, "The Projective Expression of Needs: Part III, The Effect of Ego-Involvement, Success and Failure on Perception," *Ibid.* 27: 311-330, January-April, 1949. Parts I and III of this work report research investigations of the effect of hunger and failure on perception.

Molbert, Doris, "A Personal Concept of Democracy," *Progressive Education* 34: 25-30, January, 1957. Personal recollections of democracy in action in several schools.

Ohm, Robert E. and Harold Howe, "How May Smaller-than-Usual Student Groups and Individuals Be Taught More Effectively?" *National Association of Secondary School Principals Bulletin* 43: 10-15, April, 1959. Flexibility, pupil self-direction, avoidance of lecturing and formal recitation, and working with individual pupils are offered as answers.

Oliva, Peter F., "High School Discipline in American Society: A Primer on Democratic Discipline in Its Social Context," *Ibid.* 40: 1-103, January, 1956. An expansive study of the role of discipline in high school.

Passow, A. Harry and Gordon N. Mackenzie, "Research in Group Behavior Shows Need for New Teaching Skills," *Nation's Schools* 49: 71-73, April, 1952. Stresses the need for teachers to be effective in providing group leadership.

Regan, John Francis, *The School-Connected Fears of Children Under Authoritarian and Democratic Teachers.* Doctor's thesis. New York: New York University, 1958. Abstract: *Dissertation Abstracts* 18: 2079, No. 6, 1958. Finds that authoritarian teachers increase children's fears, which may result in permanent emotional damage.

Tyler, Ralph, "Permanence of Learning," *Journal of Higher Education* 4: 203-205, April, 1933. Reports findings in studies of college students on retention of factual matter versus retention of generalizations and principles.

Wright, Grace S., "Core Curriculum Development—Problems and Practices," U. S. Office of Education, Federal Security Agency, Bulletin No. 5, 1952. Washington, D. C.: U. S. Government Printing Office, 1952. Provides a picture of what core curriculum is and how it is actually practiced.

Wrightstone, Jacob W. "What Research Says About Class Organization for Instruction," *NEA Journal* 46: 254-255, April, 1957. Discusses briefly ability grouping, nonpromotion, departmentalization, and extracurricular activities.

8

GUIDANCE
PROCEDURES

In 1950 over five hundred Connecticut parents were asked
what improvements they would like to see made in the secondary
school program. One of the three most frequently stated
desires was for increased guidance for adolescents. Other surveys
have indicated that the Connecticut response was typical.
An improved guidance program in the secondary schools is
a concern of parents, adolescents, and school staffs. How to
provide the guidance is not as clear as the demand for it.
Much of the difficulty in improving the guidance program lies
in disagreement concerning the nature of guidance. Some
people, including many parents, conceive of guidance in the
form of an adviser to whom pupils can take their problems and
obtain answers. Others, including some administrators, see
guidance as a data-collecting function. In their opinion,
guidance personnel should be used to administer tests,
prepare and maintain cumulative record folders, and supply
information concerning the results of the testing program.
Others expect guidance personnel to assist pupils in thinking
through their personal problems. Some specialists in the field

163

disciplinarian

claim that guidance is a specialized function that can be performed only by highly trained personnel. Guidance, from their point of view, is distinct from the curriculum. Some curriculum workers, on the other hand, find it impossible to distinguish between the curriculum and guidance activities. As they understand it, a good curriculum constitutes a good guidance program.

Out of these different interpretations have come misunderstandings and, in some cases, antagonisms. Individuals in planning groups, faculties, and communities have talked past each other without realizing that a semantic problem existed. It has become increasingly necessary to state the definition of guidance that is being used if communication is to be facilitated.

Guidance, in this chapter, will be used to mean helping students to learn about themselves and establish goals, to become informed about the school and community, to plan how to use the available resources to achieve their goals, and to formulate and follow standards of conduct. Any action by an administrator, a counselor, or a teacher that contributes to any of these phases of guidance, whether it is in the classroom, counselor's office, or playground, is guidance. No attempt will be made to distinguish between curriculum and guidance because guidance is an aspect of the curricular organization. If pupils become more intelligently self-directing in a school, the guidance function of the school program or curriculum is effective. A particular activity or action may be guidance for one pupil and not for another. Planning to improve guidance in a high school involves looking at what is happening to individual pupils to see what assistance they receive in becoming better able to meet their problems and does not necessarily involve examining a stated program of activities and a listing of qualifications of personnel.

GUIDANCE THROUGH PROGRAM PLANNING

The basic element of guidance for the student is helping him make the choice of the experiences available in the school he attends that will be most beneficial to him and to society. The wrong decision concerning courses to be taken or activities in which to engage will keep a pupil from getting what he could out of the time he spends in the secondary school. Thus selection of program is the phase of a pupil's school career in which the guidance program should be organized to help most. (See Chapter 6.)

Each student should have one staff member, a counselor or a teacher, who guides him throughout his high school career. This person should get to know the student well and as far as possible become acquainted with the adolescent's parents. He should have access to all information concerning the student. He should have time in his schedule to get acquainted with the student and his parents and to have consultations with them when important decisions are to be made.

At the time of decision about the student's program, the counselor should see his role as helping the student to become clearer about his goals, to see the full range of choices and the consequences of each. He should supply data about the program and the student's achievement and abilities that may be unknown or overlooked by the student or parent. It is not his job to plan a program for the student; it is his job to help the student make more realistic, more intelligent choices.

The success of this aspect of the guidance program should be judged by whether a student learns to know himself better and develops greater intensity of purpose because of an increasing awareness that he is making the decisions that shape his life.

GUIDANCE THROUGH THE HOMEROOM

Not all of the guidance needed can be provided in the program-planning conferences. Much must be secured through day-to-day contact with members of the faculty. One point of impact in many high schools is the homeroom.

The homeroom has been developed in the secondary school to supply a type of assistance that was not available in the ordinary classroom. In a typical secondary school the students met from four to six teachers a day, all of whom contacted over one hundred students per day. The close relationship between the students and one teacher, typical of the elementary school, was lost. No teacher felt particular responsibility for a given child. The homeroom was developed to eliminate this shortcoming.

The homeroom, as it has been envisioned, has six major purposes. They are: to help students learn about the school and adapt themselves to its program; to develop self-expression and skill in planning and executing; to develop desirable social and civic behavior; to develop leadership and followership skills; to provide information and assistance on personal, vocational, and scholastic problems; and to assist the pupil in developing a sense of belonging. If a teacher accepts the homeroom as a major responsibility, it can be an effective device for pupil guidance. If he sees little value to students in the homeroom or if he considers it an extra burden, he can slight the job, and the homeroom is useless as a guidance procedure.

As the homeroom has developed in many high schools, it has not contributed as much as anticipated to the guidance function of the school. Sometimes the time allocated has been so short—five to ten minutes—that only announcements can be made and attendance-taking done. In other situations, even though there is sufficient time provided, the program has been repeated from year to year, and after the first year students have lost interest in the discussions. Other homerooms failed because the teacher had not worked out a routine for conducting administrative details, and the time of the homeroom group was spent fussing over such details or sitting quietly while the inefficient teacher served as class clerk. A major weakness of the program has thus been that many teachers did not know what to do with the homeroom period. Teacher-training institutions, for the most part, have done little to prepare beginning teachers to use the homeroom.

Probably the most common error has been use of the homeroom for a study period. If it is used for a last-minute skimming of lessons prior to students' going to classes, the homeroom is a wasted portion of the school day as far as guidance is concerned, and the time could have been better spent in class activities. In some junior high schools spelling has been crowded into the period. In such schools the homeroom has thus become a regular class and does not serve the guidance function for which it is intended.

A difficulty in some schools has been that the programs for the homerooms have been prepared by an outside agency and handed to the homeroom teacher as a syllabus. The homeroom became another class for the teacher to teach, and it became impossible for him to develop the self-direction and pupil-planning that are the essence of homeroom group guidance.

Some administrators have allowed homerooms to be disrupted by permitting students to be excused from the period. As these students were taken away to engage in other activities, the lack of importance

167

attached to the homeroom by the administration was emphasized both for those who went and for those who were left behind. Seeing how little value the administration attributed to the homeroom, students begin to take it less seriously.

If the homeroom is fulfilling its guidance function, the teacher is responsible for attendance, informing the student about the school, and the social guidance of the group with which he works. He is the faculty member who assists each student assigned to his homeroom to solve the difficulties encountered as he progresses through the school. Each member of his group is helped to feel a sense of belonging and to recognize that he has a contribution to make.

To be of most help in the social development of pupils, the homeroom should be composed of a heterogeneous group of students. Its population should spread across the socioeconomic levels of the community and the ability levels of the school. In this way, the homeroom becomes a laboratory where students have the opportunity to learn to know the people with whom they may not ordinarily associate and to work out skills of living together with people who are different.

If the homeroom teacher takes his job seriously, he will observe each child in many types of activities to detect strengths and weaknesses. He will watch during student planning in the homeroom in order to learn as much as he can about each individual child. He will be tactful, gentle, and calm, realizing that his function is not to direct, but rather to assist and to counsel. He will plan with the members of his homeroom, the type of organization needed, the method of choosing officers, the types of activities, and the social program. In his guidance functions he will help students discover requirements, make their own judgments, and develop the habit of evaluation of actions. Another major responsibility of the homeroom teacher is helping pupils in their relationships with other teachers. Policy concerning the role of the homeroom teacher should be agreed upon at faculty meetings. If this is not done, the teacher about whom the student talks may feel that the homeroom teacher is interfering in business that is not his. Agreement should be reached among members of the faculty that each teacher has the right and the responsibility to help each pupil in his homeroom to work out any difficulties that may arise with any other teacher.

In planning the homeroom, there are a number of topics that a class may wish to consider. Some of them are: how to succeed in school; how to study; how to select electives; how to choose a job;

how to select a college; how to use the library; how to budget time; how to get along with people; what satisfactory school conduct, parliamentary procedure, manners, dress, and sportsmanship are; how to select friends; and how to choose and devise proper means of amusement. These are only indicative of topics that have frequently been selected by homerooms. Any particular group may feel that these are unimportant and wish to discuss others that seem to them worthwhile. In schools where the homeroom is used more intelligently, these personal guidance functions are supplemented by opportunity to study school problems and develop proposed solutions, to acquaint pupils with the student activity program, to plan and hold social activities, to discuss human relations problems, and to serve as a basis for intramural activities.

One of the major values of the homeroom is the informal, casual pupil-teacher conferences. The homeroom teacher becomes someone to whom a student may take an inconsequential question or a serious personal problem. The teacher is constantly alert for the kinds of cues that indicate the need for referring the student to someone who is better trained to help meet the particular kind of difficulty.

It is helpful if the teacher remains with the same homeroom group for more than one year. In this way, the teacher becomes better able to know students and provide guidance, and students have the opportunity to develop a strong *esprit de corps*. But, due to the importance of the guidance aspect of the homeroom, it should also be possible for a student to be shifted to another homeroom when there is strong disagreement between him and the teacher. If the pupil is forced to remain in the same homeroom even though there is a strong personality clash with the teacher, he will not derive the guidance benefits from the situation that he should. No shift should be looked upon as detrimental to either the teacher or the student. It is simply a recognition that a person may work with one individual better than with another, and the administration, in seeking the best possible guidance situation, places people together who work in greatest harmony.

A faculty will do more effective work in the homerooms if there is a faculty committee with definite responsibility to work for improvement of homerooms. Such a group should coordinate the efforts of the total faculty, offer suggestions to other faculty members, and serve as a clearing house for ideas for possible organization of homerooms and for good guidance techniques. The committee should foster cooperation and experimentation. Some schools have found the following to be fruitful:

1. Holding meetings of homeroom teachers with guidance counselors for case study conferences. The trained guidance person
summarizes the information available about a pupil, and the
teachers involved plan the next steps that they feel would be
most helpful. This procedure not only increases insight into
the needs of the student under study, but also promotes the
teachers' sensitivity to the needs of all children.
2. Providing opportunities for students to rate their homeroom
periods and having the results presented without identifying
individuals involved. Students' dissatisfactions and criticisms
provide additional data for teachers to consider in planning
better ways of conducting the homeroom.
3. Encouraging teachers to have student committees visit other
homerooms. Through this student intervisitation good ideas
about operation and organization can be spread throughout
the school.
4. Recommending books dealing with homeroom activities for purchase for the teachers' professional library. The magazine *Student Activities* contains many ideas that teachers may want
to adopt.
5. Encouraging homeroom groups to plan and share programs with
each other. In this way the homeroom not only serves a guidance function, but also provides an opportunity to bring more
creativeness into the school. It can be used to give students
opportunities in writing, acting, and production.
6. Preparing a self-evaluation checklist that homeroom groups
and their teachers may use to evaluate the success of their
own operation. The groups may not accept this checklist, but
in a discussion as to whether they feel the criteria are important and being met they get ideas for improvement.

Students will feel that the homeroom is more important if it serves as
a basis for the organization of student government, student activities,
and the intramural sports program. If representatives on the student
council are chosen by the homeroom and issues before the council are
brought back by the representatives for discussion in the homerooms,
students will have the opportunity to learn more about the school and
to develop norms of behavior which will guide their actions. Making
the homeroom the basis of activities and intramurals gives the teacher
an opportunity to become a cooperative planning member of his group
in an important phase of school life. It enables him to adopt a role

which increases the possibility that students will accept him and turn to him with their problems.

The homeroom is a major unit in the guidance program of a secondary school if it is a social unit helping each student in the school to feel that he belongs there and that he has friends; if it is a place where students may examine together the activities of the school, make value judgments concerning them, and plan social activities; if it is used for planning dances and social programs, for discussing types of behavior that are acceptable, and for evaluating together the events that have transpired.

GUIDANCE BY THE CLASSROOM TEACHER

Guidance and teaching cannot be separated. Teachers do not operate as guidance workers one moment and teach subject matter the next. As a teacher teaches subject matter to one student, he provides guidance for another. As he teaches, he guides. The teacher's role is to help the individual and the group to become more self-directing. Further, he should work with the group in such a way that guidance may come from the total group or from various persons within it. As a teacher makes it possible for pupils to state what they believe or for the class to establish standards of behavior for itself, he is providing a guidance experience.

Self-direction consists of three major ingredients: knowing and accepting oneself, determining what one believes and the goals to which one is committed, and having the skills with which to work for the goals sought. Teachers can contribute to all of these types of pupil growth, or they can teach in ways that avoid having the pupil consider his strengths or weaknesses in any of these areas. The way the teacher works determines the degree of guidance he provides. If a teacher works with pupils in such a way that they are constantly asking themselves: "What am I like?" "What do I want to do?" "What are the resources available in the school?" "How can I improve what I am doing?"—then effective guidance is being carried on. If classes are conducted in such a way that the students have little to do except carry out the directions of the teacher, not much guidance is provided. If, however, the teacher constantly relies on questions such as: "What is the most important thing for us to do?" "What is the best way of doing it?" "How well have we carried out our purposes?"

"What change should we make in our purposes and our procedures?"
—then guidance is being carried on in every class period. Guidance
is the process of helping a student achieve increasingly intelligent
self-direction.

Knowing a pupil is basic if the teacher hopes to be an effective
guidance worker. Some teachers use a party or a class excursion as an
occasion to study pupils. By observing students in a social situation in
which they are relatively free, the teacher gains a more accurate
picture of the behavior of the individual and is better able to make
plans for the types of experiences which will help the youngster to
know himself. Some teachers do much to help pupils know and accept
themselves. They hold individual conferences to discuss goals and
plans; they listen to pupils' statements of aspirations, needs, plans, and
experiences; they share test results, which enables a pupil to gain a
realistic appraisal of his strengths and weaknesses; they help the pupil
keep a record of his products so that he can have a basis for making
judgments about his own progress; they call to the pupil's attention his
socially acceptable potential; they express their faith and confidence
in his ability to be successful.

The use of the sociogram technique within a class helps the teacher
discover which youngsters are accepted and which are isolated. When
he knows which pupils lack the social skills to secure acceptance, the
teacher is in a position to hear and understand the kinds of questions
such pupils raise. Knowing a student's concerns and needs is necessary if the teacher is to help him select instructional material.

> In one New York City high school, teachers found that they
> could perform guidance functions better by using projective
> techniques which enabled them to know their pupils. They had
> students write stories of their happiest and their most upsetting
> experiences, or they asked them to finish a story. Writing stories
> about pictures was another device. Students were shown a
> picture and were asked to write the story of the picture. What
> each student wrote was important because of what it told about
> his needs, his wishes, and his purposes. As teacher and student
> discussed what the student had said in his story, the student
> could collect information that he could apply to the solving of
> his own problems. Or if he felt secure enough in the discussion
> he could state his problem directly.

The writing of autobiography has proved to be another technique
for helping students know themselves. As the student is asked to look
back over his life and describe the important events, he goes through
a process of selecting the important from the unimportant. If the

autobiography is not merely another writing assignment, he learns more definitely what he values. Time taken by the teacher and class to discuss criteria for use in selecting facts and incidents to describe, and time taken to develop a clear understanding that recording of thoughts and opinions is as important as reporting actions, helps students make their analysis more vital.

Many regular classroom projects have guidance possibilities. Let us look at some examples.

> In Tuscaloosa, Alabama, some ninth grade English classes provided time for boys to list "What I like about girls" and for girls to list "What I like about boys." The process served two functions: it gave the students an opportunity to clarify what they thought about the opposite sex and to learn what qualities the opposite sex valued in them. The norms that the peer group makes evident in such listings constitute directives and guides to action for the members of the classes involved.

> In Jacksonville Beach, Florida, an English teacher was attempting to improve speech habits. She brought a tape recorder to class and sought a topic in which boys and girls in the ninth grade would be interested. She found it when the students began to discuss how to behave on dates. Interest was high, and students soon forgot their shyness and reserve. Not only did the topic serve as a way of helping youngsters to talk freely and to hear themselves as the tape was played back, but it also gave them an opportunity to consider different viewpoints with regard to their own behavior. The pupils' comments gave the teacher an opportunity to ask questions the youngsters could examine. The same tapes were useful at parent meetings. As parents heard ninth-graders discussing behavior on dates and their problems with parents, they were stimulated to examine together the problems of dating and to learn from each other different ways of working with adolescents.

> In Sarasota, Florida, parents and adolescents had been having disagreements over the time to come home, behavior on dates, and the proper amount of spending money. Differences in the way various parents dealt with these problems caused dissatisfaction among the boys and girls and disapproval on the part of the parents. The home economics teacher and one of her classes attempted to do something about the problem. They invited parents who were interested and adolescents who were willing to participate to sit down together and think through parent-teenager difficulties. After meeting and talking together a number of times, the group agreed upon a statement of principles which should guide both parents and adolescents. The code worked so well that when four years later other parents and children in the same community re-examined the statement

to see what changes should be made they agreed that the answers were still good and were ones that both parents and
adolescents should be content to follow.

The classroom teacher makes his contribution to guidance through
planning with pupils, helping them evaluate their progress, helping
them develop self-control and self-reliance, and helping them revise
the plan in light of the evidence they collect. In-service training in
teacher-pupil planning techniques and evaluation procedures constitutes basic help to the classroom teacher in performing his guidance
function. Equally helpful is a study of the emotional needs of youth
and methods of meeting them. Being able to accept and understand
adolescents is essential if the high school teacher is to be an effective
guidance worker.

To be able to help in guidance, all of the school personnel should
be sensitive to the problems confronting youth. They should know
the concerns and motivations of youth. They should be sympathetic to
the problems youth encounter in seeking more adult status. They must
be willing to take the time to talk with boys and girls who seek their
counsel. But being sensitive is not enough. Teachers must also be
aware of the symptoms of difficulties with which they are unable to
help students. They should know the signs of emotional distress and
deterioration of personality that require more skilled treatment. One
of the major problems for classroom teachers is to learn to distinguish
between the problems with which they can be of assistance and the
ones that require treatment by a specialist. It helps if they are familiar
with the principles of mental hygiene and have an understanding of
the reasons for the prescribed treatment. In carrying out treatment, it
may be necessary to place the mental health of the student above
scholarship within a certain subject-matter area.

A basic element of planning for guidance in a school is for each
teacher to examine himself to see what types of pupils he has difficulty in accepting. Teachers are unable to provide guidance for those
whom they reject. If the guidance program of a school is to be
strengthened, each faculty member must continually extend his own
range of acceptance. When he finds that he cannot accept certain
students, he must be willing to admit it to himself and others and
to work out ways in which these students will have opportunities to
work with teachers who can both accept and assist them in solving
their own problems.

GUIDANCE THROUGH NONCLASS ACTIVITIES

A secondary school provides guidance for the student whether he wants it or not. It may be a negative kind of guidance, but the way the faculty works, the kind of courses offered, the attitude of the administration, all constitute guidance for individual pupils. In a typical school, students are helped to learn about the school through a handbook, an orientation program, the school paper, and the advisement program; they are helped to plan their school experiences through preregistration counseling, homeroom discussion, and pupil-teacher planning within the various classes; they are assisted in their postschool planning through career conferences, vocational materials and college catalogs in the library, try-out work experiences, and interviews with representatives of various colleges.

School publications provide guidance. The handbook tells about activities and describes the organization and regulations of the school. It helps the new student become acquainted with the accepted pattern of behavior. The student paper is equally important. Through the editorials, student opinion and standards of behavior are formed. The cartoons that appear help students decide what is funny and what is unwise. The type of news that receives the biggest amount of space and headlines helps to form the opinion of the student body as to what is important. The recognition that is given to certain students indicates the kind of values that are important in the school.

The orientation week helps students become acquainted with the building, the staff personnel, the student leaders, and the activity program. In most orientation programs, the new students are provided with excursions around the school conducted by teachers or upperclassmen. These help to decrease the feeling of strangeness and provide them with more information and knowledge of sources of help and the location of service facilities. Some schools use talks by upperclassmen to explain the program to newcomers, believing that students are better able to put themselves in the new pupil's place and to interpret the school in his language. In some schools the counselors and representative students go to the feeder schools and talk to prospective entrants about the program of the high school. In still other systems, students in their last year at the feeder schools are brought to the high school for a full day's visit to get acquainted with the program before they enter. As new students have these experiences they begin to set their goals concerning the position they want to assume in the school they are entering. They decide which activities seem important, which social groups desirable.

The library contributes to the guidance program, too. If the library is a place that is attractive and comfortable, students are encouraged to go there. If it is formal and dreary, it is a place to avoid. If the library has a good selection of materials describing various vocations, students have the opportunity to secure the information that enables them to make better choices. The range of fiction helps to shape the reading tastes of youth. A good autobiography section, in which students can read about great men past and present, assists students in setting their own goals and standards.

Classroom appearance and the art displayed in the building also serve as guides. If the classrooms are littered, dirty, and unkempt, certain standards of neatness and appearance are being taught. The reverse is promoted if the rooms are well organized, materials are kept in the appointed places, the colors used in the rooms are harmonious, and the furniture arrangement is conducive to the types of activities underway there. The types of pictures, ceramics, or craftwork displayed in the cafeteria, hallway, or showcases also contribute to the formation of standards that students acquire. Lack of any such exhibits teaches something about the place of art desired in the life of the individual. The displays on library, corridor, and classroom bulletin boards are also guides. A school's values are revealed by its displays. Students learn from the indirect approach as well as from the direct statements of people. The types of books recommended, the type of humor represented, the type of art displayed, all constitute information that a student uses in forming his own standards.

Many phases of the school program provide informal guidance of one type or another. Assemblies give students clues as to what is desirable. The kinds of programs presented indicate what the administration and the student government consider important. The points of view and questions advanced by speakers or movies used in assembly serve as a basis for discussion in classes and homerooms. The assemblies also teach how to behave in a large group. If the staff is skillful, assemblies may be used to teach how to participate in discussions in a large group situation.

One of the primary outcomes sought in a modern secondary school program is student self-knowledge. As the research of Carl Rogers indicates, being increasingly accurate about himself is one of the major factors in student achievement of emotional health. Many techniques have been developed for helping students learn about themselves. Perhaps the most common way is by providing opportunity for the student to talk with his counselors. Some schools schedule a talk between each student and his counselor once each semester. In less structured situations no routine is established and the student is free to seek counseling when he wishes it. Another method is the discussion group, in which members talk about the problems that confront them as adolescents. As students listen to their peers present their viewpoints they learn to analyze their own feelings and values. Common topics are dating, relationship with parents, daydreaming, and career-planning.

The testing program, in which a student has the opportunity to compare his own responses with the countrywide norms that have been established for his age, gives him a clearer picture of his own capabilities. He has a better basis upon which to judge his own performance and to make judgments about the possibility of attaining various goals that he is considering. The testing program guides. Although the statement that the person who controls the testing program controls the curriculum of the school is probably an exaggeration, certainly the tests used do make clear to students what the faculty deems important. Even when a faculty disclaims a belief in the value of a test, its use convinces the student that the faculty considers the skill or information sampled to be important. If the testing program is for the most part the kind that helps the student explore his capabilities and his interests rather than tests that are looked upon as hurdles that must be cleared, the testing program becomes one of the most important school experiences in helping a student know himself. It encourages the student to look for both his strengths and his weaknesses rather than to attempt to deceive both the teacher and himself about his weaknesses.

Vocational guidance is provided through career conferences in which students have the opportunity to talk with persons from various occupations. The information supplied helps the student learn about a range of vocations from which he may choose. Too many times students are unaware of the variety of job opportunities. Their vision is restricted by the contact that they have had with persons from a few occupations. The increase in information supplied by a career conference may lead to a wiser selection of vocation.

The student government is also a form of group guidance. The policies that are developed by the government are more important than any control that it exerts. To the extent that the student government involves a major portion of the student body in thinking through problems and forming new policies, the guidance function is enhanced. Individual students form their own standards as they assist in the formulation of schoolwide standards.

> In Niles, Illinois, the students, with the leadership of the student council, drew up a code of behavior for Niles High School students. Council representatives took the problem to each homeroom and obtained suggestions for items that should be included. After suggestions from the total school had been secured, a rough draft was formulated, and each homeroom was given an opportunity to analyze the draft. In terms of the criticism that came from the review of the draft by the homerooms, a final statement was prepared and adopted. This statement told each member of the student body what other members of the student body thought was suitable behavior and what was expected of him. It gave each student a clear definition of acceptable behavior.

> In the 1930's Wilson Junior High School in Hamilton, Ohio, took a week to write a constitution. Regular classes did not meet. Students and teachers, organized into committees to develop special sections of the constitution, met together in a convention. They then brought their proposals back to the constitutional assembly and carried through the processes of forming a constitution. Students gained a knowledge of how governmental organization is achieved, but they also learned how people become self-directing by formulating the principles that will guide their behavior.

The club program guides by providing activities in which students have the opportunity to explore ideas and techniques with which they are not acquainted. Hobby clubs, interest clubs in subject-matter fields, service clubs, all constitute opportunities to develop leadership skills and to discover or deepen interests in a particular field.

> In a New York City junior high school, a teacher provided guidance by organizing charm clubs that girls could join if they wished to learn more about dress and makeup. The underlying assumption was that if students became able to make themselves more attractive, they would become more secure because they felt more certain of themselves.

> In a Florida senior high school, time was provided in the schedule for free activity periods one hour a week in which a student might pursue his chief interest. By this procedure it was possible for teachers to discover what students' real concerns were and to be in a better position to assist the student in thinking about his purposes and his use of time. The students had

proof under this plan that the school was concerned with providing them opportunity to pursue their own interests.

The school award and honor system gives indirect guidance. The types of activities for which honors are given indicate the phases of the school program that are valued by the staff. The extent to which honors are restricted indicates the types of leadership that are recognized. If a faculty has established an awards system that is inconsistent with the philosophy of the school, students are influenced more by the emphasis on awards than by a faculty statement of ideals.

The attitudes of teachers constitute guidance cues for pupils. If teachers let students know directly or subtly that they believe that the college preparatory course is the best course and that a general course is for the misfits in the school, they exert a powerful guiding force. They influence those children with whom their opinion counts to take the approved program whether the pupils need it or not.

The appearance of teachers is a phase of group guidance. If teachers wear clothes with good design and colors that harmonize, students are assisted in formulating their standards of good taste. If, on the other hand, they are nondescript and careless in their dress, their influence is negative. Style shows held by student groups also affect the development of taste in clothes. As students plan what they will include in the style show they are developing standards of taste. Students who attend the performance may go only to see their friends, but they are confronted with certain standards of dress that they evaluate and accept or reject.

ORGANIZATION FOR GUIDANCE

In the organization of a high school guidance program, the principal is responsible for developing an attitude in the faculty that will make guidance a part of the school program and for the selection and training of the personnel, counselors, and others who act as leaders, coordinators, and consultants in the guidance activity.

The guidance staff of trained counselors provides leadership and support for the remainder of the faculty. Its function is to stimulate and assist the classroom teacher in the performance of guidance activities. In addition, the staff is responsible for conducting the program of testing and recording, for working out articulation between the elementary school and the high school and the high school and the college, for providing assistance to graduates and drop-outs in securing employment, and for counseling students concerning scholastic, vocational, and personal problems.

In some large schools grade advisers may be added to the counseling personnel. They help the classes to which they are assigned plan classwide social activities, select class symbols and equipment, and advise on registration procedures.

Many schools have found it advisable to have a guidance committee. The committee's function is to discuss the present guidance policies and make recommendations to the total faculty. It is not their job to decide on details of administration. Procedures will be worked out by the guidance specialists after a policy has been agreed upon by the faculty. The guidance committee should also serve as a continuing evaluation group, collecting evidence and making judgments concerning the existing guidance program. Obviously, the committee should contain classroom teachers as well as guidance personnel. If the committee is comprised entirely of specialisits, it will be deemed impractical and unrealistic by the faculty. It will be under suspicion because the staff will believe that these outsiders have a special interest to promote. A faculty believes wholeheartedly in a program that it has developed, and it will do everything in its power to make that program succeed.

The guidance program is good if the staff realizes that guidance is where students find it and not where the staff says they can find it. Each person chooses his own counselor. For a given student, it may be the school nurse, the custodian, or another student. If guidance is to have any meaning, it must be provided by teachers whom students accept as their counselors. Too often schools have not recognized that other students are probably the most important guidance factor in the entire school situation. In the Grand Rapids, Michigan, English workshop described earlier, good students served as counselors. Other students came to the selected students for help and advice on their English problems. But the assistance did not stop with grammar and literature. New students and less well-adjusted students in the school asked their student advisers how to become participants in certain activities, what to wear to dances, and how to get along with certain teachers. At times the difficulty with English served only as a convenient approach to talking over a more personal problem with a student whom the questioner respected.

Department meetings may be used to plan guidance activities. At one time the Business Education Department of a Norwalk, Connecticut, high school spent one meeting a month discussing the pupils whom they taught. They discussed each pupil enrolled in the department, listed his strengths and weaknesses, and told what they had been doing for him and the additional help they believed they should provide. At a meeting all of the teachers working with an individual gained more information about him, and the staff was able to develop a more reasonable and consistent approach to dealing with the pupil.

All school personnel have a responsibility for performing guidance functions. The principal, the teacher, the custodian, the lunchroom supervisor, and the bus driver can assist pupils to know themselves and to use the school environment better.

The organization of the guidance program must be one in which the local faculty believes; the personnel involved must be people the faculty and the students accept; time must be made available for the counselors to conduct the guidance activities. Guidance cannot be accomplished if it is viewed as something extra to be worked at whenever there are a few spare moments.

SUMMARY

Guidance is the process of helping a pupil to know himself, his purposes, his strengths, his weaknesses, his values, and his needs; to discover and use the resources in the environment that will further his purposes and satisfy his needs; and constantly to evaluate and revise his purposes and plans. In short, guidance is the process of helping a pupil to become increasingly self-directing by being better able to recognize and solve his own problems. Better guidance is provided for the pupil only to the extent to which the living together in the school assists him to identify and work out solutions to his own problems.

SELECTED READINGS

Adams, Georgia S., "Employment Service Serves the School," *Occupations* 30: 668-669, May, 1952. Describes some of the ways in which state employment services can cooperate with the schools in helping pupils prepare for and find employment.
Allen, Charles, "What Have Our Drop-Outs Learned?" *Educational Leader-*

181

ship 10: 347-350, March, 1953. Asserts that better counseling and meeting the needs of all youth can reduce the rate of drop-outs.

Andrew, Dean C. and Ray DeVerl Willey, *Administration and Organization of the Guidance Program*. New York: Harper & Row, Publishers, 1958. Describes the role of the school administrator in developing an effective guidance program.

Arnholter, Ethelwyne G., "School Persistence and Personality Factors," *Personnel and Guidance Journal* 35: 107-109, October, 1956. Provides evidence that there is a significant difference in personality adjustment between students who drop out and those who graduate.

Association for Supervision and Curriculum Development, *Guidance in the Curriculum* (1955 Yearbook). Washington, D. C.: The Association, 1955. Views guidance as an inseparable part of the school curriculum.

Barry, Ruth and Beverly Wolf, "The Genesis of Guidance Personnel Work," *Teachers College Record* 58: 382-396, April, 1957. Studies the development of guidance as a response to social and economic changes in our culture.

Carlson, Mabel B. and T. Earl Sullenger, "A Study of Certain Areas in Which High School Youth Desire Counseling," *Journal of Educational Sociology* 31: 179-182, January, 1958. Points out some of the areas of counseling that are often neglected.

Cook, Edward S., Jr., "An Analysis of Factors Related to Withdrawal from High School Prior to Graduation," *Journal of Educational Research* 50: 191-196, November, 1956. Concludes that withdrawal from school stems from a multiplicity of factors that appear insurmountable to the student.

Farwell, G. F., "Continuity in the Guidance Program," *Educational Leadership* 18: 338-342, March, 1961. Advocates use of a developmental approach in providing continuity in the guidance program.

Froehlich, C. P., *Guidance Services in Schools*. New York: McGraw-Hill Book Co., Inc., 1958. Outlines the basic guidance services that should be available in every school.

Hutson, P. W., *The Guidance Function in Education*. New York: Appleton-Century-Crofts, Inc., 1958. Reviews the development of guidance and its role, practice, and purposes as part of the modern school program.

Jersild, Arthur T., *When Teachers Face Themselves*. New York: Columbia University Press, 1955. Focuses on the relationship of a teacher's self-acceptance and self-understanding to his ability to help others know themselves and develop healthy personalities.

Johnson, Mauritz, Jr., William E. Busacker, and Fred Q. Bowman, Jr., *Junior High School Guidance*. New York: Harper & Row, Publishers, 1961. Provides an historical, philosophical, and administrative background together with current practices and principles of guidance in the junior high school.

Kelley, J. A., *Guidance and Curriculum*. Englewood Cliffs, N. J.: Prentice-Hall, Inc., 1955. Emphasizes the integral role that guidance plays as part of the total educational program.

Kvaraceus, W. C., "The Counselor's Role in Combating Juvenile Delinquency," *Personnel and Guidance Journal* 36: 99-103, October, 1957. Urges the school and the community to work together more closely in combating juvenile delinquency.

Livingston, A. Hugh, "High-School Graduates and Drop-Outs: A New Look at a Persistent Problem," *School Review* 66: 195-203, Summer, 1958. Suggests that such factors as school "climate," home backgrounds, pupil motivation, and relations with school staff all play a part in drop-outs.

Murphy, J. F., "The Guidance Program and Curriculum Improvement," *National Association of Secondary School Principals Bulletin* 43: 31-36, May, 1961. Outlines the major purposes and tasks of the guidance program in helping to improve the curriculum.

Pry, H. C., "Home-Room Teacher's Responsibility for Curricular Guidance," *Ibid.*, 43: 19-25, October, 1959. Discusses the role of the home-room teacher in providing guidance for his students.

Reeves, J. M. and Leo Goldman, "Social Class Perceptions and School Maladjustment," *Personnel and Guidance Journal* 35: 414-419, March, 1957. Reports an experimental study which found that disturbed relations with peers can be a basis for maladjustment in school.

Rogers, Carl R., Bill L. Kell, and Helen McNeil, "The Role of Self-Understanding in the Prediction of Behavior," *Journal of Consulting Psychology* 12: 174-186, May-June, 1948. Concludes that the best index to the later adjustment of a delinquent is his own self-adjustment.

Spellman, C. T., "Curriculum Guidance for High School Students," *School and Society* 89: 183-185, April 8, 1961. Describes many of the services that guidance can provide for high school students.

9

THE OUT-OF-CLASS
CURRICULUM

The first thing I noticed as we stopped in front of the attractive
high school building in a western city were the small holes in
various window panes. Rocks had been hurled through them.
As we walked the forty yards to the door, I saw two fights in
progress, one to my left and one to my right. Inside the door
I was struck by the black surface of the hallways and the
yellow stripe painted in the exact middle the full length of
the corridor. At intervals of approximately fifty feet stood boys
wearing Sam Browne belts. They were insisting that all traffic
keep to the right. The bustle of passing students was great and
the noise at a high level.

Upon entering the principal's outer office, my attention was
caught by two long lines of students, girls in one and boys
in the other. The separation of sexes was being enforced by
a secretary yelling in a shrill voice to any who chanced to
get into the wrong line. Getting an admittance slip after being
tardy or absent was the major concern of many that morning.
Four boys came into the office and began to make shaming
signs at four others seated on the "mourners' bench." It was

obvious that the seated quartet was in trouble. The leader, seeing us waiting, arose, sidled over to me, and asked out of the corner of his mouth: "Are you a cop?"

We could not get to see the principal immediately, so we wandered down the hall to the art room. No one was there, but we entered and looked. All of the drawings and paintings were done in small, tight lines, and only dark blues, purples, blacks, and browns were used. Not a broad stroke or a pastel color was in the room.

On the way back to the principal's office we passed a door with the sign "Guidance Office" above it. Seated at the desk was an attractive woman talking to a lovely girl of about fourteen, who was standing. Both were smiling at each other. But as we passed, the girl turned to leave. When her face was turned away from the counselor the smile left her face, and her lips formed the words: "I'll be damned if I will!"

As we re-entered the administration suite, a stout teacher in her fifties emerged from the principal's office, walking with angry steps.

The principal motioned for us to enter. He closed the door, threw himself in his chair, put his head in his hands, and said: "That is the fifth one this morning. Look!" He handed me two pages filled with small, firm handwriting. The one thought elaborated upon for the full two pages was that a boy was insubordinate because he had refused to remove his jacket when the teacher told him to.

We left as quickly as we politely could. In the thirty minutes we had been in the building we had received many clues concerning the nonclass curriculum of the school.

Later in the day I was speaking a hundred miles away and felt that, if I did not name the school, it would be safe to describe it to illustrate a point. To my chagrin, the first question in the discussion period following my presentation was: "You were describing ————— High School, weren't you?"

A school curriculum is more than classes. It consists of all the experiences of a pupil under the supervision of school authorities. In the secondary school a large portion of the day is spent in nonclass activities in which the student also learns. This phase of the curriculum includes the social and physical environment, the personnel services, the student activities, and the student government. The contribution of these elements (except student government and student activities which will be examined in the next chapter) to a student's values and to his conception of a desirable way to live constitutes the content of this chapter.

THE PHYSICAL ENVIRONMENT

As one visits secondary schools throughout the United States, one is impressed by certain common characteristics, but even more by the uniqueness of individual schools. All have classrooms, laboratories, gymnasiums, cafeterias, libraries, and administration offices. Some are beautiful; others are drab. Some are restful; others are noisy. Some are stimulating; others are uninteresting. Some are sumptuous; others are meager. Each has its distinctive qualities which contribute to desirable or undesirable learning. Size and newness are not the determining factors. The way in which the existing facilities are used is much more important. Persons concerned with improving the curriculum should look carefully at the plant that houses the student body. Is it a place where a boy or girl or teacher enjoys spending the day? Does it suggest that interesting things are happening there? Is it appealing or repelling in its appearance?

The appearance of the building is the first thing that students notice, so a school should be attractive. If the building is dark, dingy, and unattractive, they are not proud to enter. If it is dingy, it suggests that the curriculum is dingy and unimportant. Youth resists the dull, the dingy, and the dusty. They are attracted to light, to brightness, to color. *The appearance of the school should give the impression that the school is a place where it would be fun to live and work.*

For too long, school buildings had been brown or gray or neutral in their appearance. A city in upper New York State had a two-million-dollar high school building with an outside of stone, marble, and brick that gave an appearance of stability, strength, and culture. On the inside, even though the building had been occupied for ten years, no classroom had been painted. The walls and ceilings of the hallways and classrooms were a dirty gray where dust and dirt had accumulated on the white plaster. After sitting in a classroom in this building for an hour, the casual observer began to wish for the end of the half-day that he was assigned to be there. A coat of paint that would have cost very little would have completely changed the appearance of the building. Instead of looking like a run-down institution, it could have been a school that students would want to show to their friends. With industrial research showing the influence of color on morale and production, school people fail in their responsibility if they do not make the community aware that penny-pinching on paint decreases the effectiveness of the total program. (It should be noted that in the city mentioned above many of the industrial plants made the most modern use of color dynamics.)

Lighting is a second aspect of the physical facilities affecting learning. It contributes to appearance, but, even more important, poor lighting also prevents youth from doing their best class work. If the wattage is insufficient, reading produces tension and strain, and the pupil avoids it where possible. When this happens, he seeks satisfaction in some manner other than reading. When consideration is given to how much of school work is reading, the importance of adequate lighting is readily apparent. A revealing experience for most curriculum committees is to use a light meter and make a survey of lighting conditions in their building.

The noise level also affects learning. Research in industry has indicated that much fatigue is due to excessive noise. To create a desirable learning situation, effort should be exerted to reduce to a minimum the noise created by students moving around and working together. Some faculties have sought to secure relative quiet by reducing activity and regimentation. This approach also reduces learning. The proper procedure is to recognize that learning involves activity and to adapt the housing to accommodate it. Acoustic tiles for the ceiling absorb much of the noise. Rubber taps on the chairs and tables decrease nerve-jarring sounds. Arranging the room in a way to create alcoves for different types of work decreases interference of small group work with the total class operation. *Steps taken to decrease the amount of noise by structure, furnishings, and room arrangement increase the effectiveness of the instruction and improve the quality of learning.* Groups working on curriculum improvement should study the noise level in different portions of the building. Sometimes a shift in room assignments to group noise-producing classes in the same section of the building improves the situation.

The building should be neat. Are classrooms cluttered with materials not in use? Are hallways used for storage? Do offices have the appearance of rats' nests because of papers strewn about? If so, pupils gain the impression that the school is a haphazard sort of experience, lacking in organization and structure. Students from well-ordered homes are repelled, and those from homes where poor management and poor housekeeping are typical do not have an opportunity to become acquainted with a different way of living. If the school wishes to teach good management of materials, the staff organizes the building in such a way that there are inconspicuous storage places for the items used in instruction and maintenance.

The school building should be livable. It should be a place where youth feels at home. Classrooms with drapes or gay curtains and space where students may display the products of their work contribute to a sense of possessing and belonging. Nooks around the building where students can relax during free time, and lounges to which students may go for small group meetings or for activities make the school a more desirable place to be. Schools in the warmer climates often provide patios where students may sit and relax. Many schools place chairs and couches at various locations around the building where students may converse. Some schools station receptionists with tables and chairs, desks, and table lamps at the entrances. These devices make the school a place to live as well as to attend classes. How the student feels about the school affects his effort and what he learns.

The extent to which a school building is kept flexible is indicative of the staff's willingness to work in terms of the purposes and needs of the people who inhabit it. Rigidity and fixedness in the operation of a building indicate that the staff believes that curriculum should be prestructured and that teachers and classes and individuals should conform to the existing structure without bringing their purposes and their desires to bear on changing the environment or the curriculum to fit their needs. If classrooms are fixed and seats are fastened to the floor, it seems evident that the individual is supposed to conform to the environment. If, however, the furniture in the rooms is movable and can be rearranged to meet the varying activities of the class, it is evident that the purpose that a group has is the important element, and that materials and room structure are flexible and subject to change in order to facilitate the purposes of the class.

Beauty should be evident throughout the building. As the student walks the halls, does he see more space assigned to the trophy case than he does to paintings and ceramics? Is there a student mural in the building? Are flowers or plants used for decorating? *The school teaches appreciation for beauty by the extent to which art is a part of the life of the school.* If art is restricted to the studios, the student learns that it is a hobby or occupation for a few, not a functional part of everyday life. Pictures, sculpture, draperies, and flowers should be a part of the living space for all. If the school has a special work of art that the student body and faculty value it adds to the quality of living in the school. The sculpture, *The Burning Bush,* in the central patio at the

Austin, Minnesota, High School is an excellent example of the contribution of a work of art to school living.

Classrooms should be large. Human relationships and learning effectiveness deteriorate when people are crowded. Classrooms should have adequate space for students to move about, to do committee work, to engage in creative activities in various media, and to present creative expressions of points of view and interpretations of experiences. It is not sufficient to have space for desks for the teacher and each pupil. Classrooms that are so crowded that it is impossible to do group work limit the quality of curricular experiences provided in the school.

The classrooms should be separated from each other as much as possible. If classrooms are so close together that each class must be constantly concerned about the ways in which its activities may affect nearby groups, the range of possible learning activities is limited. If land is available, a *campus* for a high school is preferable to a single building. In a campus situation the noise of the two or three rooms that are located together do not affect the entire school. A second desirable plan is a building on one floor with a series of wings extending away from the central unit. By this plan the number of rooms adjacent to each other is decreased, and the activities in one room are less likely to interfere with the class in another. If a compact building is necessary, the rooms should be situated in such a way that the windows of one room do not face directly on the windows of another room. Plenty of space for committee work, for informal group living, and for nonclass activities should be provided.

The physical environment facilitates desirable student growth or handicaps the faculty's efforts to promote it. No staff should make the mistake of assuming that the plant is not part of the pupil's curriculum. In fact, the building shows what someone believes about curriculum. Is the plant for physical education large, modern, and well supplied? Is the band room larger and more generously endowed than the library? Are the shops better equipped than the science laboratories? Is an undue portion of the building devoted to space for the administrative suite? Do teachers have lounges and offices, but students no gathering places or rooms for their out-of-class activities? Values are taught by housing and equipment as well as by teachers' statements.

THE SOCIAL ENVIRONMENT

Each school has a
distinctive social climate that can be felt. Some student bodies greet
all newcomers and visitors with friendliness; others ignore or insult
them. Some student bodies pass cheerfully through the halls, calling
greetings to friend; others seem sullen and subdued; others are rowdy,
shoving and pushing. Some schools seem friendly, happy places; others
are cold, indifferent, or hostile. The youths who attend a school live
in its social atmosphere and absorb values and behavior patterns.

The principal plays a major role in determining the social climate
of a school. In a leadership study conducted at the University of
Florida a positive correlation was found between the way a principal
worked and the human relations in the faculty and the student body.
If the principal behaved democratically, there were fewer fights and
quarrels in the student body and more willingness to accept persons
who were different. *If persons responsible for high schools want youth
to acquire increased ability to live and work with others, they should
seek administrators who consult before taking action, cooperate in the
decision-making process, and seek generally to increase their own
sensitivity to the feelings of others.*

Teachers also contribute to the social climate. The extent to which
teachers understand and accept adolescents affects pupil-teacher relationships. Bush, in his book *The Teacher-Pupil Relationship,* a report
of a research study, states that "teachers have a strong personal liking
for the academically inclined pupil who learns his lessons well, who
conducts himself well, and who agrees with the teacher on social
issues." But teachers must go beyond this point if the social curriculum
of a school is to be good for all youth. Bush suggests that

> . . . a strategic task for the teacher is the cultivation on his part
> of the personal liking of his students for him. This requires a
> teacher who is skilled, sensitive, and adjusted in the area of
> personal relationships and who is able to handle his relations
> with pupils objectively rather than as a source of meeting his
> own personal inadequacies. Learning is enhanced markedly
> when teachers make themselves personally acceptable to pupils.

> More effective relationship between pupils and teachers will
> probably result when teachers carry with them in their minds
> an individualized picture of each pupil which encompasses
> some accurate information about his (1) health; (2) abilities,
> aptitudes, competencies, and interests; (3) ambitions, purposes,

desires; (4) special blocks, stresses, or strains; and (5) the cultural milieu, including the home situation from which he comes. [Robert N. Bush, *The Teacher-Pupil Relationship* (Englewood Cliffs, N. J.: Prentice-Hall, Inc., 1954), pp. 189-191.]

This research leads to the conclusion that *one way for a staff to improve the curriculum is to take time to learn about the pupils enrolled in their classes and to try to get an accurate picture of the way in which they, as individuals, relate to pupils.*

The phase of the social climate that students feel most is the way their peers treat them. A sense of belonging and of being wanted are vitally important. Some student bodies make an inclusive approach: newcomers are welcomed; many social functions are open to all. Others display exclusiveness: newcomers must prove themselves; small groups form which consider themselves superior to others and try to prove it by striving for favored roles and status positions. Sororities and fraternities accentuate the problem in some secondary schools. The social activities of a school reveal much about the social climate. Are the parties held by exclusive groups? Are dances so expensive that a large portion of the student body cannot attend? Are the students who are deficient in social skills assisted in acquiring them? Answers to questions such as these reveal whether the social curriculum needs improvement.

A faculty that wants a highly productive student body will promote friendliness and inclusiveness. Studies of drop-outs in the Grand Rapids, Michigan, high schools showed that students who had friends in the student body and who participated in some status activity did not leave school. Orientation weeks, big brother and big sister plans, and social activities open to all are ways of promoting a good social environment.

A faculty concerned with the social environment must be alert for evidences of tension. A very simple thing to look for is the kinds of remarks that people make to each other in a class or on the school ground. Do students of one racial group make disparaging remarks about another? Do members of one religion call members of other religions derogatory names? Do gangs in the school attack other students on the way home or in the evening? Are rocks hurled through the windows of nearby synagogues and churches? Are inscriptions that belittle and deride scrawled on walls in public places?

The faculty that is alert to human relations problems takes preventive steps. Aggression toward another usually starts with a feeling of insecurity or inadequacy. A first step is to work for the kind of acceptance and the feeling of belonging that make it unnecessary for a person to exercise aggression toward another. The staff should attempt to help youngsters acquire this sense of adequacy. One of our larger cities maintains a special school to which youngsters who have had difficulty in other schools are sent. In this school teachers police youngsters. They always take the position in a classroom where they can watch, catch, and punish offenders. When I spoke in an assembly in this school on the topic of democracy, teachers patrolled the aisles of the auditorium facing the pupils rather than the speaker. By this action they made it very clear to the pupils that the staff did not believe that they could be trusted or would be interested in the topic. In such a situation, where the youngsters feel inadequate before they come and where teachers increase their sense of insecurity by giving visual proof that they are not trusted, it is to be expected that acts of aggression toward other people will take place. And they do. It is to be expected that minority groups will be subject to attacks by majority groups in the attempt of the members of the majority groups to develop their own sense of security and adequacy. *As much is taught about human relations by the way the staff attempts to relate to pupils as by teachers' statements.*

A second step the staff can take is to emphasize the value of differences. Too many times differences are looked upon by pupils and teachers as something to be minimized and even overcome. Actually, differences as well as likenesses can be assets. Values and beliefs held in common can be bonds to hold people together while differences are examined. Through the examination of differences new insights can be obtained which will enrich the lives of all. Youth need to have an opportunity to examine this concept. Many have been taught that the person who is different is a person to be suspected or persecuted.

Some secondary schools are confronted by drastic problems in human relations. Open conflict between racial, religious, or economic groups exists. Two common problems are the exclusion of individuals or small groups (because of race, religion, or some factor in their background) and conflict between two approximately equal groups. Of the two, the latter problem is the more difficult. In the situation where members of a minority are excluded, the solution lies in helping the people who are in the majority to obtain experience that will help them to overcome their prejudices. In a situation in which two groups of approximately equal size are in conflict, the first step is to seek leaders in each group who see the desirability of reaching agreement. Improvement depends upon supporting and aiding the students who see the need for harmony.

The school alone cannot resolve problems in human relations. What the staff finds in the high school population is a reflection of the tensions and terrors of the entire community. Because representatives of all groups attend school, the difficulties are brought out into the open. Community planning is necessary, and the student government or the faculty can assume leadership in bringing the community resources together to formulate a plan for improvement.

THE LIBRARY

The school library is another place in which important out-of-class experiences are provided. In the past, too many libraries have been considered places where books are kept. The librarian has been judged by whether or not the books were kept in good condition, a practice that has led many conscientious librarians to put primary emphasis on protecting the books. Students were kept from handling materials without permission. Fortunately, many faculties now see the library as the center of the school and recognize that it should be one of the most attractive areas in the building. More and more libraries are being furnished with reading nooks, easy chairs, open shelves, magazine racks, attractive drapes that add color and life, displays of book jackets and other types of material that entice pupils to sample and read. The library should not only be a place where a student can come to prepare an assignment. It also is a place where people develop their leisure-time reading habits, where committees go to work on projects, where students are welcome to browse and explore. In a good high school library great emphasis is placed on having students come into contact with all of the materials to be found there. The librarian sees her role as a resource person and curriculum leader. She trains student assistants and counsels students in their reading. She is available to work with student committees or individual students who come to the library with a problem. She goes beyond locating the material the student requests and suggests other suitable sources.

The librarian is also an important person in the curriculum development program of the school. She aids teachers in collecting materials that they need for new activities, serves as a coordinator in the collection of recommendations for new purchases for the school library, and secures student recommendations for improvement of the library. In the curriculum committees, she calls the attention of the staff to new publications that have been added to the library, and she plans with teachers the types of materials that they need for use in their classes. She assists in securing books for the professional library. As new professional books are published, she calls them to the attention of teachers and committees who may wish to have her purchase them. The librarian also expects that teachers want to know about curricular innovations and will continually recommend newly published material that they should consider.

In the modern school library, the librarian works with more than printed materials of learning. She coordinates the collection and organization of tapes, records, film strips, motion pictures, books, or programed learning. Another important library service in the development of an up-to-date curriculum is the formation of an extensive vertical file. No matter how fast books are published they are not able to keep up with the latest information in the various fields. It is necessary to clip from current professional periodicals, magazines, and bulletins the latest information in the areas in which the classes of the school are working. The librarian who knows the curriculum of the school serves an essential function in this respect.

Many schools improve their curriculum by having collections loaned to the classroom by the central library. The materials may be on permanent loan with a record of their location filed in the central library, or small collections of books may be assigned to a class while it is studying a particular unit.

If the library is operated as a learning center, students come to know books as usable tools and sources of pleasure, and they develop the habits and skills that enable them to use the community libraries in continuing their education after leaving the secondary schools.

HEALTH SERVICES

The development of the physical health of the individual is one of the stated functions of the secondary school. Usually it is assumed that health will be developed in physical education classes. However, the major portion of the health curriculum will be found in nonclass situations.

The secondary school should have a health center to which students can go for first aid and advice. In the operation of the center, the school nurse should consider counseling to be one of her major functions. She should be the kind of person with whom students can feel free to discuss their physical problems. A basic outcome of the experiences should be the development in students of the habit of going to competent people to discuss health problems that they face rather than concealing them and failing to secure necessary treatment.

The health program should help a student know himself better and secure treatment if necessary. Annual physical and dental examinations are essential. The results of the examination should be used to determine the kinds of physical activities in which the student may engage and the corrective activities that are needed when deficiencies are found. Without an annual examination the health activities provided in school may be doing more harm than good. Reports should be made to parents of the condition of their children's health and of any necessary remedial treatment. In cases where the parents are not able to afford the medical and dental care needed, the school should seek help from local service groups that make funds available to provide for needy individuals. Although some persons have raised serious objection to the school's providing this service, the objection appears to be very shortsighted. The major resource of any nation is its citizens. If the citizens are in poor health or physically unfit, the nation cannot be strong. The development of a sound body is a basic preparation for good citizenship, and the school that ignores the physical side of the pupil's development is handicapping the pupil and the nation and failing to fulfill its function of developing adequate citizens. When the induction record for boys in America during World War II was examined, it was found that one out of every three persons was physically unfit for service in the military forces—even when the requirements were lowered. Surely the school must do all it can to provide a strong health program for all youth and assist individuals to secure aid where necessary.

Information about the health of a pupil should be used to determine his work load. If his sight is impaired, extensive reading may be harmful, and sightsaving help is indicated. Any adequate secondary school makes special provision for such youth by having adults or other students read for them or work with them to save their eyes.

The lunchroom is another element of the health program. Nutritious lunches at a low cost should be available to all students. The lunches offered should be served on a cost basis. Any school that has a catering service which makes a profit on the school lunches is conducting a program that is contradictory to the philosophy and point of view of a free public education system dedicated to developing better citizens for the nation. It is inconsistent for the staff in all other portions of the school to be providing the best education possible with the funds available, while the food program is being used to make a profit out of an essential need of youngsters. In the lunchrooms, posters and other informational devices should be used to help students become more aware of the benefits of the balanced diets they are served.

The schedule of the school is an important phase of the health situation. If students are given a lunch period of twenty minutes, in which they must stand in line ten minutes to go through the cafeteria and then be back in the classroom ten minutes later, the school is creating a condition where youngsters may not engage in essential health practices. Such a schedule keeps the youngsters from washing their hands before they eat, and it forces them to rush their eating, thus contributing to inadequate digestion.

Physical education class activities certainly should be adapted to meet the needs of individual students. Not all youngsters should play basketball or engage in strenuous physical activity. Some youngsters need corrective exercises. Some need rest during the gym period. Some should play games with limited physical activity. A good health program means that someone studies the record of each pupil and secures necessary adjustments in his program.

The sports program reflects the importance the school attaches to the health environment. *If health is a major consideration of the faculty, the sports program will place as much as or more emphasis on the intramural program than it does on the interscholastic competition.* In a school with a large number of students, an interscholastic program can serve only a minor portion of the student body. Too many schools place the greater portion of the facilities and staff at the service of the few youngsters who are the most completely developed in the total student body. When this is done, the student who is average or below average physically is neglected. The very ones who need the benefits of the sports program most are denied proper guidance and experience because the facilities and the staff are concentrated for the most part on a few youngsters who need it least. The sports program of the school should be for all, and the only way that this can be adequately achieved is by putting a strong emphasis on an intramural program in which all who are physically able participate.

The health aspect of the school environment extends into the classroom. Classroom teachers affect pupil health. Fleming's study of teacher acceptance of pupils indicated that increased teacher acceptance decreased the incidence of certain types of pupil illness. Health is affected by the emotional and social, as well as the physical climate.

When persons concerned with improving the curriculum look at the health phase of the school program, it is necessary to examine the cleanliness of the building, the lunch program, the sports program, the health services provided in the school, the type of schedule, and the pupil-teacher relationships.

THE CAFETERIA AND HALLWAYS

The student learns as he lives in the cafeteria and the hallways. His experiences in these portions of the high school curriculum affect his attitudes and his behavior.

Food service plays a major role in the secondary school. If cheap, nutritious lunches are provided, a contribution is made to efficient learning. The student who has a satisfactory lunch is better able to work at full speed for the entire day. If the food served is too expensive or so poorly prepared that students go elsewhere to eat, the school fails in supplying a needed service and loses the opportunity to provide another educative experience.

In the cafeteria the student should learn much about nutrition and attractive food service. If the cafeteria table is organized so that sweets come first and other dishes later, youth's craving for sweets is emphasized, and he is encouraged to select an unbalanced diet. If the desserts are all served in attractive form and the other food is served haphazardly, poor food selection habits are taught. If food is displayed properly and posters about the food help pupils to select a balanced menu, the school is teaching good nutrition. If the lunchroom is managed well, the lunch period is a time to learn good manners. If an attempt is made to have flowers on each table each day, something important is taught about the way a table should be set. If the lunchroom is attractive, the staff can make lunch an enjoyable social occasion and conversational skill is increased. A number of schools attempt to develop an appreciation of music by providing music during the dining period. Instead of being a necessary break in the day, the lunch period can be turned into an activity in which many different kinds of learning are fostered.

The attitudes of those who supervise the dining area are critical. If they see their job as helping and counseling children, as providing a pleasant atmosphere, they promote desirable learning. If they see their role as controlling children and supplying food, the learnings of pupils may be undesirable.

The way in which traffic between classes is handled educates either positively or negatively. Some schools have students who serve as traffic officers, report other youngsters for misdemeanors, and bring them before the administration or student court for punishment. Others have hosts and hostesses who serve in the hallways. These students, selected for their good manners and for their way of working with others, greet and assist visitors to the school and counsel and help other students. When they see traffic disorders they talk with the other students and help them recognize the rights of others and the dangers of bad traffic habits in the halls. The success of this type of approach depends upon the backing of the student government and the selection of the kind of people whom other students respect to serve as host and hostess.

Schedule plays a part in the traffic problem. If the time for passage from class to class is too short and students are penalized for being late, students think more of getting to class on time than of safety and courtesy.

When schools make their hallways attractive, fewer traffic problems occur. Some faculties see the hallways as an instructional area. They use them for display of student art work or exhibits that are brought to the school. As features such as displays are added to the hallways, it becomes worthwhile for students to stop and to look and to discuss what they see. Less crowding and running occurs. The hallway is thus also a part of the curriculum. The students learn what they live where they live it.

THE NONTEACHING PERSONNEL

A student's school life is affected by what happens to him on the school bus, in the library, in the cafeteria, and in his relations with the custodians. Nonteaching personnel contribute to the learnings of pupils. But the nonteaching personnel may be working with or against the teaching faculty. The opposition may not be intentional. It may come out of lack of understanding of what the school is attempting to do. *When staff begins to think of curriculum improvement, investigation should be made of ways in which people who service the school can understand and perform their functions better.*

To be very specific, bus drivers are in need of in-service training as much as the teachers. Not only do they need instruction in safe operation and maintenance of the bus, as is customary in some states, but they also need in-service experiences that will help them understand the school program and the nature of adolescents. The way they treat youth affects pupil attitudes and behavior. If the student riding a school bus is subjected to adult aggression against which he is not free to retaliate, it will affect and condition his behavior and his relations with the teacher in the classroom. On the other hand, if the bus driver understands the youth with whom he is dealing, he may serve as an important counselor in the school situation.

Custodians are also in a position to help or hurt adult-adolescent relationships. If the custodian understands the needs of boys and girls, he is in a position to think with them and advise them as they bring problems to him. In one school in Ohio the custodian served a greater guidance function than any other member of the staff. When the boys had problems on which they wanted help, they talked with the custodian in his office by the furnace room. Although no one realized it, the custodian was doing more to help pupils form their values than any member of the teaching staff.

If a faculty wishes him to make his greatest contribution to pupils, the custodian should have an opportunity to participate in in-service activities and in curriculum development activities. Understanding of what is being done would eliminate some opposition. Sometimes custodians work against making the school program more flexible. Some do all in their power to make life disagreeable for the teacher who leaves chairs in some arrangement that interferes with the cleaning. When they do not understand why things are done in a certain way, they resent it. If there were an appreciation of different methods of teaching, the cooperation would be greater.

If the school building is to be used to its fullest extent, it is necessary for the custodian to see his and the teacher's jobs as parallel service roles. Custodians have an important task. They are responsible for the operation and maintenance of plants costing millions of dollars. The way they treat the building and the way they work determine whether or not the community receives full value for its dollars spent and whether or not students find adults working together to provide a consistent environment.

SUMMARY

Learning does not begin when a student enters a classroom door, nor cease when he exits from it. Each minute that a youth is in the secondary school he is learning. Values, ways of behaving, and beliefs about himself and others are absorbed from the physical and social environment that the school provides.

SELECTED READINGS

Bush, Robert N., *The Teacher-Pupil Relationship*. Englewood Cliffs, N. J.: Prentice-Hall, Inc., 1954. Reports extensive study of teacher-pupil relationship.

Butler, George D., "School-City Cooperation in the Planning of Recreation Areas and Facilities," *Recreation* 46A: 34-37, April, 1953 (continued in May issue, 98-102). Outlines and describes ways in which school and municipal authorities have cooperated in the acquisition, planning, construction, and maintenance of areas for use by both the school and the community.

Coleman, James, *Social Climates in High Schools*. Washington, D. C.: U. S. Government Printing Office, 1961. Reports on the influence of high school status systems on the behavior of adolescents.

Fleming, Robert, "Psychosomatic Illness and Emotional Needs," *Educational Leadership* 9: 119-123, November, 1951. Shows how the social and emotional climate of the school affects student health.

Gordon, Calvin W., *The Social System of the High School: A Study in the Sociology of Adolescence*. Glencoe, Ill.: The Free Press, 1957. Reports that high school pupils have an effective social system that influences not only dress and behavior, but also school achievement.

Hill, Thomas J., "Dating Patterns and Family Position," *Clearing House* 29: 552-554, May, 1955. Reports a definite relationship between dating patterns and family social position.

Keislar, Evan R., "Differences Among Adolescent Social Clubs in Terms of Members' Characteristics," *Journal of Educational Research* 48: 297-303, December, 1954. Finds a relationship between grades received in school and club membership.

National Association of Secondary School Principals, "Camping Education in the Secondary School," *National Association of Secondary School Principals Bulletin* 37: 41-48, May, 1953. Outlines the place of camping in the secondary school program.

Phelps, Harold R. and John E. Horrocks, "Factors Influencing Informal Groups of Adolescents," *Child Development* 29: 69-86, March,

1958. Reports that the socioeconomic status of the family is closely related to the attitudes and activities of adolescents.

Scandrette, Onas C., "Social Distance and Degree of Acquaintance," *Journal of Educational Research* 51: 367-372, January, 1958. Finds that a strong degree of acquaintanceship and the possession of acceptable traits are both necessary for friendship to develop.

10

STUDENT ACTIVITIES

Although student activities are not a part of the regular
daily schedule in many secondary schools, they constitute
a major portion of the student's high school curriculum.
Students enter them with a positive attitude because they
choose to engage in them. Students assume more responsibility for them; they have a greater control over them.
Students consider them important; they wear insignia, which
proclaim their participation and publicize their membership.
At least one study reports that success in an activity is important in keeping students in school. No evaluation of a
secondary school curriculum is adequate that does not give
major consideration to the student activity program.

THE ROLE OF STUDENT ACTIVITIES

For many years
student activities were not considered a part of the secondary
school curriculum. In the early part of this century students
organized and conducted sports contests, debating societies,
glee clubs, and orchestras. Faculty members showed little

or no interest. Later, the school recognized the activities and began to provide some help. For example, a member of the community might be paid a part-time salary to coach a football team or direct a band. A teacher might be asked to give some time after school to work with a club. Out of this period in the development of the secondary school came the term extracurricular activities.

By the thirties it was widely recognized that working with nonclass groups required special skill and training. School administrators sought to provide staff counselors and advisers for each activity. Bus schedules were arranged to allow students to stay after school and participate. State and national organizations came into existence to assist in the initiation, encouragement, and control of the various activities. Records were kept of the individual's participation in activities and were included in his transcript. No credit was given, and the term cocurricular activities came into use.

Since about 1935 the sentiment has been growing that a cocurricular status for activities is not sufficient. Studies of leadership have found a greater relationship between successful participation in nonclass activities and later community leadership than between a high scholastic average and subsequent community leadership. Some schools have begun to give credit for music, publications, and dramatics, for example, even though the credit may not be equal to that given for the same amount of time in other subjects. Other schools have placed activities in the regular schedule. Thus recognition has spread that all of the experiences in the school educate, and only the adult attempts to make the classification of some as curricular and others as extra- or cocurricular.

The term student activities has gradually replaced extracurricular and cocurricular, and new responsibilities are entailed for staff and students. Student activities as a part of the curriculum can no longer be considered merely as ways of keeping students happy and amused. They have a right to administrative and budgetary support and a responsibility to make a major contribution to certain types of growth that the secondary school seeks to promote, such as self-direction, ability to communicate, and the discovery of an avocational interest. Student activities constitute a portion of the school program where students learn the skills that are essential to democratic participation, where they may pursue their own purposes and work on activities that they consider significant.

PRESENT STATUS OF THE ACTIVITIES PROGRAM

Most secondary schools have extensive activities programs. Although developed as extra- or cocurricular activities, the school staffs have seen them as a vital part of the program.

The degree to which secondary schools provide activities is illustrated by a survey of the junior and senior high schools in Connecticut. In 1950, nine out of every ten schools had intramural athletics; three out of four had interscholastic athletics; nine out of ten had a band or orchestra; nineteen out of twenty had a glee club or chorus; nine out of ten had a school paper; nine out of ten had a student council; nine out of ten had clubs. But not all students participated in the activities. One out of two students engaged in intramural sports; one out of five participated in interscholastic sports; one out of twelve played in a band or orchestra; one out of five sang in a glee club or chorus; one out of thirteen worked on the school paper; one out of ten took part in dramatics; one out of twenty had the opportunity to be on the student council; and one out of two enrolled in clubs. This rundown is still typical today.

In spite of the size of the program and the degree of participation, few high school faculties are satisfied with the activities program. Many teachers object because students are taken out of their classes for an activity. Others feel that too much attention and publicity lead the community and students to believe that activities are more important than classes.

Few teachers consider activities as valuable a use of time as classes. The administration in many schools verifies this belief by not including sponsorship of activities as part of a teacher's load. Teachers may be asked to assume responsibility for an activity because of a special interest or skill, but little attempt is made to equalize the extra work the activities program entails. If teachers were asked to name the least successful phase of the high school program, a high percentage would indict clubs and other activities, usually excepting interscholastic sports, bands and glee clubs, and publications.

Johnston and Faunce conclude their book *Student Activities in the Secondary Schools* with the following list of shortcomings in student activity programs:

1. Many schools have adopted the forms of an activities program without any real understanding by teachers and pupils of the function it should perform.

2. We have been afraid of democracy. We have lacked faith in the abilities of pupils to plan, to make intelligent decisions, and to accept responsibility. Too frequently student councils have been only thinly camouflaged agencies of administrative domination or attempts to shift the onus of discipline to pupils' shoulders.

3. Participation in the activities program has been limited to too few pupils, both through regulations denying opportunity to pupils scholastically unsuccessful and through failure to provide for appropriate distribution.

4. The competitive aspects of the program have been overemphasized. The winning of contests has been allowed to overshadow more important outcomes.

5. In some instances, national organizations developed to encourage a particular phase of the activities program have devoted energy to promoting the organization and have lost sight of more inclusive objectives.

6. Organizations representative of special groups in the community or engaged in promoting one point of view on controversial issues on which public opinion is divided are permitted in some instances to function as school organizations. (Sponsorship by the school should be limited to those organizations representative of the entire community and under the direct control of the school and school personnel.)

7. The activities program has not been vitally related to the curriculum.

8. There has been no consistent effort to evaluate activities in terms of fundamental objectives.

9. Teacher-training institutions have failed to provide appropriate experiences for prospective teachers to prepare them for responsibilities in relation to student activities.

10. Duties in relation to the activities program have not received adequate recognition in considering the teacher's load.

Clearly, much thinking remains to be done if activities are to make the contribution to pupil growth that they hold promise of providing.

STUDENT GOVERNMENT

The student gov-
ernment should be the most important student activity in the school;
it should be the keystone of the student activities program and the
index to the quality of living that the faculty seeks. The student government serves many functions: It builds a sense of responsibility in
students; it provides opportunity for learning how to become self-directing; it contributes to the improvement of morale; and it enables
students to learn democratic procedures. The latter is the most fundamental reason for having the student government. The school exists to
prepare citizens for a democracy. By having an opportunity to make
democracy function in the school government, students exercise and
increase their competency in the use of democratic skills.

In every school there is a way of life. The faculty has the opportunity to set the stage. If decisions are restricted to the administration
and teachers, pupils gain only one picture of the way that adults believe they should relate to students and the degree of responsibility
that youth should have. If many decisions are shared with students,
they assume a responsibility for the program and have concrete evidence that the faculty is concerned with helping them become more
mature people. When people are left out of the decision-making process, they know that they have little responsibility for what happens.
When they have a part in the decisions, they assume a responsibility
for the successful execution of it. If the faculty decides what students
will do and how they will do it, students do not have the opportunity
to learn self-direction. The dependency is prolonged. If, on the other
hand, the school faculty is seeking more and more areas in which
students can be self-directing, the school becomes a place in which
students have the opportunity to develop the necessary skills to direct
their own affairs successfully. If students do not have a part in decision-making, they have no way of seeking improvement of the irri-
tating factors in the situation. If they have a government that has
some authority and responsibility, they have a device by which they
can secure greater personal satisfactions. When people have channels by which they can work on decreasing their dissatisfactions, their
morale is higher.

No student government can make all of the decisions that will
affect the students in the school. Each school unit operates within
many outside limitations, such as regulations from the state board of

education, the local board of education, and the central administration of the school system. In addition, each student body lives within a program in which many policies have been formulated by the faculty of the local unit. But many phases of the school life are not covered by either outside regulations or the policies established by the faculty. If the staff wishes, students can make many decisions that are important to them. A faculty that wants student government to be effective will identify the areas in which it is willing to allow students to make decisions.

There are many things faculties can do to encourage students to make decisions. They must make clear to the students the areas in which they are willing to abide by student decisions. Second, the faculty members working with the student government must see themselves as advisers on process rather than as bestowers of solutions. It is very easy for an adult working with a group of students to give the impression that he is manipulating them to reach certain preconceived answers. If this is done, student government fails. The adviser performs his role as he helps the students think through the problems to determine their possible ramifications. He suggests ways of working on the problems, assists with procedural difficulties that arise, and he suggests a number of solutions that the student group will want to consider. Third, the faculty must not exercise the veto over decisions that they have said will be in the area of student responsibility. A veto is a clear indication that no responsibility for decision existed at all. Whenever a veto is used it is evidence to the student government that they are free only to make the type of decision the faculty would make anyway.

In a high quality school program the student government is the central element in the student activities program. It has responsibility for working with the faculty in planning and operating the activities of the school. Although students cannot make all of the decisions regarding the activities program, they can and must have a voice through their chosen representatives. For example, the student government should have responsibility for developing policies concerning the operations of the various organizations and clubs and for participating in the formulation of regulations concerning student behavior. It should play a key role in developing a school tradition and spirit. It should have the leadership in formulating codes of behavior and a way of student life in the school. The student council should see its role as evaluating student life and leading in the activities that raise the norms of the student group.

Careful thought should go into the organization of the student government. The faculty and the student body should attempt to develop a structure that will make possible the representation of all students and the maintenance of communication between the members of the student government and the rest of the student body. A representative in the government should be representative of some group of students and be responsible to that group for seeing that their wishes and desires are recognized and attempts made to fulfill them.

As soon as students have the need and desire for student government, the first step should be to develop an organization. Typical committees that can be established for this purpose would be: a committee to study the constitutions of other student governments; a committee to investigate the areas in which student government can be most useful; a committee to study the way in which student government can best fit into the local school organization; a committee to determine the best method of representation; a committee to investigate parliamentary procedure; a committee on election procedures. Recommendations from the committees should then be placed before the student body. After the students have had an opportunity to study the recommendations, a draft of the constitution should be prepared and submitted to the student body. This constitution should: include a procedure for nominating and electing officers; carefully define the areas in which the student government will function and the jurisdiction that it will have; provide for a fair and adequate method of student representation; delineate relationships with the faculty and administration; provide for supervision of such school activities as the club program, the sports program, social events, discipline, safety, assemblies, and finances.

After the government has been organized, the members of the government group should collect information about the problems that trouble the student body. This can be done by having the representatives meet frequently with the group that they represent. If representatives are chosen on a homeroom basis, the process is easy. The representative from the student government asks for time in the homeroom session to secure ideas as to problems and activities with which the student government should deal, brings them before the council, and then reports back to the homeroom group.

The reporting is one phase of the government operation that frequently fails. Some schools have overcome this difficulty by not attempting to resolve any problem at the session at which it is introduced. After the problem is presented to the government, the representative takes it back to his homeroom group to see what solutions they would propose. Opportunity is provided within the homeroom to talk about the problem and possible ways of dealing with it. Each student has the opportunity to present his thoughts on and criticisms of the various proposed actions. When the representative goes back to the government meeting, he carries with him the knowledge of the point of view of all the members in his group. By using this procedure, it is possible for each student to have an active part in the student government. The meetings of the student government should be scheduled during the regular school day, and all representatives should arrange their schedules so that they are available for the period in which the government meetings are held. Only when a regular time is provided for serious thought and deliberation can students assume real responsibility in the policy-making process. A sure way to guarantee failure is to depend upon the student government's operating when it can find occasion to meet.

An important consideration is the relationship of the student government to the faculty. Both are involved in policy-making. Some schools have attempted to solve this problem by having representatives of the student government meet with the faculty in regular faculty meetings. Others have depended upon the faculty representatives' sharing with the student government the faculty's thinking. A Miami high school holds a meeting once a week in which all of the department heads sit down with the principal and with the officers of the student government to talk through the actions that should be considered during the week and the problems that have been brought to the last meetings of the faculty and of the student group. This weekly meeting serves as a channel of communication between students and faculty.

Whatever the structure, neither group can go it alone. Both students and faculty live in the community that comprises the school. Each has a different responsibility, and each perceives the situation in a different way. It is necessary for each to talk with the other about the things that they feel are important and to arrive at joint conclusions as to what needs to be done.

Student government can succeed only when it has the support of the administration and faculty and when students have the opportunity to plan and think with the faculty or its representatives. The thinking together must be on a peer basis. If students feel that they are there only to advise and do not have a real part in decision-making, they soon learn that the student government is only a tool of the administration and faculty. When they reach this conclusion, the student government ceases to be a vital force in the life of the school.

CRITERIA FOR THE STUDENT ACTIVITIES PROGRAM

As faculties recognize the importance of student activities as an element of the curriculum, it becomes necessary to examine more carefully the way in which the activities are operated. As long as they have an inferior status, shortcomings can be ignored. Once recognized as curriculum they must have standards as high as those applied to classes.

What criteria should be applied by the faculty to the student activities? *The administration should give wholehearted support to the activities program.* Much of the value of activities depends upon the attitude of the administrator. If he sees them as important educational experiences and is willing to give his executive leadership to them as he does to other portions of the curriculum, the activities will be productive. If he does not, this phase of the curriculum may be its weakest area.

Student activities should be controlled by the school administration, perhaps through a committee composed of pupils and faculty. The group responsible should determine the objectives and coordinate the activities of the program as a whole. In some schools, the student government with its faculty advisers serves this function.

Both teachers and pupils should have a part in planning the activities program of the school. The planning together can be a guidance activity and a means of developing standards of judgment in which the thinking of different age groups is involved. It is not satisfactory for teachers to plan for students what the activities will be; neither is it satisfactory if the information and judgments of teachers are ignored.

A wide selection of activities should be available. Traditional patterns of activities should not limit the thinking of students or faculty concerning student activities. Whenever a group of students decides that an activity is important to them, the governing body should be willing to consider their petition for the addition of the new activity, and an attempt should be made to find the facilities and the sponsorship that will make its success probable.

The range of activities should be broad enough so that there is at least one organization in which each pupil is interested. This ideal should be sought. Too frequently student activities are restricted to sports, music, publications, and clubs, which only supplement regular classes. Opportunity should exist for the development of activities that will expand the existing curriculum. In many schools too little thought is given as to which activities should be included in the program. Sometimes the faculty draws up the list of activities that they are willing to sponsor. In other situations the students are given a blank sheet of paper and asked to name the activities in which they would like to participate. The assumption in either of these cases is that if a person puts down something he is willing to sponsor or in which he would like to participate, it is a satisfactory activity for the secondary school.

Each activity should be operated for its educational value. Although it is hoped that the activity is fun and interesting to students, it must contribute to desirable pupil growth. A proposal for a new activity should be subject to as careful a scrutiny as a proposal for a new course. It should be subjected to the same criteria that any class must meet. Any activity that does not contribute to the purposes of the school has no place in the curriculum. Any activity that cannot be justified in terms of its educational value should be eliminated in the same way that a class which is no longer functional is dropped from the curriculum.

The activities must be open to all students. Restricting the right to participate to students from certain economic groups may deny the very students who need the activities most. Secondary schools must look carefully at the cost attached to various activities. Are the incidental fees prohibitive?

In studies that have been made of the costs involved in participating in clubs and activities in schools, it has been found that sometimes these go as high as seventy-five dollars a year. Youngsters from less privileged homes cannot participate fully. In a New Jersey high school, it was found that girls were not invited to join certain social clubs in the school unless they could entertain twenty girls in their homes. This demand eliminated many of the girls who would have profited most. In *Elmtown's Youth* it is reported that few students from the lower economic classes participate in the activities program of the school, that certain activities are associated with certain social groups. Any school faculty should look at its program of activities carefully to see what portion of the student body is being shut out and the extent to which the activities decrease social mobility in the student population.

211

A scholastic average should not determine the eligibility of students to participate in activities. It would be just as logical to ask that students have a certain activities average before they were eligible to enter a class. Regular classes and activities are educative experiences. Some students will derive most benefit from certain classes and from certain activities. Other students will profit from other classes and activities. The school regulations should not restrict the areas from which a student, his parents, and his counselor may select a valuable experience, by requiring a certain level of performance in one activity before a student may enter the one that he chooses.

One exception to not requiring a certain average in academic classes is necessary for interscholastic athletics. The student must secure a minimum level of marks in academic classes before being allowed to compete against other schools. This exception is made, not because of lack of educational soundness of the principle of nonrequirement, but because high schools have been compelled to establish this item in the code governing interscholastic competition to be sure that all will use bona fide students.

Student participation in activities should be voluntary. Much of the value is eliminated from an activity if it is required. Little hope can be held for the development of self-direction in an activity that a youth has been compelled to undertake. Students should be allowed to make their own choices of activities and to refrain from participation if they so desire.

Opportunities for leadership in the various organizations should be available to many. The program is not good if only a few students in the school hold most of the leadership positions. Some schools have found it desirable to establish a point system, which limits the number of leadership positions a single pupil may have. In this way more opportunity is provided for all to have some experience in holding office.

Records should be kept of student participation in activities. If activities are a real and vital part of the school curriculum, the student's work in them is entitled to the same recognition as his participation in scheduled classes. The student's cumulative folder and permanent record and the reports to parents should include evidence of his participation in activities.

Each activity should be supervised by a member of the faculty trained in informal group leadership. In his role as sponsor or adviser the staff member should stay in the background, serving as a resource person to the students in working out the problems that confront them.

He should raise questions that help students see the implications of their actions and enable them to plan more intelligently. Students should be given as much freedom and initiative as they can use wisely.

The school should provide a time and place for the meeting of student activities in its daily schedule. Inclusion of the activities in the regular schedule is particularly important in a situation that requires transportation for a number of students. If the activities are conducted after the school day is over, the majority of students who are transported are eliminated from participation. The activity should be part of the scheduled day for the teacher just as it is for the student. If an activity sponsorship is added to an already full work load, the activity will suffer.

Parents and lay people should be used as resource personnel in the activities program. Many times adults within the community have greater skill in the area in which a particular organization needs help than any member of the faculty. Bringing these lay people in to help with the organizations in the school is one way of bringing the school and community closer together. Usually the community member will serve as a resource person to an organization for a short time. If the staff member serving as sponsor does not have all of the skills needed and the community member has the time, interest, and ability, it may be advisable to use cosponsors, a teacher and a layman.

In-service education in student activity sponsorship should be provided. The quality of an activities program is dependent upon the ability of the advisers. Since many teacher education institutions do not include activity sponsorship in the preservice program, in-service experience may be more essential for this work than for others. It may be obtained by weekly meetings at which sponsors of similar activities discuss how they are working and the results that they are achieving.

The finances of all organizations should be under school control. Students within each organization should be encouraged to develop their own budget, but the administration, perhaps through student government, should exercise a supervisory function. A member of the faculty with skill in accounting should assist with the supervision of the finances of the various organizations in the school.

Each activity should be evaluated annually. It should be judged on the basis of its contribution to the school program. If a particular activity does not measure up to the standards that have been established, its charter should be removed. In judging a specific activity, the following questions should be asked: What is its aim? What needs of the students does it meet? What values are derived from participation in it? What contribution does it make to the welfare of the school? the home? the community.

The student activities program should be flexible. Students and faculty should be able to change the type of student activities program when they find that the present activities are not satisfactory. If constant evaluation is in progress, the clubs, sports, and social activities that are no longer meeting the needs of the students and the ones that are not suitable should be dropped. Additional ones should be added as students and faculty see the possibility of a more adequate program.

DESIRABLE ACTIVITIES

The typical activities program places major emphasis on sports, clubs, music, dramatics, and publications (see Chapter 4). Size of school affects the completeness of the offering in each area, but most high schools provide students with some opportunity for participation.

Much controversy rages about the activities in sports. Critics complain that: interscholastic sports are too competitive; overpublicity is harmful to students; interscholastic sports take an undue proportion of the sports budget and staff; the students who need physical development most are neglected, while those who are most developed get all the attention; sports monopolize the school press releases; athletes do not have enough time for their important studies. If the sports program is to meet its critics' charges, it must provide activities that will appeal to all (including a variety of individual and small group sports such as tennis, swimming, and golf); contain intramural leagues and competition which offer opportunities for most of the student body to play; emphasize fun and good sportsmanship above winning; center publicity on service and school spirit rather than on individual excellence.

Music offers real opportunities for development of skills, appreciation, and lasting interest. Difficulties have arisen when those in charge have stressed showmanship. In some schools undue amounts of money spent on glittering uniforms and flashy instruments for marching bands have restricted the parts of the program with more lasting benefits. Provision for many types of vocal and instrumental groups, for public performance by large groups, for frequent sharing of productions within the school, for community singing, for good music in the cafeteria and recreation areas, and for music within the other school activities is essential if the music program is to make its contribution to the growth of adolescents. Like sports, music must be for all.

Dramatics in many schools are conducted by a small dramatics club, or the total program consists of four class plays. If dramatics is to be a real force in the school, these should be supplemented by an experimental theatre group that writes and produces plays; shows prepared by homerooms and class groups and shared with other groups; pageants, style shows, and radio productions that grow out of class activities.

Publications should be the expression of the creative life in the school as well as a communication channel and record. Too many high schools publish only a paper and yearbook. Poems, short stories, and essays written by students go unnoticed or are not published because no media of expression are available. Collections of student writing should be as much a feature of the school's publications program as a yearbook.

The activities that have caused administrators and teachers to feel most hopeless are probably the clubs. Scheduling has always been difficult. Clubs rise or fall with the enthusiasm and ability of the faculty sponsor. But the time has come to put the clubs into the regular schedule, to provide adequate leadership, and to have students elect them as they do classes—or else to abandon them. Clubs should be viewed as a part of the elective curriculum which makes possible exploratory and depth experiences in avocational interests. Experiences in radio writing and production, operating a business, and photography, for example, should be available to students through clubs.

The activities offering should be reviewed frequently and revised in terms of its effectiveness, appeal, and contribution. Participation should give pupils experience in policy-making. Each organization faces new problems and needs to work out procedures and standards. If this function is left to the organization within the limits set up by over-all school policy, all members will have the opportunity to gain this valuable experience.

One of the problems that the sponsor must face is the development of leadership within the organization. Some students have gained the impression that leadership is a quality that only a few possess, and if these few do not go ahead, the club will fail. Actually, the reverse is true. To the extent that participation in policy-making is restricted to a few, the vitality of the organization wanes. For example, members of the group should be given the opportunity to participate in the preparation of the budget. Learning how to plan expenditures is one of the by-products of a good activities program.

The content of a student activity should not be standardized. One of the values of the activities program is that it gives pupils and sponsors an opportunity to be creative. Pupils should be encouraged to make new plans, try projects that have not been undertaken before. Classes may feel compelled by syllabi and textbooks to cover the same content that previous classes have studied, but clubs do not have similar limitations. Any attempt to have one group of students engage in the same activity that the preceding group followed limits the creative possibilities of the situation.

SUMMARY

The activities program constitutes a major portion of the social structure of a school. It should be developed in terms of the quality of living that the faculty seeks and in terms of the contribution that each activity can make to the social attitudes and skills of the entire student body.

In looking at the total activities program, students and faculty should ask themselves these questions: Is the range of activities offered great enough to meet the interests of all students? Is the program gradually changing? Is the change taking place as the result of careful evaluation and planning? Is greater participation being achieved now than in the past?

SELECTED READINGS

Benerd, Gladys, "How Do Pupils Benefit by Participation in the Cocurricular Program?" *National Association of Secondary School Principals Bulletin* 37: 103-111, March, 1953. Outlines the many ways in which pupils benefit from the cocurricular program.

Bush, Robert N., "The Proper Place of the Extracurriculum in High School," *California Journal of Secondary Education* 34: 257-262, May, 1959. Urges that the proper balance be found between the curriculum and the extracurriculum.

Davis, Paul and Jerry J. Gerich, "What Is a Defensible Activities Program for the Senior High School?" *National Association of Secondary School Principals Bulletin* 43: 167-171, April, 1959. Stresses the need for continuous development and evaluation of the activities program.

Delaney, A. A., "In Selecting a Faculty Adviser," *School Activities* 32: 12-13, September, 1960. Stresses the need for careful selection of faculty advisers for student activities.

Fulcher, Tyler, "Extracurricular Activities Can Supplement the Academic Program," *Nations Schools,* 66: 67, November, 1960. Discusses ways in which the activities program can supplement the academic program.

Grinnell, J. E., "Our Most Dangerous Neglect," *Phi Delta Kappan* 41: 213-216, February, 1960. Outlines an action program for character education based largely on student activities.

Hamilton, H. H., "Educational Value of the Extracurriculum," *National Association of Secondary School Principals Bulletin* 43: 132-136, December, 1959. Reports, on the basis of a questionnaire research project, that extracurricular activities have a definite and positive value.

Hollingshead, August B., *Elmtown's Youth.* New York: John Wiley and Sons, Inc., 1949. Portrays high school experiences of youth in a midwestern town.

Johnston, Edgar G. and Roland C. Faunce, *Student Activities in Secondary Schools.* New York: Ronald Press Co., 1952. Discusses the place, purpose, and benefits of student activities in secondary schools.

Karner, E. F., "Check Points for Improving School Activity Programs," *School Activities* 32: 133-135, January, 1961. Presents a list of check points by which a school can evaluate its activities program.

Keislar, Evan R., "Differences Among Adolescent Social Clubs in Terms of Members' Characteristics," *Journal of Educational Research* 48: 297-303, December, 1954. Points out the influence of grades on club membership.

Maas, Henry S., "The Role of Member in Clubs of Lower-Class and Middle-Class Adolescents," *Child Development* 25: 241-251, December, 1954. Presents evidence that social class is closely related to role perception and role fulfillment of club members.

Miller, Franklin A., James H. Moyer, and Robert B. Patrick., *Planning Student Activities.* Englewood Cliffs, N. J.: Prentice-Hall, Inc., 1956. Presents the purposes, principles, and best practices of the cocurriculum.

O'Neil, H. R., "Let's Limit Participation in School Activities," *School Activities* 32: 21-22, September, 1960. Warns against the danger of letting students overload themselves with extracurricular activities and proposes that a "point system" be adopted to prevent such overloading.

Shelly, G. N., "All This and the Three R's, Too," *Illinois Education* 48: 274-275, March, 1960. Describes the activities program in a junior high school that devotes the last period of the day to cocurricular events.

Taba, Hilda, *School Culture.* Washington, D. C.: American Council on Education, 1955. Describes human relations and the climate of school life as they affect pupils.

Tompkins, Ellsworth and Robert C. Story, *The Activity Period in Public*

High Schools. U. S. Office of Education, Bulletin No. 19, 1951. Washington, D. C.: U. S. Government Printing Office, 1951. Reports activity period practices widely found in public high schools.

Willman, C. A., "Activities at the Expense of the Program?" *Educational Leadership* 18: 213-216, January, 1961. Suggests ways of maintaining a balance between the curricular and cocurricular offerings in high school.

Yon, J. F., "How May Extracurricular Activities Contribute Most Profitably to Education?" *School Activities* 32: 266-267, May, 1961. Relates the value of student activities to the Seven Cardinal Principles of education as set up by the Commission on the Reorganization of Secondary Education.

III

THE PROCESS
OF CHANGE

The extent to which desires are realized depends upon the depth of understanding of the individuals involved. But transformation is not achieved by wishing for it. Those who want curriculum improvement need to know the organizational structure, the roles played by various groups and individuals, and the factors both inhibiting and facilitating change. From this knowledge they must then devise a plan of action that gives promise of achieving the desired goals.

11

INDIVIDUAL
AND GROUP ROLES IN
CURRICULUM CHANGE

As people work together in curriculum change,
as in other human cooperative enterprises, they need to have
relatively common role expectations and need to feel free to
perform the functions inherent in those roles. Unless roles are
understood, conflict develops because individuals feel that others
are either not concerned or are presumptuous, that they lack
good will or common purpose. If curriculum change is to
progress smoothly, agreement on roles is essential.

THE SOURCES OF CURRICULUM DECISIONS

Decisions con-
cerning curriculum are made in many places. Some are the
prerogative of state departments of education. These
statewide decisions provide the framework within which
all local systems must operate. Some curriculum decisions

221

are made by the local boards of education. Their decisions, within the policy established at the state level, delimit still further the area of choice for professional people working in a local school system. Within the legal framework, the school system staff makes curriculum decisions. Some of these are made by systemwide committees; others are the prerogative of individual schools within the system. Each faculty may make some decisions about curricular organization (assuming that the principal is willing to share his authority). The individual teacher makes certain curriculum decisions as to how he will organize and operate his classes—subject always to the limitations imposed by the state, the local board, the system, and the local faculty. And the pupil, too, decides what he will emphasize and what he will achieve.

THE ROLE OF THE BOARD OF EDUCATION

The board of education plays a major role in curriculum change. It establishes as one of its primary goals the improvement of the school program and takes steps to secure a chief administrator and staff that will work for constant evaluation and experimentation in seeking better schools.

If they are to promote curriculum improvement, the members of the board of education keep informed about the program. They do not wait until some citizen or group begins to question or criticize. They consider that they are as responsible for knowing about curriculum issues and instructional practices as they are for understanding the tax structure and financial needs of the schools involved. Board meetings are scheduled to hear what is being done in the school curriculum and the evidence of its success or failure. The curriculum director is as well known to them as the business manager.

The members of the board seek the best professional advice available. They consult with the professional personnel they have employed and secure consultant help from the outside if they cannot agree with the recommendations of their staff or if a certain problem is one on which regular staff members do not feel sufficiently competent.

As efforts to improve the curriculum continue, the board members must assume responsibility for the cost of investigation, study, and in-service education. Program change is not bought without effort, and the extra expenditure of time and energy must be underwritten.

To fulfill his role in curriculum change, the board member must stand for support of curriculum study and in-service education activities.

THE ROLE OF THE CURRICULUM DIRECTOR

The curriculum director, be he called assistant superintendent in instruction, general supervisor, or curriculum director, is responsible to the board of education and the superintendent of schools for developing the curriculum structure, securing proper instructional materials, and constantly improving the quality of instruction. He has responsibility for all of the decisions not established by state laws and regulations that are related to these problems. He will not make all of the decisions. He cannot. But he has the task of taking the necessary steps that will insure that the decisions made are wise ones.

To perform his role he will establish a districtwide organization to supply him with information concerning the problems, feelings, and ideas of administrators, teachers, pupils, and parents that will be used as evidence in making decisions. He will want each school represented. If he wishes to increase the commitment of the staff to the curriculum decisions made, he will operate the district curriculum organization in such a way that he shares information and decisions. He will select and develop a staff of supervisors and consultants who can help to provide the information that school faculties and individual teachers need in making curriculum decisions and conducting curriculum experimentation. He will develop procedures for collecting evidences of the effectiveness of the existing program in producing the type of pupil growth sought. To do this will require that he secure agreement on goals and establish a testing program that will keep his office informed of strengths and weaknesses in the existing curriculum and pattern of instruction. He will assume responsibility for developing an in-service education program that will constantly increase both the curriculum insights of principals and the competency in leadership that will enable them to guide their faculties in making wise curriculum decisions.

The role of the curriculum director is a coordinating, facilitating one. If he operates in terms of existing evidence, he encourages each high school faculty (elementary, too) to develop the unique program that most effectively produces the desired results with the students and community it serves.

THE ROLE OF THE PRINCIPAL

The principal of a school is the central figure in any curriculum development program. He can block it, or he can promote it. His attitudes and actions can encourage or frustrate his faculty and can either negate all of the efforts of supervisors and central office staff or facilitate the use of their contribution.

The major assistance that a faculty needs from a principal is *a manifestation of concern for curriculum improvement.* If he works in such a way that the staff sees him as only being concerned with the routine of administration, reports, and administrative details, curriculum work will have to be done on an individual or undercover basis. On the other hand, if the principal constantly emphasizes that his main function in the school is improving the quality of living and the learning experiences of pupils, teachers will use his strength and put their efforts toward the improvement of instruction and curriculum. Curriculum work will be the approved activity, and many teachers who would hesitate to undertake it on their own will become active.

If curriculum work is to succeed, the principal sees it as a cooperative function. Every principal has the legal responsibility for making decisions concerning the school program. He can make these decisions alone, or he can share them with teachers. The University of Florida leadership project, conducted in the Hillsborough County Schools in Florida, collected data which led to the conclusion that schools where principals make decisions by themselves do not make as many curriculum changes as schools with principals who share decisions with their faculties. Schools in which decisions concerning curriculum were shared made a greater number and variety of changes and used the help of available supervisors much more than schools in which the principals kept the decisions to themselves.

If the principal sees supervisors as a threat to him, he will not perform his role as a curriculum leader well. Sometimes conflict develops between supervisors and principals. The supervisors feel that they have a responsibility for developing a program in their area in each of the schools in the system. The principal, on the other hand, believes that he is the person primarily responsible for the curriculum in his school. Out of failure to talk through these differing perceptions concerning respective functions, difficulties emerge and curriculum work is blocked by personality clashes. *The principal should see himself as the person responsible for curriculum work in the school, but he should also recognize that he has a responsibility for helping the staff use the resources that are provided for them in the system.* He should take the initiative in talking through with supervisors the kind of program the faculty is attempting to develop and the type of contribution that can be expected from each supervisor.

Another phase of the principal's role is the formation of a structure for curriculum change. In a small faculty, this structure may be the planning committee of the faculty, which takes the initiative in planning faculty meetings and in-service education. This group, using the suggestions that come from the total faculty, can project the kind of curriculum study that makes improvement possible. In a larger faculty, it may be desirable to designate a curriculum coordinating committee apart from the planning committee. Such a curriculum coordinating committee has the responsibility for looking at the total program and recommending projects for the faculty to undertake to bring about an improved curriculum. Its focus of attention is on evaluation and the proposal of projects in areas in which the school is not adequate. Whatever the necessary organizational structure, the principal should take the initiative in helping the faculty plan, organize, and execute curriculum work.

In his position as liaison between the central office administration and the board of education, the principal is better acquainted with systemwide policy than any other member of the faculty has the opportunity to be. He knows the kinds of policy limitations that are placed upon the local school. He knows the areas in which he is free to make decisions. To prevent frustration within the faculty he has the responsibility of informing them of the limitations of their authority. He needs to say quite frankly that certain curriculum decisions are not theirs to make, and he must indicate the areas in which the faculty may make changes without securing permission from the central administration, the board of education, or the state department of education. *This definition of the areas in which he has authority to make decisions that he is willing to share with the staff is a part of the principal's role in curriculum-making.*

The principal more than anyone else on the faculty must be concerned with processes used by the faculty. *He must use his authority to guard against decisions being made on the basis of whim or without thinking through all the aspects of the problem.* He will want to help the faculty establish procedures by which problems are defined and time provided for collecting evidence and making proposals before any final decision is reached. If he recognizes the data-collecting and -analyzing period as the time in which faculties will make the greatest growth, he will see the curriculum development procedures as a major portion of the in-service program and will not be frustrated by the time spent in arriving at proposals and decisions.

In the decision-making process, the principal fulfills his role as he helps the staff provide time for members to express their opinions, to question, and to propose alternatives. He will not want to rush decisions. An illustration of this function of the principal can be seen in the operation of a college faculty.

> A committee had proposed the establishment of a curriculum for the training of guidance workers. After discussion in the faculty meeting, a vote was taken. There were eighteen in favor of the program and eighteen against it. The Dean, since he was chairing the session, was in a position to cast the deciding vote. He told the faculty he would do so if they insisted, but that he would prefer not to, that he felt the faculty was too divided. He suggested that a committee of six—three for and three against—be established to re-evaluate the proposal and, if possible, come back with an agreement. The Dean's suggestion was followed, and six months later the faculty took unanimous action to approve the new proposal. The Dean, as would a good principal, used his position to help the faculty arrive at an agreement rather than himself making a decision that would leave a large number of his colleagues unconvinced of its wisdom.

A final phase of the principal's role is *implementing the decisions reached.* Curriculum work will bog down in schools in which decisions are made but no action is taken. Faculties lose interest after two or three such experiences. Unless steps are taken to put the ideas into operation, the whole process of thinking through curriculum improvement seems useless.

THE ROLE OF THE CLASSROOM TEACHER

Each teacher can make a contributon to improving the curriculum in his school. In a school where the total staff is interested in curriculum improvement he may do this by *willingness to participate in schoolwide projects and committee activity.* But he is not limited to curriculum work that he can do with other people. There are steps that he may take as an individual when the total staff is not concerned with curriculum improvement.

He can study the pupils in his class. If he does, he will be able to examine the items in the course of study with the immediate personal problems of his class members in mind. He will then be better able to make an intelligent interpretation of each pupil's interaction with other pupils in the class and with the material being studied. Knowing each pupil will also enable him to recommend available material in the classroom and library suited to any student's purposes and needs. Knowing his pupils will also provide him with a sounder basis for deciding what new materials to requisition.

Each teacher can strengthen the curriculum in his class by *bringing students in on the planning*. Even though the class is restricted to following a preplanned course of study, the teacher, by planning with pupils, can decide which phases to emphasize in making the activities more worthwhile for a given group. Students will be able to say what they want to know about a particular topic and the ways they believe they can best work on it. Such planning will make possible a more efficient use of the materials and time available, and *any increased efficiency in use of time and effort is an improvement in the curriculum*.

He can share equipment with other teachers. As he institutes joint use of equipment, he increases the resources that are available to him and to his classes. This makes possible a richer program for students in all classes.

He can participate in community groups. He will grow as a person and as a teacher as he shares ideas with community members. He will discover opportunities for his students to participate in community activities because he knows the projects that are being undertaken in the community. He will gain greater support for new undertakings in his class because his contacts with the adult members of the community have increased their confidence in him and in his ability to provide good guidance for their children.

He can keep up-to-date with ideas in his field. By reading the professional journals that deal with teaching procedures and practices that are being tried in other schools, he gains greater insight into possibilities in his own situation. As he reads what other teachers are doing under similar circumstances he discovers new ways in which he may take advantage of assets in his own school that he may be overlooking.

He can keep a file of materials that he wants. Unless he keeps a record of the things that he needs, he finds himself faced with opportunities to requisition additional materials and the ability to remember only those for which he has felt a need within the past few weeks. If, however, he has kept a record throughout the year of the shortages he discovered as students investigated the various problems in his field, his record enables him to secure a greater supply of materials because he has evidence which he can present to support his stated needs at requisition time.

He can establish a close working relationship with the librarian. No one can keep abreast of all of the new materials that are coming out in a field while he is carrying a full-time teaching load. The librarian, more than any other person on the school staff, has the responsibility for keeping informed about new materials. If the teacher works closely with the librarian and keeps her informed about the instructional materials he needs, the librarian is alert to these needs as she checks the new materials and will inform the teacher of the teaching aids she discovers.

Each teacher can *try out new ideas and procedures* and evaluate the results in terms of the objectives he seeks. Constant testing of new procedures is a way of improving the curriculum within the individual classroom. He can discuss his ideas with congenial faculty members and parents. In this way he will gain greater clarity and avoid many of the pitfalls that he would encounter if he attempted to institute some of the ideas without careful analysis. As he talks over his ideas with others, he stimulates them in the process and promotes curriculum improvement within the school as other individuals begin to experiment, even though there is no total faculty curriculum work.

The area for innovation should be carefully determined. It is easier to continue to do most things in the way to which one has become accustomed. If the present procedure is satisfying, a teacher's resistance to change is understandable. The experimentation undertaken should be with the phases of a person's work which irritate him or in which he fails to reach his goals. Experimentation is a device for seeking greater satisfaction with one's procedures or results.

For most teachers the degree of experimentation should be rather small. Too drastic a change frequently results in lowered effectiveness and, hence, frustration. If a teacher can select one phase of his teaching—such as increasing the degree of pupil-teacher planning, instituting some group work, developing a new procedure of evaluation, or substituting certain experiences for those listed in the syllabus—and experiment with it while continuing to operate as usual in the other aspects of his teaching, he will have greater security and more opportunity to evaluate carefully the success of the innovation.

When, as a result of new insight which brings dissatisfaction with present practices, or of lack of pupil growth, or of pupil expressions of resentment or resistance, a teacher decides that a certain portion of his teaching needs improvement, he should formulate an hypothesis concerning the way to achieve amelioration. The hypothesis may be formed by analyzing past failures, by consulting research, or by talking with fellow teachers; but it should be stated definitely enough to define the new procedure that will be tried and the types of evidence to be collected. For example, a teacher may conclude that pupil interest is too low in his class. He may decide that use of group work in class will increase the motivation of pupils. He may hypothesize that providing a portion of each period for small group discussion will result in more pupil reading, more animated class discussion, more unrequired creative activity undertaken by class members.

If the teacher is going to be able to make valid judgments about his experimentation, *he must collect evidence* that can be used in the decision as to whether the new procedure is better. If evidence is to be collected, the types of behavior expected must be defined so clearly that they can be observed and recorded. The defining of the behavior observed serves to delimit the amount of evidence to be collected. It frees the teacher from attempting to record extraneous data. Unless the data-recording process can be simplified and made a part of the teaching-learning process, the teacher will soon discard this phase of experimentation as entailing too much effort, and the validity of the research process will be destroyed. In planning the recording of procedures and pupil growth, consideration should be given to the part that pupils can play. Much of the recording may be done by class secretaries or by the individual pupil in his own record of his progress.

In the process of experimenting, the teacher needs to be alert for unexpected results. Changes much more significant than those originally anticipated, but of a different type, may occur. Unless these unexpected developments are examined, much of the value of the experimentation may be neglected.

The major benefits of research by the individual are the changes that occur in him. He becomes more exact and clear in his definitions, more objective in his treatment of data, obtains greater insight into the teaching-learning process, and becomes more confident and self-directing. Thus he improves the curriculum as he becomes a better scholar and a more effective guide of student thinking.

If he is a member of a faculty working to improve the curriculum, *the teacher can exert leadership by taking a positive stand for curriculum work, by participating actively in problem identification, by accepting committee responsibilities readily, by expressing his opinions in decision-making, and by implementing the decisions reached.* A teacher's neutral or negative attitude toward curriculum work hinders the program. Not only does he fail to carry his load, but he influences others to shirk. Failure to express his perception of the problem may result in the faculty's collecting the wrong data. Acceptance of committee tasks encourages others to do their share. If opinions are objectively and honestly stated, the faculty will make wiser decisions. And whether the program succeeds or fails depends upon each faculty member's executing the decisions made. The principal is not the only one who must put the decisions into force. Unless each faculty member does his part to make the decision effective, the thinking and studying together are useless.

THE ROLE OF THE SUPERVISOR

Unless all concerned are clear regarding the role of the supervisor in curriculum development in the individual school, intense problems can arise. The supervisor may feel that it is his responsibility to institute changes in the program, whereas the principal and the staff may feel that the supervisor is stepping beyond his prerogative in insisting that they undertake programs of which they do not approve.

The supervisor should see his role as a resource person to a faculty. He needs to discuss with the principal the way in which the two of them will work together, to find out what the faculty wants and expects from him, and to make known the kind of help he is able to provide. As he participates in faculty meetings and discussions he must be careful not to take the leadership away from the principal or faculty members. *He is a person available to help, but he is not meant to direct.*

Much of the supervisor's contribution is through conferences with the principal. He helps the principal analyze situations by talking through difficulties that arise, provides support and encouragement when the program is not moving as expected, and, when requested, offers suggestions as to how the organization and process might be improved.

If he is the supervisor responsible for a special area of the curriculum, he is not expected to be in on all faculty deliberations in all schools. In fact, his services should be enlisted only by schools working on that phase of the program and he should not feel any need of attending faculty deliberations in other schools.

The supervisor helps in the evaluation of the present program. The principal should seek his reaction to what he sees, and staff members should use him in making judgments about what they are doing. One of the supervisor's special contributions is sharing what he finds in other schools. Although he should not draw invidious comparisons, his descriptions of what is being done in other schools enable the principal and faculty members to have a better basis for making judgments about their own activities. To perform the sharing function well, the supervisor collects material from other schools in the system and from other school systems concerning the way in which they are meeting the needs of youngsters in the subject-matter area that is the supervisor's particular concern.

The supervisor can perform a valuable function in faculty sessions when the faculty is organizing and interpreting data. *Work committees use the supervisor as a resource person to collect ideas concerning the possible ways of solving problems.* In fact, he makes some of his most valuable contributions to faculty growth through his face-to-face interaction in these small study groups.

A major phase of the supervisor's role is participation in the trying out of new content and methods. He should be available to assist in planning the tryout and in undertaking the project. If he can work as a teammate in the group trying out a new plan, he is in a position where he can share his insight, can give support, and, because he is a part of the project, can be honest in his evaluation.

Another phase of the supervisor's role in curriculum improvement is *explaining innovations to the community.* If he has a part in developing new programs, he understands them. Since he is in a position where he is called on frequently by the community to share ideas concerning the school program, he can tell the community about how and why things are being tried. As he explains the reasons for the project, the care that has gone into the decision-making, and the way in which all phases of the program are being constantly evaluated, he can do much to build the confidence of the community in the curriculum that is being developed.

THE ROLE OF THE CURRICULUM CONSULTANT

Curriculum consultants are used by some faculties to assist in improving the curriculum of the schools in which they work. These consultants may be regular members of the staff of the school system, or they may be brought to the school on a part-time basis from nearby institutions of higher learning.

The Outside Consultant

The curriculum consultant who is brought in from the outside performs a unique role. He is not a member of the staff and does not have the responsibility for living with the results of the decisions. He is there to be used by the staff and not to direct the staff into the development of the type of program that he deems desirable. If he performs his function correctly, he does not identify the problems or argue for particular solutions. Instead, his role is a helping one. He helps the group in the process of identifying problems and considering alternate courses of action.

Some school systems secure or employ part-time curriculum consultants from institutions of higher learning, state departments of education, foundations, or other agencies. These persons are selected as advisers because the school administration feels they have a special competency not available in the full-time staff. Or the consultant may be secured because of the prestige his name will add, because the task to be done will arouse opposition that will make it difficult for the person spearheading it to continue to work in the community, or because so much conflict and disagreement exist that a neutralizing force is needed. Whatever the reason for his employment, the outside consultant can have a higher degree of objectivity because he has no vested interest to protect and no empire to build. He is in the situation as a supplier of additional evidence, as a facilitator of decision-making, as an expert on research or curriculum design, as a trainer to assist in the development of certain skills. *He is not a decision-maker.* The persons who will carry out the program should secure all of the help they can from outside resource people, but if it is to be successfully implemented, the final decision must be the prerogative of the local board of education and staff.

The consultant is a curriculum expert, a resource person to whom both parents and staff members can turn for suggestions and reactions. His reactions, however, do not commit either parents or teachers. He seeks to improve communication and help the group know the problem. He may, through his reactions, fall into disrepute with either parents or teachers, or both. But he serves a function. He is the factor in the situation against whom aggression can be directed and who, because he knows he is playing this role, is able either to continue work in the situation or, if it seems advisable, to withdraw. Neither parents nor teachers can withdraw; they have a continuing stake in the situation. Although he serves as a stabilizing force, the consultant is not brought into the situation as a human relations expert. He is there to help the teachers and parents plan and implement some phase of the program. His primary purposes are to help people define their goals more accurately, to increase the number of alternative courses of action, to assist the persons involved to see the relationship between each possible choice and its underlying or inherent values, and to refrain from attempting to predetermine the outcome.

The curriculum consultant differs from the regular supervisor in one major respect. He is always expendable. He has no vested interest in the local school and is there to be used only as long as he proves helpful to the faculty. When he has fulfilled his function, whether it is stimulating, participating in problem solution, or assisting with evaluation, he should be ready to have his services discontinued. He must constantly recognize that he is able to perform certain tasks better than other people, but that they are able to help more with different phases of curriculum development than he. He must not allow his ego to get involved. If he does, he may move from being of service to the system to being a hindrance. Above all, he must not attempt to compete for the leadership in the group. He is there to assist the official and emerging leadership in the situation. If he seeks a leadership role for himself beyond his service function, he loses his value as a curriculum consultant.

A skilled curriculum consultant works in a number of ways. He participates in faculty discussions and raises questions that probe the unstated assumptions that faculty members make. He listens and from time to time attempts to reflect in other words what staff members say so that they may see how it sounds when it is presented by an outsider in words other than the accustomed clichés used by the faculty. He suggests possible courses of action that other members of the group do not mention. He does not advocate. He does not lend support to one faction of the faculty against the others. He helps the people recognize differences and agreements. He assists the chairman of the meeting to take the steps that help people to reach conclusions. He does not use the weight of his position or his prestige to get the staff to move in a particular direction. He does not act as a critic or an evaluator. His chief role is to help the group remain task-centered.

The curriculum consultant works with committees. When a particular faculty group has been assigned the responsibility of working through a problem and coming up with a proposal, he is available as a resource person to that committee. He brings to the meetings descriptions of programs that have been developed in other schools. He cites references. He supplies information concerning recent research with which the faculty may not be already acquainted. He may be asked by the committee to bring a proposed plan of operation. In such situations he will usually bring several alternate plans, with arguments for and against each, and leave to the committee the decision as to which proposal it will make to the faculty.

A *major role of the curriculum consultant is to supply information.* Usually he has knowledge of experiences in other situations that the ordinary teacher does not have. As he moves from school to school and from teacher to teacher he shares the things that he has discovered. He is able to refer faculties and individual teachers to other persons who are already working on a similar problem. When a teacher asks, he suggests possible ways of implementing an idea that the teacher already has.

The curriculum consultant is available to individual teachers for consultation. When a teacher has an idea that he wishes to try out on an experimental basis, the curriculum consultant serves as a listener. He gives his full attention to the teacher's proposal. He questions. He reacts. He adds additional ideas. He suggests ways of evaluating the experimentation. He calls the teacher's attention to sources of help of which the teacher may not be aware. *He is available to the teacher to serve as an observer* as the teacher tries out some of the ideas. In his observer role, he seeks to make an accurate record of what occurs and to look at the record objectively with the teacher who has asked him to assist. If he is wise, he avoids making any value judgments about what he has seen, and he certainly does not tell others of difficulties and failures that the teacher encounters. He serves a supporting role and is a source of strength and counsel when the teacher needs it.

235

The Inside Consultant

In some of the larger high schools, a post of curriculum co-ordinator is established in the staff organization. He has a continuing relationship within the faculty and a responsibility for the execution of decisions reached. Usually he has a responsibility for assisting the curriculum committee in organizing the curriculum work of the school and in coordinating the activities of the various work committees. He, too, serves as a resource person for committees and for the faculty, and he supplies data and help as they are needed. He is a constant instigator of curriculum work in the school. He is an aid and support and a source of encouragement to faculty members who are working on a particular type of curriculum problem. He is a service person. He helps secure materials of instruction and evaluation. He helps collect and analyze the information to be used as the basis for decision. He helps build an organization for curriculum improvement and facili-tates in every way he can the successful operation of the organization. He is a member of the work group with special functions to perform, but, unlike the outside consultant, he should propose and advocate when he believes that a particular solution is desirable. However, he must exercise care to make sure that his actions do not threaten others or interfere with his performing the stimulating and coordinating role.

THE ROLE OF PUPILS

Pupils have a role in curriculum change if the staff will invite them to participate. Pupils, like teachers, have much valuable information to supply if those or-ganizing and directing the program of change will seek their help. Evidence can be secured concerning the success of instructional pro-cedures and the value of content used if the judgments of pupils who have experienced them are sought. The real curriculum is what pupils perceive it to be, not what adults expect or hope. To know what the curriculum is like for pupils means that they should have an oppor-tunity to evaluate freely, without fear of reprisal if their opinion happens to disagree with that of the staff. It is not the pupil's role to decide what should be included or deleted from the curriculum, but the adults who ignore the evidence of pupil judgment will make a less wise decision.

THE ROLE OF PARENTS

Too often in the past the curriculum has been determined by the school administration and teaching staff without participation of other groups. While these professional people are highly trained as educators and sincere in their desire to develop the best curriculum for the pupils placed in their charge, curriculum improvement is more lasting when the pupils, parents, and outside community agencies have a part in its planning.

Some school staffs have brought parents into curriculum planning to sell them on the school program. They have assumed that it is their job as professional people to know what is good for youngsters in our society and to plan a program that will bring out the qualities that a good citizen in our society should have. The staff members in these schools feel that they have been technically trained to educate children and that it would be just as inappropriate for a parent to tell teachers and educators what a school program should be as it would for a layman to tell a dentist how to fill a tooth. They attempt to sell parents on a school program by bulletins, by having school nights, by lectures, by any of a number of devices that they have found to convince parents that what the school is doing is good for their youngsters.

The process of selling is not an easy one today. The school faculty in such a situation is competing with the best hucksters available in our society. Parents are constantly subjected to selling programs devised by the advertising agencies and presented through magazines, over the radio, in television programs, and by billboards and newspapers. Various organized groups within our society attempt to convince other people of the rightness of their point of view. Editorial writers and columnists are constantly attempting to influence people to believe as they believe. Parents are sophisticated about the techniques of selling, and if teachers conceive of their role with parents as a selling role, they often find that they can be outtalked and outsold by groups within the community who have entirely different points of view.

In some situations there has been a fear that parents would try to assume control of the school. When this concern is present, parents are usually excluded, if possible, from the planning. But even in some schools where parents are participants in planning, the role they play is carefully restricted. The ground rules vary from school to school, and the role of parents is hazy and often misunderstood.

Before a staff begins to work with parents it needs to look at its assumptions about them. Does the staff believe that parents know what they want for their children? Does it believe that they have a contribution to make in deciding what is good for their children? Is it really willing to plan with parents or is it attempting to persuade them of the value of its program? Is the staff attempting to use devices which make parents believe that it is planning with them when it is actually ignoring them and following procedures that attempt to convince them of its rightness? Only if the staff seriously accepts the assumption that parents are concerned and have a contribution to make can they play an effective part in curriculum development. The big problem then is to find the most effective method of obtaining their contribution. Unfortunately, there are no neatly packaged plans for curriculum improvement that will work in all school systems. Each school must examine its own program and use the means that best accomplish the purpose.

Parents are busy people. They have many other activities. Not all parents are able to participate actively in curriculum development. Some are so deeply involved with earning a living that they are unable to find time to work with a staff. On the other hand, there are many members of the community who do have the time, who are concerned, and who want to think with teachers about the kind of education provided for their youngsters. As a staff works with a group that does have the time, the opportunity, and the willingness, it needs to help them see the importance of finding out what the other parents who are unable to participate believe.

Parents are not professional educators, but they can state the types of growth they want their children to achieve and can supply evidence of the results being obtained by the present program. Some can assist with the collection and organization of data. But they are not professional technicians. The choice of procedure to be used in obtaining the desired results is a professional decision. If this distinction is carefully delineated for staff and parents, the roles will be complementary, not conflicting.

Whenever parents are used as resource people, the important thing is that they and the professionals are working together. As people work together they get to know each other and to appreciate the contribution that each can make. Joint curriculum planning increases the respect of the parent for the teacher and vice versa. Better education for youth results, because home and school work together to provide the learning experiences that have been accepted as desirable.

Parent participation is of two types: informal, routine relationships with the school and formal, organized, lay advisory committees. The informal participation is much more widely used and has a greater variety of uses if the faculty wants to secure parent assistance in planning.

The first step in bringing parents into any planning is to make them feel welcome in the school. Too many times parents have had unsatisfactory experiences with the school when they were students. They have come to look upon teachers with a feeling of distaste or distrust. It is easy to understand why this is true if it is recognized that one-half of all the parents who started to high school failed. School has been a place where they have met with failure, and no one particularly likes to return to the scene of such experiences. Teachers must take the first step (maybe several first steps) before parents become convinced that teachers sincerely want parents in on the thinking about the school program. Many parents expect rebuffs and artificial, hypocritical welcomes. A staff needs to take all of the steps that it can to help the parent feel that it welcomes him, that it believes he has a contribution to make, and that it accepts him and his contribution. Verbal welcome is not enough; asking him to take a seat is not enough. It goes further. It involves obvious sincerity, honesty of actions, continued listening, willingness to let all parents in the situation evaluate the suggestions rather than having the staff make judgments about their ideas, ruling some as good and others as inappropriate. It involves thinking together. It involves social activities where parents and staff have an opportunity to get to know each other well.

Parent participation may start in many ways. Probably the most common method is through informal suggestions. Teachers may get the suggestions by merely listening, polling by questionnaire, or recalling conversations concerning the curriculum that occurred in a social situation. If this relatively unplanned approach is used by a faculty to secure real help, it is important that all comments be turned over to someone working on curriculum improvement so that they can be considered.

A practical place to start in planning with parents is through the homerooms. In many schools, homeroom mothers for each room are elected or appointed to be spokesmen for the parents. The ones chosen are usually people selected for their leadership ability and a manifestation of genuine interest in the welfare of their youngsters. Too often their role consists of baking cookies, chauffeuring groups to picnics, planning parties, and serving as chaperones. School personnel miss a good opportunity when they allow a genuine interest in the school to degenerate into social errand-boy services.

If the role of the homeroom mother has been strictly social, the teacher can suggest that the parent help secure the suggestions of all the parents of children in the homeroom concerning ways to improve the school curriculum. If some feel that parents have no interest in curriculum planning, the teacher should show with sincerity and honesty that he wants to know how parents feel so that he can provide better experiences for their children. If this appeal for help is rejected, and the chances are slight that it will be, the teacher can always find other approaches.

Homeroom groups offer real hope for the beginnings of cooperative curriculum planning. Parents and teachers have a common interest in a particular group of boys and girls. If an informal relationship is started, communication will be achieved more easily. Problems considered can be more concrete because they deal with certain children. Agreements can be reached and steps taken to implement them immediately. If progress is made in the small homeroom group, both teachers and parents may be ready to consider a joint effort on a schoolwide basis. Planning on a homeroom basis can make a difference for a specific class, and it serves as a situation in which parents and teacher can test each other and learn if it is safe to proceed or wiser to withdraw.

Some school systems believe that the best way to poll parent thinking is through individual parent-teacher conferences. These conferences give the teacher and the parent the opportunity to appraise each other and to discuss the child in terms of home and school situations. This will provide a means of better meeting the needs of an individual child within the existing framework of the present curriculum. If a parent has suggestions for the improvement of the school's curriculum they can be noted by the teacher and referred to the curriculum committee.

A parent-teacher conference can mean more. After the initial period of getting acquainted and discussing the particular child, some time can be spent in which the teacher honestly and tactfully asks the parent for suggestions for improving the program. To start the discussion the teacher may ask questions regarding specific aspects of the curriculum. The suggestions he receives may turn out to be wholesale criticisms of the school, or they may be helpful ideas. In any case the teacher will know more about the parent's feelings and will better understand his values, beliefs, and desires for his child.

Whether a parent-teacher conference has value for curriculum improvement depends upon what is done with parent suggestions. They must not be filed away and forgotten. The teacher should compile the parents' comments in some usable fashion and pass them on to some individual or group designated by the school to plan for curriculum improvement. If parents do not see results based on their suggestions, they become reluctant to continue making them or resentful and aggressive toward the school personnel.

The PTA can be another means of bringing parents into helping plan improvement of the school curriculum. Too often the true potential of this organization for securing parent participation is not realized. How many times parents and teachers groan at the thought of another PTA meeting. Parents sometimes feel that PTA meetings are set up expressly to give the school a chance to sell its program, that it is a once-a-month ordeal where the school tells the parents how good the existing program is and how rosy the future looks. If the PTA meetings are planned properly they can provide a good opportunity not only to inform parents about their school, but also to provide an opportunity for them to take part in the planning. Plenty of opportunity must be provided for honest reaction, criticism, and suggestion. Schools defeat the entire effort if they become defensive or ignore comments and criticism.

Many times parents are too busy or have little desire to undertake serious study of the total school curriculum. When the school staff has a real desire to find out how parents feel about the school program but fear they would be frightened by a large-scale attack on the problem of curriculum improvement, it is often better to start small. For example, a home economics teacher may know that her pupils are concerned about acceptable manners and dress which may be conflicting with their parents' ideas. This teacher may start by having her students invite their parents to a meeting that they have planned. The students can tell the parents some of the problems they are facing in the home economics class and ask for the parents' viewpoints. In this type of situation the home economics teacher has an excellent chance to poll parents for suggestions for improving her particular course program.

Students in a social studies class may find that certain controversial issues they are discussing in class are conflicting with the ideas expressed in their homes. Or some parents may feel that the school is giving their youngsters only one side of a social issue and wish that all sides would be presented. Inviting parents to come to the class and express their views gives the teacher a way of finding out how parents feel about the particular course. It gives both teacher and pupils a chance to explain what purposes they have and will thus develop more parent understanding. Helpful suggestions for improvement may come from using parents as resource people in the classroom.

Most high schools undergo periodic evaluations to maintain their accreditation. Usually the Evaluative Criteria or a variation of them are used to guide the evaluation committee, which may or may not, under present regulations, include parents. Some secondary schools have found that a worthwhile step is the inclusion of parents in the Evaluative Criteria process. When the parents become a part of an evaluating team their judgments become known to the staff and they begin to assume responsibility for improvement of the program.

A school that wants parent participation in curriculum planning can bring them into two phases of the evaluation process. Parents may be asked to work with the committees of the local faculty as they study the school and make judgments about its strengths and weaknesses, and the visiting committee may be asked to include parents in its organization.

Within the local faculty study parents can be invited to serve on each committee. As members of study groups they can collect data and participate in judgment-making. Parents who are asked to undertake this role must understand that the study will continue throughout the year and will take a number of hours. Only parents who agree to be available for as much time as needed should be included on the work committees.

The parents selected for the visiting committee will only need to be available for the few days that the visiting committee is at work. During the evaluation they should participate as any other member of the visiting committee, working through the organization, the collection of information, and the preparation of the final report. Through their activity they will become informed as to the way their high school compares with others and can be valuable assets as they help other members of the committee form a more accurate appraisal of the quality of their school.

THE ROLE OF THE LAY ADVISORY COMMITTEE

In schools where lay advisory committees have been used, the undertaking has not always looked the same way to parents as it has to professional educators. A parent from a New York community that was planning the program for a new consolidated high school described her experiences as follows:

> I was the only parent from our school. Seven of us, all from different elementary school districts, met in a town twelve miles from my home. When we arrived at the first meeting I asked what we were to do. A woman from the school office who sat with us said: "That decision is up to you!" We began to discuss what we believed about high schools. No decision was reached. At the second meeting and the third it was the same. Talk, talk by people without information. No decisions were reached. Before the fourth meeting winter began, and the roads became so icy over the mountains I decided it wasn't worth the effort. At the end of the semester the report for our committee was written and presented by the woman from the office who had sat in at the meetings. Why didn't she write the report for our approval in the first place? It would have saved a lot of time and we are all busy people.

The school personnel undoubtedly saw the meetings very differently. They would say:

> Parents really took the lead in developing our high school program. Representatives from each elementary school district formed the curriculum committee. No attempt was made to control their thinking. Help and consultation service were provided if desired, but nothing was forced on the committee. Due to bad weather conditions, one of the parents from an outlying district had to miss many of the meetings, but the group produced a splendid report that was accepted by the community. Parent participation taps a wealth of resources and produces a parent commitment to the school program.

Certain difficulties are apparent in the situation. At least one member of the parent group was not clear on the functions of the committee. She expected to advise, not to tell. Neither did she understand the working relationship between lay and school personnel. Who was the woman from the school office? Was she meant to record, lead, supply information, listen, or what?

What is the role of a lay committee concerned with the curriculum?

How should it work? How should professional personnel be related to it? It would seem obvious that any lay committee cannot be more than advisory. Legally the board of education is responsible for the school program. The board may seek advice, but it must make the decisions that school officials implement.

If a lay committee on curriculum is advisory, how can it best perform its role? The committee may be systemwide, as it was in the incident described, or the committee may serve one school. In either case it is formed by some official or official group and should have its role defined at the source. Usually its role consists of analyzing the problem referred to it, isolating the issues, collecting information, and making recommendations. If the committee is a standing one, it will call the attention of school officials to issues that concern the community of which the administration may be unaware. But in all cases committee members should recognize that they are to recommend, not to direct. The recommendations should be on policy and should not attempt to prescribe specific techniques of implementation. Decisions concerning how to implement fall within the responsibility of the professionally trained person who has spent years learning the skills of his profession. The distinction between formation of policy and its administration and implementation should be carefully examined and fully understood by all if friction between advisory committees and school personnel is to be avoided.

In organizing an advisory committee, decisions must be reached about membership. If it is too large it cannot function. If it is too small it will not represent many people or have much influence. Usually groups from ten to twenty work well. Members are chosen in many ways. Sometimes the principal or superintendent organizing the committee makes the choices. If he does, he must be careful not to choose only those who agree with him or he will not have a group that increases his vision or makes wiser decisions by bringing in more data. Sometimes the school official asks groups to appoint representatives. If so he will want to be sure that organizations representing most segments of the school population are included. Under this procedure, it is evident that the people in the community who do not belong to organized groups will not be represented. Some claim this segment to be thirty per cent or more, and to overlook them would be a grave mistake. Whatever the method, the curriculum advisory committee, if it is to have major value, must represent an adequate sampling of the various opinions in the community.

In most cases the committee will advise an individual administrator or a single school faculty. A Connecticut town had a number of committees advising the board of education, with a member of the board participating in each advisory committee and bringing to the board both the thinking of the committee and its official recommendations. During a curriculum improvement program in a lower New York community, three members of the parent advisory committee served as members of a committee planning a curriculum study. By this arrangement the parents were kept fully informed of steps being taken in the system, and professional personnel were influenced by lay reactions. A Texas principal had the parent committee for his school meet with and advise him. He served as the link with the faculty. Channels of communication must be established and given recognition, and some official must play a major liaison role.

As school personnel work with lay committees they are likely to find one of two conditions: either the group will be dependent and want direction, or it will be filled with a desire to decide and direct. In curriculum improvement the advisory committee must:

1. Stimulate the staff by calling parent dissatisfaction to their attention.
2. Serve as a sounding board for ideas and programs that are emerging.
3. Sample the variety of opinions in the community.
4. Inform the community of issues being examined and ideas being advanced.
5. Provide support for those attempting change by providing a lay group in the community who understands and can explain.

THE ROLE OF THE STAFF MEMBER WORKING WITH THE LAY ADVISORY COMMITTEE

The role of the school person working with the advisory committee should be defined by the school administrator as the purposes of the group are being discussed. Most frequently his role is that of executive secretary: he helps organize the meetings; he brings pertinent information to the meetings; he collects the data and materials requested; he provides service in recording decisions and progress; he does what seems desirable as a good group member to assist in defining the problem, in sticking to the problem, and in reaching a consensus; and he communicates the outcome to the professional personnel. If he is to function effectively he must not be merely a listener, observer, and recorder. He must be an active group member with a service function to perform.

As he works, the staff member must avoid certain dangers. First, he will fail if he tries, however subtly, to get the committee to accept his answers. If he has a preconceived solution that he wants the committee to support, he will find himself withholding some data and emphasizing others; passing value judgments on the group members and their contributions; attempting to override, undercut, or ignore certain persons; being hypocritical in his relationships. Any of these actions can destroy his usefulness and, perhaps, the work of the committee. Second, he must not direct the work of the committee. If he does he will cause others to become too dependent upon him or to rebel against him. If the committee becomes too dependent it will have no greater vision than the staff member had in the beginning and no reason for existence. If the committee is forced to rebel, the gains made by initiating the committee become losses because negative emotions will have replaced the desire to cooperate. Third, he must not remain passive. His lack of action and withholding of comment are threatening. Committee members are forced to wonder whether he is ineffective, a spy, or an evaluator. In any case, the committee would function better without him.

Much of the success of the lay advisory committee depends upon the insight with which the staff member assigned to it interprets his role and the skill with which he implements it.

SUMMARY

Unless individuals involved in curriculum improvement have common perceptions of their various roles, any program of improvement will be hampered. Principals, teachers, supervisors, curriculum consultants, and parents should explore together the expectations that each has of the others and the mutual help that can be provided.

SELECTED READINGS

Alexander, W. M., "Cooperative Action for Curriculum Improvement," *Educational Leadership* 16: 268-270, February, 1959. Emphasizes

the need for closer cooperation among state, regional, and local
educational units in promoting curriculum development.
Association for Supervision and Curriculum Development, *Balance in the
Curriculum* (1961 Yearbook), Chapter 8. Washington, D .C.:
The Association, 1961. Devotes itself to a discussion of the roles
played by various persons and groups in reaching curriculum
decisions.
Beggs, W. K., "Types of Jobs Citizen Committees Should Undertake," *School
Executive* 71: 55, January, 1932. Outlines several roles that citi-
zen committees can fulfill.
Bostwick, Prudence and J. A. Dahl, "The Specialist and the Curriculum,"
Journal of Secondary Education 36: 107-111, February, 1961.
Deals with the relationships between the professional educator
and lay representatives in the legislatures and boards of edu-
cation.
Christensen, D. C. and Sterling G. Goplerud, "What Role for the Principal in
Improving the Instructional Program in the Junior High School?"
National Association of Secondary School Principals Bulletin
44: 211-214, April, 1960. Specifies some of the responsibilities
and tasks of the principal in fostering curriculum development.
Educational Leadership 15: 334-363, March, 1958. Entire issue devoted to
staff participation in curriculum development.
Ibid., 15: 398-430, April, 1958. Entire issue devoted to lay participation in
curriculum development.
Ibid., 19: 2-43, October, 1961. Relates, in turn, the roles of teachers, school
board members, state departments of education, legislatures, citizens, and organized interest groups in planning the curriculum.
Gross, Neal, Ward S. Mason, and Alexander W. McCachern, *Explorations in
Role Analysis*. New York: John Wiley and Sons, Inc., 1958.
Analyzes and examines the role of the school superintendent.
Jenkins, Clifford D., "The Work of Lay Advisory Councils" (Abstract of
doctoral dissertation), *Penn State Review of Educational Re-
search* 4: 19-25, May, 1953. Discusses the organization, opera-
tion, functions, and evaluation of lay councils.
Kennedy, R. H., "Teacher Readiness for Curriculum Improvement," *National
Association of Secondary School Principals Bulletin* 45: 70-74,
September, 1961. Discusses the relationships between teachers
and administrators in promoting curriculum improvement.
Krug, Edward A., *Curriculum Planning*, rev. ed. New York: Harper & Row,
Publishers, 1957. Describes the rationale, principles, and pro-
cedures of curriculum planning.
Lawler, Marcella R., "Role of the Consultant in Curriculum Improvement,"
Educational Leadership 8: 219-225, January, 1951. Emphasizes
the importance of the consultant's competence in his area of
specialization and in human relations.
Leese, Joseph, et al., *The Teacher in Curriculum Making*. Harper & Row,
Publishers, 1961. Considers in detail the role of the teacher in
curriculum planning.
Mackenzie, G. N., "Role of the Supervisor," *Educational Leadership* 19: 86-

90, November, 1961. Stresses the need for clarifying the role of the curriculum supervisor.

Morgans, R. D., "The Administrator and the Curriculum," *Journal of Secondary Education* 36: 103-106, February, 1961. Suggests steps that the administrator can take in promoting curriculum improvement.

Pratt, W. E. and D. G. McGarey, *A Guide to Curriculum Improvement in Elementary and Secondary Schools*. Cincinnati, Ohio: Public School Publishing Co., 1958. Describes the activities of both administrators and teachers in promoting curriculum change.

Pritzkau, P. T., *Dynamics of Curriculum Improvement*. Englewood Cliffs, N. J.: Prentice-Hall, Inc., 1959. Emphasizes the part played by teachers, supervisors, and administrators in planning curriculum change.

Rasan, N. A., "The Principal and Curriculum Improvement," *National Association of Secondary School Principals Bulletin* 44: 103-105, February, 1960. Describes the role of the principal in bringing about curriculum change.

Stembridge, A. W., "Curriculum Advisory Committee," *Ibid.*, 45: 75-79, September, 1961. Outlines the work of a curriculum advisory committee.

12

BARRIERS TO CURRICULUM IMPROVEMENT

As plans are being made for instituting a program
of curriculum change, it is necessary to look at the difficulties
in the situation. They may be so great that the first steps in the
curriculum improvement program consist of attempting to
decrease some of the handicaps that exist.

HOW THE PUBLIC MAY HINDER CURRICULUM IMPROVEMENT

The conception of
education held by the public may serve as a block to curriculum
improvement. Whenever the public looks upon any change in the
school program as a move in the wrong direction, it serves as an
effective pressure to prevent improving the school. For example,
if some members of the public voice the opinion that success is
achieved only by encountering unpleasant and extremely difficult
learning experiences, they may feel that it is unimportant to add

248

counseling and guidance services to the school. In one community certain citizens objected seriously to adding vocational counseling and placement to the school program because they felt that such services would decrease the sense of independence and initiative that constitute the American way of life. When the public believes that something must be hard in order to be beneficial, when it is operating in terms of an outmoded, formal discipline concept of learning and is unaware of the results of current research indicating that there are different theories and more effective methods of learning, it serves as opposition to any changes in the school program. If those who oppose change based on research are vocal enough, they intimidate all except the brave within the school faculties and may be effective enough to eliminate from the local scene those in the schools who hold viewpoints different from their own. When teachers lose their jobs as a result of working in terms of the best research that they know, all teachers are threatened. They tend to decrease the amount of effort they put into program improvement, and any experimentation becomes something that is illegal and must be bootlegged into the school situation.

Curriculum improvement is sometimes prevented by community pressure groups. Within the past few years various groups have attempted to restrict what will be taught in the schools. Some have tried to dictate what should be taught about power and housing and taxation. Great pressure has been exerted to control what is taught about world citizenship and international organizations. Efforts to restrain the school from dealing with certain topics not only affect what is done in the area in which the group attempts to force its ideas on the school, but also serve to inject fear into the situation as a whole. Many faculty members are intimidated and want to teach what is accepted by a method that is approved or to work more in line with the things that are tried and proved. Criticism and attacks by community groups decrease the willingness of teachers to take a chance with ideas in which they believe but which they have not tried sufficiently to determine what the exact results will be.

If there has been criticism of certain practices in the school, and if sufficient communication between parents and teachers has not been established, the more fearful teachers will be intimidated by caustic comments of the parents. If a substantial portion of the public in the community is demanding a return to the fundamentals, and if the public relations program of the school has not made clear the place that fundamentals presently have or the amount of pupil achievement in those areas, teachers will be insecure and will hesitate to attempt innovations.

Teacher fear will be especially prevalent where the administration has not supported teachers when parent criticism has arisen in the past. If the administration accepts criticism without attempting to explain and support, teachers feel very much alone and faced with the necessity of doing only those things in the classroom which parents understand from their own experiences in school a decade or two previously.

An administration that is afraid of the public is a serious liability for curriculum improvement. Sometimes administrators are not secure in their position or lack confidence in their ability to lead curriculum work. If an administrator is afraid he will lose his position his fear is conveyed to teachers, and they know that they will not have support should they undertake experimentation that the public questions. Or, if the administrator does not want to jeopardize the building program or some other project by undertaking instructional change that the public may not understand, the teachers know this and view any positive suggestions he may make regarding curriculum change as insincere. If an administrator lacks knowledge of curriculum and instruction and is unable to discuss what the school is doing with the curriculum and why it is doing it, any major change is a remote possibility. Teachers need the strength that comes from having an administration which can represent them adequately in discussions with the public. Teachers know that any change will result in public questioning, and a scared administrator spreads fear and insecurity throughout the entire staff.

A homogeneous community may also prevent curriculum improvement. If the present program is representative of the point of view and values of a homogeneous community, little change will take place. If, however, the community is one in which there are many groups with different points of view and different values, the difference of opinion among the various groups serves as a lever to move the school program forward. Each group will want the school program to represent more nearly the thinking of its members and will provide the kind of stimulation, maybe irritation, that forces the school to make curriculum changes. Homogeneity may produce harmony, but may at the same time result in a complacency that defies change.

Indifference or hostility toward the school on the part of the general public also acts as a barrier to curriculum change. If the public has never felt a part of the school and is indifferent to the kinds of

Those who can, do.
Those who can't, teach.
Those who really can't, teach
teachers to teach.

schools that exist within the community, it decreases the teacher's sense of importance and makes him feel that his job is a routine one without significance. If the community is actively hostile, the teacher may feel inadequate and insecure to the point where he will follow the line of least resistance and deal only with the kinds of problems that he is sure will not disturb any powerful force in the community.

HOW PROFESSIONAL AGENCIES MAY HINDER CURRICULUM IMPROVEMENT

Colleges, whether it is recognized or not, play a big part in determining the content of the secondary school. The education that they provide for teachers determines in large degree how and what teachers will teach. Most teachers tend to teach the way they were taught, and they are likely to put an emphasis on the things that have been emphasized for them in their college training. The knowledge that teachers have as a result of their college education does much to determine what the content of a high school program will be.

In still another way the colleges tend to force a continuation of the same type of curriculum that the school has had. The entrance exams and requirements that colleges establish tend to freeze the curriculum and prevent change. Many schools place a major emphasis on giving their students the kind of education that will make it possible for them to be successful in college. If teachers believe that a foundation in a certain subject matter is necessary for students to be successful in college, they attempt to provide youngsters with that knowledge. The beliefs that teachers have concerning what information is important restrict curriculum change and continue the emphasis on subject matter that has traditionally been considered college preparatory.

Still another way in which the college constitutes a pressure to continue the present program of the secondary school is through developing organizations for teachers around the subject-matter areas in which the teachers have majored in college. College people are not anxious to lose their status, and one of the ways to continue the prestige and importance of a department is to stress organizations that are devoted to continued study in that department. Language teachers form one group, science teachers another, and English teachers still a third. Each of these associations of teachers in a subject-matter field serves as a vested interest group to continue in the high school program the kind of education provided by work in their area. Members of these organizations place their attention on how to do a better job of teaching English or modern languages or science or mathematics and leave to further study the question of whether or not portions of the content of their field should be dropped from the high school curriculum.

Accrediting agencies also tend to perpetuate the status quo. High schools seek to become accredited. To become accredited, they must meet certain standards that have been set up by the accrediting agencies, and thus there is a movement in the direction of existing standards and things that have been labeled "good." To depart too much from the existing program as described in the standards of the accrediting agency jeopardizes the position that the high school hopes to attain (or to retain if it is already accredited). It should be said, however, that some of the accrediting agencies are now encouraging experimentation by establishing as one of the standards for continued accreditation a plan of experimentation designed to bring about continuous improvement of the program.

Statewide testing programs have been another block to curriculum change. The tests that have been devised have not only served the purpose of helping students and schools to judge the amount of pupil achievement, but they have also, perhaps without their authors intending to do so, focused the work of the classes in the school systems using them on certain bodies of subject matter. In order to do well on the statewide or systemwide tests, teachers and students have studied previous tests and have organized their work around the material that was included in them. When this practice is followed, teachers look backward to determine what the content of the courses should be. They look at the tests that have been given in the past rather than assuming that they are on the frontier, where they should be constantly seeking new information and working with new types of problems that are more appropriate for students growing up in our society. Statewide tests encourage all teachers to work in all schools on the same content. When achievement tests are given on a statewide basis, teachers do not feel free or have the time to experiment with new material that may not be included in the tests. The pressure is increased when colleges refuse to admit students who do not score well on these achievement tests.

State laws which require certain types of content for the curriculum keep the program from developing. For example, when a state requires all teachers to teach safety or conservation, the curriculum is frozen by the number of minutes per subject matter required by law. Each piece of legislation compelling the teaching of certain knowledge restricts the freedom of the teacher or the school to develop the program that seems most important for the students for whom they are working and decreases the possibility that curriculum change will take place. We should recognize, however, that all legislated curriculum has been an attempt at improvement and that it may have brought about curriculum change in the right direction at the time the law was enacted. But eventually, curricular legislation serves as a restrictive force working against further advance.

One of the reasons that there has been a lack of real public support for curriculum improvement is that teacher education institutions have failed to produce teachers and administrators prepared to work with the community in curriculum development. Much of the preservice education for school personnel has been the kind that prepares teachers to conduct the present program with little emphasis on the techniques of change and improvement. Few teachers and administrators have had the opportunity to discuss ways of working effectively with the public in curriculum improvement. In fact, in some teacher education institutions curriculum improvement is something that is not discussed or studied in any detail.

Without intending to do so, the plan of federal support for vocational education has hindered curriculum improvement, for it has brought a degree of federal control. Vocational teachers in some schools have contended that their program is not subject to the thinking of the rest of the staff, that their program has been outlined in Washington or in the state capital and that they have a responsibility to execute it without change. Some vocational supervisors deliberately attempt to keep teachers from making any change. Another aspect of the problem connected with vocational education is that federal support has resulted in the vocational teachers being paid more in some schools. The additional pay has brought resentment on the part of other teachers, which has interfered with cooperative thinking about total curriculum improvement. An added interference to joint action has been the feelings of superiority found in some teachers who receive extra salary, which has made them less willing to think with other teachers in the school concerning any change that should be made in their program. Persons with superior status frequently tend to resist change, which may leave them in a less favored position.

HOW LOCAL SCHOOL OFFICIALS MAY HINDER CURRICULUM IMPROVEMENT

Sometimes local boards of education prevent curriculum improvement. They may keep curriculum improvement from occurring by not appropriating the funds necessary to carry on the continued research and in-service training that make curriculum improvement possible. They may not make time available for teachers to work on curriculum improvement as a part of the regular job. In some schools, any attempt made by a faculty or a group of teachers to improve the learning situation must be done outside of the regular school day. In other cases—and these are the most harmful—the school board operates in terms of a concept of education that is no longer useful. They look with a halo effect at the kind of education that they have had, and they assume that all youngsters will profit by having the same type. As a result of this feeling, they insist that the schools stick to teaching the fundamentals by the old-fashioned methods. They place restrictions on the schools they control without realizing that the fundamentals and the accepted methods they insist upon are merely the courses that they studied in school being taught as they have always been taught. A board of education that looks backward on a previous educational concept is one of the major hindrances to curriculum improvement.

A further liability is teacher fear of the administration. All systems do not have harmony between administration and staff, and in the worst situations a real fear is developed. Whenever people are afraid, they seek security. Fearful teachers will follow the ways that already have administrative approval or will openly rebel and resist any authority or change that is administration approved. Teacher fear develops when instances occur in which the administration does not support teachers who have undertaken new procedures, when teachers are mistreated if they disagree with the administration, when the person who disagrees is transferred to a less desirable situation or is given a less pleasant schedule or is placed with youngsters whom he considers more difficult to teach. The most fearful teachers hesitate to undertake any instructional change that they are not sure the administration will approve. This fear is crippling to any growth within the staff or to any improvement in the program.

Closely allied to teacher fear of the administration is lack of confidence in the school leadership. Unless the staff believes in the competence of the status leaders in the system staff members will hesitate to undertake any curriculum work under their guidance. If administrators make statements about curriculum and instruction that teachers know cannot be supported by research evidence, they refuse to participate in projects that the administration advocates. They do not want to be in the position of giving support to practices in which they cannot believe. If the administration takes positions and advocates directions for the school program that teachers know are in error, they will seek other leadership or avoid any kind of activity that calls for more effort than merely teaching classes. If principals and supervisors have been appointed on a favoritistic basis or through political pressure, teachers know this and resent it. They lack confidence in the persons so designated and are unwilling to exert effort to help them be successful. Or if previous administrators have used teachers' efforts in curriculum work to get advancement for themselves, teachers seek to avoid a repeat of the situation. If they have seen one principal after another use their curriculum work for personal aggrandizement and promotion, they become suspicious of efforts to improve the curriculum. If there has been inadequate planning for successful implementation of the program in previous attempts at improving the curriculum, teachers lose confidence in their school officials and have no interest in working on new plans. If the administration insists that teachers work on problems that the administration considers important and the teachers do not, little more than formalities are followed. The teachers do what they feel they must, but their heart is not in it. No administration is capable of carrying through a curriculum improvement program alone. No change will take place in the classrooms as long as the problems being worked on are the administration's problems alone.

HOW CONDITIONS IN THE LOCAL STAFF MAY HINDER CURRICULUM IMPROVEMENT

Insufficient financial support blocks curriculum improvement. If there is barely enough money to employ the necessary teachers and consequently those secured must carry a very heavy load, there will be little chance that they will find the energy or the time to work on program improvement. They will be so busy simply meeting the demands placed upon them that there will be little chance for research or pioneering. Furthermore, without enough funds teachers are not provided with the consultant help or the materials needed to make many projects successful.

Low teacher morale is a liability that it is disastrous to ignore. Unless teachers are satisfied with the work situation they will be unwilling to attempt to improve the curriculum. If the administration has evidenced no interest in teacher welfare or feelings, the attention of teachers will be centered so much on resentment toward the administration that they will not be interested in curriculum work and may even actively resist it.

Lack of communication among teachers is also a liability in curriculum work. Although this shortcoming is not as apparent to the observer, it is just as real. If teachers are not in the habit of sharing, they will feel that any common planning is a waste of time. To them, time taken away from individual work in planning class activities is an added burden because they feel that it is necessary to add the group planning to the individual planning. If teachers have never experienced the support that comes from joint teacher planning, they will not know that cooperative planning enhances and promotes much individual planning. Some teachers will be selfish about materials, for example. Teachers who have developed devices that enable them to make their classes interesting will hesitate to share them with their fellows. They will already have established a reputation as a good teacher and feel that if other teachers improve, their own status may be jeopardized. In schools where communication among teachers has not been established except on a social level, teachers do not feel the strength that comes through being a part of a strong faculty. Instead, strength is taken to mean being an outstanding teacher in comparison with the remainder of the faculty.

Lack of any consistent, cooperatively developed school philosophy hinders curriculum development. Unless all members of the faculty have been in on forming the statement of philosophy, it has little meaning to those who have not participated and is only a hollow form, a paper document that has little significance in determining what shall be done in the school. Unless there is agreement as to what the school is trying to do, teachers have little sense of direction in deciding upon desirable changes. Unless there is a functional school philosophy, changes that an individual teacher makes may be interpreted as a whim by other members of the faculty or by the community. If, however, there is an agreed upon statement of philosophy that indicates the direction in which the school desires to move, the teacher has security with other faculty members and with the community in making changes.

Undesirable human relationships among superintendents and supervisors and principals and teachers hinder curriculum change. When there is suspicion, distrust, and hostility among the school personnel, there is little enthusiasm for working together for improvement. Instead, energy is expended in taking advantage of the opposing faction. It is necessary to protect oneself in a situation where there are opposing forces, and this means being cautious so that the other person cannot secure evidence of inappropriate action. Unless there is a spirit of harmony among the school personnel, there is little likelihood that there will be cooperative attempts to move ahead on curriculum and instruction or that individual teachers will introduce change into their programs.

One of the big reasons that there has been little curriculum improvement in some schools is that teachers are unacquainted with educational research. They are still basing their judgment and action upon the research that was available when they attended teacher education institutions. Many school systems have not provided adequate professional libraries, which bring into each school the results of research that would reorient teachers' thinking. Unless teachers are aware of the evidence that is being found today concerning teaching methods and learning processes, they do not have the stimulus that comes from seeing where these results contradict the assumptions and procedures that they have been using. Evidence contradicting what a person has been doing either makes him withdraw or stimulates him to take action. Evidence supporting the things currently being done on a limited basis gives a person greater courage, makes him exert more effort.

Even though all the factors discussed previously are satisfactory, a curriculum program may be doomed because of lack of materials. If the school budget does not contain enough funds to provide sufficient materials to go around under existing conditions, the teachers are sure that change is impossible. If the shortage of materials is due to an inadequate budget, teachers question whether any change is possible. They honestly and sincerely ask: "Why plan change if it cannot be made because no materials will be provided to implement it?" There is no point in planning if it is known beforehand that the plans cannot be executed. When insufficient funds for instructional materials result from the diversion of monies to other phases of the program, the teachers know that the administration is not really interested in curriculum and instruction, and as a result they will not take curriculum work seriously.

Another liability is lack of time. If there is a heavy teaching load that does not permit time during the school day for planning, teachers will not have the energy or enthusiasm for curriculum work. Priority must be given to doing the things that are essential to keeping the present program going. If the administration does not recognize that planning takes time, teachers do. Any movement to make change without adequate provision of time for planning on the part of the people who will be involved in it is always recognized as being a token effort.

All of these liabilities and others may be present in any situation. To ignore them in planning a curriculum program is always foolish and is usually disastrous.

HOW TEACHERS' ATTITUDES AFFECT CURRICULUM IMPROVEMENT

The feelings of teachers about curriculum work will determine the success of any curriculum improvement effort. If teachers are hostile, they can prevent any important change. If they are indifferent or apathetic, nothing happens. If they are overenthusiastic about exploration and experimentation, the principals and supervisors will have difficulty supplying the resource help and coordinating efforts that are needed.

No generalization can be made concerning teachers' feelings about curriculum development activity. Attitudes vary from teacher to teacher. Let us examine a few of them.

Teaching classes is my job. I do that well, but I avoid all the extras they try to put on me. This teacher may or may not be an excellent operator in the classroom, but his interpretation of the teacher's role is limited to classroom work.

I would like to, but I have too much to do. They load us with so many committees and administrative duties in this system that I can't take on another responsibility. He may be right, or the comment may represent evasion tactics. But it is evident that this teacher will not enter curriculum work with enthusiasm.

Nothing ever happens. It's all talk. This man has had sad experiences. Once he may have been a willing, idealistic worker, but those days are gone. Maybe that first curriculum project on which he worked was misguided. Maybe the faculty spent the first year talking through the school philosophy and exhausted its energy before any changes were proposed. At present, he would be a skeptic even if he were coerced into curriculum work.

The present program is good. What is back of all this pressure to change it? Perhaps this man is lazy and does not want to assume any additional burdens. But he may really believe his statement. He may have helped devise the program and be deeply committed to it. He may have received so many compliments from parents about his work with their children that he does not feel change is desirable.

An expert should do it. We are not well enough informed to make intelligent decisions concerning curriculum change. This man may have a glorified concept of the curriculum. His lack of information concerning the evolution of the present program may make it seem sacred, the product of some great scholars. He has never realized that the curriculum is never more than the teacher's interpretation, that regardless of design a curriculum is no stronger than the classroom teacher's vision and skill in implementation. Until this teacher gains a clearer understanding of the curriculum and his part in it, he will withdraw from proposals that he participate in curriculum-making.

Don't let them kid you! The administration is subtle. They are criticizing our work but don't have the courage to tell us. So they institute a curriculum study to get us to change. This teacher is on the defensive. He feels that any question of any phase of the program is really an attack on him. He is suspicious of all administrative action and wants other teachers to join him in a self-protection alliance. Until he gains more self-confidence, he will not trust status leadership and will resist participation in any curriculum study.

We aren't meeting the needs of youth. Have you seen the drop-out figures for our school? This teacher is ready to work. He is dissatisfied with what the present program is doing for boys and girls and wants to be of more help. Time spent in program improvement will be satisfying to him if he can see results of his efforts.

Curriculum work has helped me more in meeting the needs of my pupils than any other part of my professional training. We worked on curriculum revision constantly in the last system in which I taught, and I miss it here. This teacher is not only ready for curriculum work but wants it. In his mind, a school that has it is helping its teachers improve. Lack of a program of curriculum development is evidence of inadequate leadership and planning.

We want to improve. I hope our system can become the best in the state. This person is ready to exert leadership in curriculum work.

Teaching to him extends beyond meeting classes and making out reports. He sees planning improvement with other staff members as part of his role as a teacher.

The opinions of the teaching personnel constitute a major asset or liability in curriculum improvement. If the majority of the staff is against it, no program can succeed. Preliminary planning must provide opportunity for teachers to express dissatisfactions, to suggest ways of working to overcome them, and to participate in developing work plans. If there is to be acceptance of the expenditure of the time and effort that curriculum work involves, the staff members must see it as their project to decrease some of their feelings of inadequacy or to eliminate some of the handicaps to successful teaching.

WHY DO SOME TEACHERS RESIST CHANGE?

Many reasons exist why high school teachers do not want to change the program. They range from real fear to insecurity to lack of the enthusiasm necessary for creative effort.

One fear is that students will not be able to meet college requirements. Teachers in some communities know that they are judged by whether or not their students are able to achieve in college, and they are afraid that any change they make may result in less adequate preparation for college. One kind of security that they can have in changing is a knowledge of the research done on the effects of program changes on pupils' success in college. When they come into contact with evidence like that produced by the Eight-Year Study, the fear of pupil failure in college tends to be allayed.

A fear of many teachers is that they will not be as successful under the new procedures as they have been with the present ones. All teachers want to be effective. They want students to believe that they are doing a good job. When they have the security of knowing that their present efforts are good, it is hard to depart from those procedures in the hope of obtaining something better. Regression rather than advance may occur.

A third fear, and a very real one for some, is the fear of being labeled. Teachers do not want to be different any more than do other members of the population. They do not want to be labeled as "radical" or "progressive" or "conservative." When the community, administration, or other teachers use these terms to deride new proposals and procedures that are recommended, people stop advancing the proposals. A teacher wants to be considered an adequate working member of the staff of which he is a part. He does not desire to be set apart by having his ideas labeled as anything other than an attempt to improve the program. This human wish emphasizes once again the need for the faculty to agree on its direction and, in terms of the goals accepted, to seek better ways of accomplishing the desired results.

A cause of insecurity is the lack of agreement on what constitutes good teaching. When a staff has reached agreement on desired outcomes of the school program, a teacher has a basis for judging his teaching. When the teachers know the desired pupil growths and frequently discuss ways of attaining them, there is less insecurity about attempting new ideas.

A teacher may lack faith in his own interpretation of ideas. When teachers have had unpleasant experiences in which their interpretations have been held up to ridicule or their implementation of ideas has gotten them into difficulty or people they respect have evidenced lack of faith in them, they lose confidence in their own abilities. Lack of confidence in themselves causes them to stick to the types of interpretations that have been approved in the past. Working in traditional ways gives them a confidence that they cannot have in their own interpretation.

Lack of training also causes resistance to change. When all of a person's training has been within a certain area he hesitates to go into another. He feels that he will not have enough knowledge to be successful in the new field. If the preservice education has been the kind that promotes skill in only one type of teaching, an in-service program in which teachers have an opportunity to develop new skills necessary for a proposed activity is essential if teachers are to have the security that makes them willing to try out the new plan. In-service education is an important aspect of curriculum development. When a work committee makes a proposal, it needs to specify the steps that will be provided to help the people involved gain the skills necessary to make the proposal successful.

If the school has not had an in-service education program of any type and teachers have not been brought into contact with new ideas, little enthusiasm will exist. Unless a teacher has been confronted by ideas that conflict with his own, he usually has not been challenged to examine his present practice unless intense dissatisfaction exists in the student body or community. Without a steady influx of new ideas from professional materials or activities, complacency comes to many.

The job becomes routine. The validity of the assumptions underlying methods and content used are not questioned. If a staff is engaging in a professional siesta brought on by lack of stimulation, it will passively resist efforts to promote change.

Resistance to change on the part of many teachers may in actuality be lack of enthusiasm for the policies and procedures of the school system in which they work. Discrimination, favoritism, lack of time for planning, a heavy teaching load, poor personnel policies cause such low morale in some schools that there is no enthusiasm for any activity beyond meeting classes.

Resistance to change may exist because a teacher is committed to the present program. He may have helped develop it. Any questioning of present practice might be considered a criticism of his own judgment. In schools in which experimentation is not expected as a part of the normal routine, loyalty to what exists usually results. Unless a commitment to seek better methods and programs is developed, a staff will resent and resist all who advocate change.

When a staff disagrees basically on what is important in education, resistance is certain to occur. A move in one direction will be looked upon by one portion of the faculty as a dangerous regression. Seeking some common ground as to desired outcomes, and making possible experimentation to see which procedure is most effective in attaining them are necessary steps when the faculty is divided. If no agreement can be reached on goals, any program for improvement is doomed to failure through interpersonal strife and hostility.

It should not be inferred that resistance to change is wrong. Passive or active resistance may be the only way in which an individual can maintain his integrity. If a teacher considers any proposed change contrary to the evidence he has been able to find about teaching-learning situations and he is continuing to seek new data, he has a moral responsibility to oppose the change. *Resistance to change is unprofessional only when it is practiced as a way of maintaining personal privilege or of avoiding an increase in responsibility.*

SELECTED READINGS

Ferris, R. W., "The Teacher and the Curriculum," *Journal of Secondary Education* 36: 100-102, February, 1961. Discusses the attitudes of teachers as a factor in preventing curriculum development.
Leese, Joseph, "Personal Tensions in Ourselves and Others as They Relate to Curriculum Planning," *High School Journal* 43: 2-7, October,

1959. Cautions that change may bring about pressures upon the staff that could easily reduce both its efficiency and its interest in curriculum planning.

Platte, DeGroff and E. M. Moore, "Curriculum Improvement, Ltd.," *Clearing House* 34: 153-155, November, 1959. Discusses barriers to curriculum improvement encountered while working on a curriculum project.

Rubin, L. J., "Curricular Senility," *California Journal of Secondary Education* 34: 426-428, November, 1959. Discusses forces that prevent curriculum development.

Sand, Ole, et al., "Components of the Curriculum: Curriculum Decisions in Secondary Education," *Review of Educational Research* 30: 233-237, June, 1960. Reviews the major studies made on aspects of curriculum decision-making.

Simons, B. L., "Obstacles to Curriculum Development," *National Association of Secondary School Principals Bulletin* 43: 26-29, February, 1959. Suggests some of the many obstacles that must be overcome if curriculum change is to take place.

Smith, D. W., "Ethnocentrism and Curriculum Change," *Education* 78: 100-103, October, 1957. Discusses the effect of ethnic feelings within the community in impeding the process of curriculum change.

Van Dyke, L. A., "Perspective and Priorities in Curriculum Planning," *School and Community* 46: 13-144, February, 1960. Emphasizes the need for a school philosophy to give direction to curriculum planning.

13

FOSTERING CURRICULUM CHANGE

Many different procedures for improving the curriculum
have been tried. Some have failed. Others have succeeded.
This chapter will present some generalizations that can be drawn
from numerous attempts at curriculum change in the public
secondary schools during the past fifty years.

INITIATING CURRICULUM CHANGE

When school leaders
begin to plan changes, they should be sure that they are not
concerned about change for change's sake, that they are not
merely trying to be "modern." They should be extremely cautious
lest they make changes simply to "keep up with the Joneses."
Too many schools have attempted innovations because they have
seen that other schools around them do so. In approaching
curriculum improvement in any school it is important to recognize
that changes should be made in terms of the needs of that
particular community and the inadequacy of the present program
in meeting those needs.

Although curriculum change should start with the dissatisfaction of people in the situation, not all dissatisfaction calls for change. The fault may lie in the distorted perception of the dissatisfied. Dissatisfaction is merely an indication that study is desirable. The study will reveal the nature of the situation and whether or not an important problem exists.

One of the best ways to bring dissatisfactions out into the open is to carry on an evaluation of the school. In a school survey, persons involved in the situation—teachers, pupils, parents, and administrators—should first seek agreement on criteria by which to judge the program. An excellent way of identifying the criteria is to look at the needs of the student population in the school, the needs of the community and society, and the democratic ideals that the school is attempting to teach. Application of these criteria to the school program will help identify weaknesses in the program. Without an agreed upon basis of making judgments, statements of dissatisfaction may be looked upon as unjustified griping by the staff or parents.

In schools in which faculties are complacent, school leadership should not be content merely to allow dissatisfactions to emerge. Steps should be taken to create dissatisfactions in the minds of the teachers. One function of the school's curriculum leadership in self-satisfied faculties is to bring to the attention of the staff any ideas that will cause dissatisfaction with the present methods of work. Opportunity should be provided in staff meetings for members to describe what they are doing so that other people will contrast these methods with their own and, in the process, see better ways of working. Resource people who advance ideas that are not currently in operation in the situation should be asked to address the staff. It is not expected that all of these ideas will receive a favorable reaction. But if many new ideas are brought into the situation, some of them will appeal to the staff, and a desire to move from their present status will be cultivated.

Encouraging members of the staff to attend conferences where they hear people from other schools describe what they are doing may foster dissatisfaction with the present program. Intervisitation in which teachers go into other schools and see things that they would like to have in their own school also helps. Giving students an opportunity at faculty meetings to present their ideas as to how the school could be improved is a way of making faculty members more aware of things that can be done to improve the situation. Holding open hearings at which parents can talk about things they would like to see the school do increases the pressure for improvement. One high school used an internship program of a nearby university as a way of increasing dissatisfaction. The interns brought into the school the ideas that they had been getting from their preservice training, and as directing teachers and interns worked together teachers began to see some new elements that might be included in their program. In other schools a child study program, in which teachers focused their attention on learning to meet more adequately the developmental needs of children, has served as the springboard for teachers' deciding that certain changes are desirable in the program.

ASSETS IN CURRICULUM CHANGE

In any secondary school those concerned with bringing about curriculum improvement have some assets with which to work. The degree to which these factors are present in the situation largely determines the success of any program that is initiated.

The most important asset is teacher dissatisfaction. Not all teachers will be dissatisfied at the same time or in the same way. Some may become dissatisfied as a result of a new vision of a good teaching-learning situation that they have developed as a result of in-service experiences or graduate work. Others may feel that the present program is undesirable because of the discipline problems that they have in their class. Some teachers may not even see the difficulty as stemming from inadequate curriculum; instead, they may feel that the children attending the school are less able and less interested than those to whom they are accustomed. Their dissatisfaction may manifest itself in resentment toward the type of child they are asked to teach rather than in questioning whether or not the present curriculum content is satisfactory. Still other teachers may be unhappy because of parent and pupil complaints that have come their way. They want to do something to decrease the amount of conflict they find in their present operation. Some may be disturbed by the number of drop-outs and feel guilty that the school is not serving all of the youngsters who enter. Regardless of the cause of dissatisfaction, the feeling of a necessity for change is the beginning of curriculum improvement.

Articles written in popular magazines that attack present-day education programs foment change. Whether such articles are an asset for curriculum change depends upon the way in which they are used. If they are viewed as attacks that must be answered, a faculty moves to a defensive posture and seeks ways of supporting the present program. If, however, they are used to raise issues that the staff needs to examine in evaluating the present program, they open the doors for constructive thinking. The articles present points of view different from those held within the profession, and they should be examined. The issues raised may bring about questioning areas in which the staff is sure of itself and enhance determination to collect evidence that will help to settle the issues.

A principal's skill in leadership is another important asset in the curriculum program. What the principal thinks and does casts a long shadow over his school. According to the leadership study conducted at the University of Florida, the principal is able singlehandedly to block or to promote the curriculum work in his school. Even though the county staff is attempting to carry on a curriculum improvement program, a principal can prevent change from occurring within his own faculty or, if he will, he can enhance and support the countywide effort. If the principal lacks skill in leadership, the school system's central office staff will be unable to make the advances for which it hopes.

A school that has parents who participate actively in the school program has a tremendous advantage in making curriculum change. When parents are in the school frequently enough to develop an understanding of the program, it gives the teachers added strength. They are able to communicate with parents with whom they work closely and can share with them their understandings and concerns. Parents who have this kind of relationship with teachers are in a position to interpret any changes that are made for other parents who may have questions. This type of support by the parents who participate actively in the school develops and maintains confidence in the program on the part of those who have less frequent contact with it. Changes made by the school personnel will not seem as threatening to them if the parents who are closely related to the school accept the changes.

A procedure for sharing teaching ideas is still another advantage in making changes. If the school has a mechanism for letting teachers know what other teachers are doing, the vision of everyone in the school is broadened. Each teacher sees a greater range of possible things that can be done. Knowing that other teachers are doing things in many different ways gives any teacher courage to make some deviations in his own pattern of work. This knowledge constitutes the first step in experimentation.

If there has been assistance provided for experimentation in the past, knowledge of this assistance is a real asset for curriculum development. Staff members will know that as they undertake new projects the administration will supply help when they need it. If staff members have had the support that comes from working with other staff members in a previous joint enterprise, they will not hesitate to undertake new ones. If the system has established committees of people working on the same kinds of problems, committee members are able to share, to help each other, and to give strength to those who have not experimented before. They will have heard from other teachers about the kind of help that such committees have given them. If the system provides consultant help, in the form either of supervisors or outside consultants ready to talk through problems when they arise, staff members know that they are not alone in experimentation. If the school system has continuously supplied materials to those undertaking new projects, teachers will not fear that they will find themselves in the middle of an enterprise without the teaching materials they need.

One of the most important kinds of assistance that teachers want is help with developing methods of evaluation by which they can collect evidence of the value of the practices being tried. No teacher wants to be in the position of having to declare that his method is good without having evidence to support his claim. Much experimental work calls for attempts to produce types of growth that the typical evaluation instrument does not measure. School systems give real support to experimentation as they make available to teachers expert help in evaluation techniques.

A little noted asset is a strong professional library. If the system has been supplying teachers with the best professional books and magazines, the staff will have developed a point of view that is conducive to change. Many changes take place as a result of teachers' trying out new ideas that they have gained from their perusal of professional materials.

One of the most important assets is time for curriculum work. If the school has some pre- and postschool conference days in which details of plans can be worked out, the staff will be more ready to undertake curriculum improvement. When a board of education provides such days it gives evidence that it will support curriculum changes. Time makes possible consulting research and discussing the evidence before decisions are made, and the staff will be more sure of their hypotheses before trying them out.

BASIC CONCEPTS IN CURRICULUM CHANGE

The curriculum is changed as people are changed. Unless teachers are changed in their beliefs, they seldom change their practice. A directive announcing that the school program is to be changed, either by legislative action or by a revised course of study drawn up by a committee of educators, makes little difference in the way a teacher teaches. He resists operating in a new way if he does not believe in it. He engages in many types of evasions to avoid making the change. If, however, the teacher has come to believe that a change is desirable, he will attempt to make it whether official statements have been issued or not.

Teachers should undertake to make an innovation only if they are convinced of the desirability of the change. No teacher can do a good job if he does not believe that the thing he is doing is right and worthwhile. A teacher forced to work in a way in which he does not believe cannot be successful, and a forced change will result in a less satisfactory program rather than an improved one.

People are changed through participation. In the past some attempts have been made to change the curriculum by having an expert draw up a new program or by statewide or local committees forming new courses of study. But it was found that the only people who made any degree of change were those who had participated on the committees. If change in people which will result in revision of curriculum is desired, staff members must be involved in curriculum study and experimentation.

Participation provides the major key to curriculum improvement. As people change, the curriculum is changed. When curriculum change is attempted by having statewide or countywide or citywide committees formulate new courses of study or new programs, little change occurs in the program except as committee members carry new ideas back into their classrooms. For the most part, the reports prepared by the committees collect dust on the shelves and make little difference in the way teachers who have not been on the committes teach. The people who are on the committees and who have been deeply involved in thinking through the revision do make changes in their method of operation. Real curriculum change occurs only at the operational level.

Teachers, administrators, parents, and pupils must be changed if a program of curriculum improvement is to be successful. It is necessary for parents and pupils to be in on the planning if they are to support any change that is made. Each person operates and judges in terms of his own perceptions and expectations and, if the perceptions and expectations of parents and pupils are too different from those of the teachers, dispute will arise that will jeopardize the possibility of making any lasting change. Cay found that teachers in four secondary schools in Georgia perceived parents and parent opinion as the biggest barrier to curriculum revision. If lasting change is to occur, both school staff and community members should participate in evaluating the present program and planning the revision.

Local school units within a system form the primary work groups for effective curriculum development. If curriculum change occurs only through change in people, a systemwide change achieved through committees is impossible. Not all teachers can participate on system-wide committees. Only by organizing the local school staffs, students, and parents into working committees can the majority of those who must change for real curriculum revision be involved in the planning. Freedom of individual schools to initiate change is essential. Unless a local school unit is free to change its program as the group immediately involved decides, then the work of committees in that school may be a frustrating experience leading to rejection of further participation. Many teachers and parents will soon see that there is no point in having a local committee take the time to work out a needed improvement if the central office staff of the school system is able to refuse them permission to put it into effect.

Officials responsible for curriculum improvement facilitate their task if they establish official channels of communication. To provide local school personnel with suggestions, it is advantageous to establish a means by which staff members in separate units can exchange ideas. One way of doing this is by providing an organization through which ideas and programs that are being developed in individual schools can be shared throughout the system. In Rockford, Illinois, a curriculum coordinating council was used to perform this function. Each school was represented on the council by two people, a teacher elected from the staff and the principal. This council had no policy-making powers. It met once a month, and representatives told of the developments within the schools from which they came. After the sharing, each representative took back to his school the ideas that were emerging in other schools.

Changes should be made to decrease dissatisfaction with the present program. It is foolish to change just to be modern. Any program has so many features with which parents, patrons, and pupils are dissatisfied that it is unintelligent to seek to discover weaknesses in the phases of the program with which all participants in the situation are satisfied. But the decision as to where to start is not easy. The individuals in any situation are dissatisfied with different phases of the program. If it is accepted that several of these can be reorganized at one time, differences of opinion as to shortcomings can provide the basis of organization of a curriculum improvement program. Persons dissatisfied with a particular phase of a school can be asked to become members of the group seeking better ways of conducting that portion of the program. Others with a different problem are provided opportunity to work on it.

When dissatisfactions are brought out into the open it is important to have an organization for doing something about them. If people are dissatisfied and have no way of doing anything about it, frustration and aggression result. But if the school has a curriculum committee to which complaints and dissatisfactions can be brought for consideration, it serves as an organizer and expediter of activities. It does not attempt to do all the work itself. Rather does it assume leadership in the formation of committees to work on particular dissatisfactions and offer recommendations to the faculty.

It is important that any proposal for major change be brought to the total faculty for discussion and decision. The process of decision-making, if skillfully conducted, is a type of in-service education for the faculty in which values are examined and tested. The evidence presented in support of the proposed change adds to the knowledge of each staff member, and the viewpoints of those who are not convinced of the worth of the suggestion promote clarification of issues and indicate additional verification that should be sought through evaluation should the proposal be accepted. Constructive cothinking is the process by which the faculty grows and the curriculum is improved.

Faculties are stimulated to undertake curriculum change if they are helped to realize that there is no one best *curriculum or method, that each school and each teacher must devise the best way of working in that situation.* This knowledge decreases any fear that a person is departing from what is good if he tries something new. It eliminates, too, the feeling that it is necessary to copy a program already rated good in another school. It puts the emphasis on each individual and each faculty evaluating for itself what it is doing in terms of the criteria that it accepts. It helps the faculty to recognize that the best secondary school program has not yet been achieved and makes clear the opportunity that each school has to make its program better than any program yet devised. It presents unlimited opportunity for change and in no way restricts the kinds of contributions that individuals can make.

If change is to be undertaken, *time should be provided for planning*. Little improvement is likely to occur in situations where teachers are expected to revise the program while attending to their regular work load. The work cannot be unpaid overtime if teachers are expected to devote their full effort to it. Time for curriculum work must be provided—either through skillful scheduling or through pre- and post-school conferences where teachers can focus their full attention on planning and evaluating.

Changes should be made on an experimental basis. No innovation should be undertaken on the assumption that it is to be permanent. All groups hesitate to make changes that may threaten their security, but almost everyone is willing to experiment if he knows that he can revert to existing methods should the new ones prove less satisfactory.

It is usually undesirable to disrupt the whole school program in the first stages of a curriculum revision. Certain faculty members should be designated by the total faculty to try out the program on an experimental basis. If the evaluation indicates that it has been successful, it can be spread throughout the entire program.

When all the faculty must make a decision to do something at the same time, it is almost impossible to achieve consensus. But it is easy for a faculty to agree that certain members try out a method or a project if it is understood that the project undertaken is experimental and will be evaluated not only by those who are in it, but by the other faculty members as well. Even the most conservative are not disturbed by an experimental activity that will be evaluated by all, with the evaluation being used as a basis for deciding whether a schoolwide change should be made. Any conscientious teacher is disturbed by being forced to move before he is ready or by having an innovation made in the curriculum which becomes a permanent feature even before there is evidence of the results of the change.

Opportunity should be provided for the group that will engage in the experimental work to plan together before the project starts. Good ideas are many times jeopardized by being undertaken before the implementation has been carefully thought out. It takes time to get ready to try something new. Tools must be assembled, procedures clarified, and a technique of evaluation devised before the experimental group will feel secure in moving ahead.

Plans should be made for continuous evaluation in terms of the purposes and procedures of the experiment. The persons involved in the new procedures need constant reassurance that they are moving in the right direction. Evaluation provides the technique for securing this satisfaction. If the evaluation is continuous, the purposes and procedures may be revised as the group works ahead. In this way a successful outcome is more likely to result.

All members of a faculty should be engaged in some form of curriculum improvement. Experimentation should not be restricted to a portion of the staff. If only a small percentage of the faculty is engaged in curriculum improvement activities, they constitute a threat to the rest of the faculty. They run the risk of being looked upon as the inner circle or the élite and of being rejected because they are different. If they are successful, they make the rest of the faculty appear less professional and less adequate, and the only type of defense that is available for the others is to look for weaknesses in the new procedures and shortcomings in those conducting them. If, on the other hand, all members of the faculty are conducting some type of experimentation, no one is threatened and each is making some contribution which may be shared with the faculty and utilized by others if they deem the contribution to be worthwhile.

Each group of teachers engaged in experimentation should have the support, encouragement, and evaluation assistance of the total staff. If all members of the staff are engaged in some form of experimentation, they will support each other. Further, if proposals for experimentation are presented to the total faculty and approval is secured for individuals or groups to undertake the experiment, all members of the faculty feel a responsibility for helping the group conduct and evaluate the new curriculum. The experimentation is thereby the property and responsibility of the total faculty.

All members of the faculty should be informed concerning the types of experimental work being conducted in the school. It increases everyone's sense of security to know what is being tried, and it makes possible the intelligent explanation to parents and students of things that are underway in the school. If members of the community ask teachers what is being tried and they are not fully informed and are able only to say "I don't know," "I can't be sure of what it is," or "I don't know whether it is worth trying or not," then doubt is developed in the community concerning at least some of the things that are going on in that school.

A committee or person must coordinate the curriculum change in a school. Continuing effort to stabilize the curriculum must be made.

Unless steps are being taken to bring the results of all of the successful experimentation into the general structure of the curriculum, the program will get out of hand. No one will know for sure what the school is doing, what its present status is, or where it is going. The coordinating committee should have the responsibility for keeping a record of the status quo, the new ideas being tested, the sharing of experimentation, and the presenting of proposals for program change to the total faculty.

If a drastic change is undertaken, agreement should be sought with college associations for recognition of the experiment. Many schools hesitate to take action that will jeopardize the opportunities of graduates to enter college. Until agreements with college associations are worked out that will encourage local schools to experiment, the high school curriculum will not progress as rapidly as it should.

If increased faculty support for curriculum improvement is to be attained, it is important that an atmosphere of permissiveness be established. Status leaders should state their conviction that improvement takes place as new things are tried, that a teacher who tries a new procedure is doing so for the entire faculty. They should attempt to promote a willingness within the group for various individuals to experiment. Instead of looking for reasons why something should not be done, they should begin to look for ways in which they can assist people who are undertaking new things. If a large number of faculty members are experimenting, there is not the insecurity caused when only a few try something new. If few teachers do experimental work, those who are not experimenting will be threatened. It will appear that they are not as alert or adequate as those undertaking experimental activities, and they will do little things to prevent innovations from being started. Out of their insecurity will emerge hostile actions against the experimental activities, and those who are carrying on the experimentation will themselves be threatened. Each faculty member should be encouraged to work on his own pet idea of improvement and to "live and let live" where others are concerned. If this attitude can be engendered toward minor types of innovations that one individual can initiate, the faculty will become better able to examine without serious threat any proposals for change involving major alterations.

A faculty is more secure if a distinction is made between minor experimentation and major change. Any teacher should be experimenting with the phases of his teaching with which he is dissatisfied. He is working to improve his own practice and should be encouraged to do so without feeling any need to gain permission from anyone. On the other hand, some changes involve several teachers and a large segment of the student body. These changes should have total faculty approval. When a proposal for a major change is made, it should have committee study and recommendation and faculty approval. With this approach, status leaders can encourage the committee to give permission to experiment rather than to see their role as prejudgers and preventers.

Sometimes permissiveness is not understood. It does not mean anarchy or lack of regulation. When a curriculum worker strives for permissiveness, he gives support to: individuals having an opportunity to question, to oppose, to make alternate proposals; individuals and groups experimenting for the faculty with cooperative evaluation of results; and groups making decisions based on evidence that will be enforced by the executive officers of the faculty. Permissiveness is not laissez-faire; it is a scientific, thoughtful, evaluative approach with a structure for implementing decisions reached.

OUTSIDE PRESSURES

Not all innovations in secondary education start with the staff. Money and access to the channels of communication through the mass media can be used to make an initial impact on the secondary curriculum. Foundations with millions to spend can affect at least the surface of the program. The Ford Foundation has been able to secure use of TV education in high schools by grants that made possible some urban systems' experimenting with education by television. Grants have also supported team-teaching projects. As long as money has been supplied to underwrite the tryouts, the changes have continued. As far as the effect after financial support is withdrawn the evidence is inconclusive, but the opportunity to secure money for a special type of project has moved some school programs in a certain direction for at least the time being.

When an organization or a person with influence makes a recommendation and there is money for mass communication of the idea, it may create pressure for change. The suggestions of Lloyd Trump advanced under the sponsorship of the National Association of Secondary School Principals with money supplied by the Ford Foundation have caused many school systems to scrutinize their programs and to consider more flexible buildings and schedules. The Conant report, *The American High School Today,* sponsored by the Carnegie

Foundation, has been more widely considered than any proposal in recent educational history. University scholars developing proposals for courses in physics, chemistry, biology, and mathematics, with financial support of the National Science Foundation, have encouraged many high schools to change their courses in these fields.

These efforts and others can secure support through the mass media and in this way force local school faculties to examine them. Almost any idea, if repeated often enough, will find some segment of the population to which it appeals. Adherents become a pressure group, and local curriculum workers and teachers must find evidence to refute it or else give it consideration in curriculum planning sessions. But the outside pressures constitute an asset and a danger. The stimulation from outside initiative increases the range of possibilities that are examined. If, however, funds and prestige cause a staff to accept proposals without thorough testing and evaluation, the school becomes a tool of the strongest pressure group.

SUMMARY

The fostering of curriculum change involves providing a climate and a structure that will use dissatisfactions, both staff and lay, to engender curriculum study and evaluation.

SELECTED READINGS

Cay, Don Frederick, *Selected Teacher-Expressed Judgments Concerning Barriers to Curriculum Improvement.* Unpublished Dissertation. Gainesville, Fla.: University of Florida, 1960. Reports teacher perceptions of barriers to curriculum change.

Crosby, Muriel, *Supervision as Co-Operative Action.* New York: Appleton-Century-Crofts, Inc., 1957. Stresses the role of human relations in curriculum improvement.

Ebey, George W., "Front Line Observations on Curriculum Improvement," *North Central Association Quarterly* 27: 273-282, January, 1953. Outlines some of the major factors involved in promoting curriculum improvement.

Fliegler, Louis E., ed., *Curriculum Planning for the Gifted.* Englewood Cliffs, N. J.: Prentice-Hall, Inc., 1961. Contains chapters devoted to mathematics, foreign languages, reading, creative writing, science, and music, as well as overviews of the entire curriculum.

Kearney, Nolan C., "Three Ways Administrators Can Speed Curriculum Progress," *School Executive* 73: 52-53, December, 1953. Identifies use of research results, end of authoritarianism, and working with the public as the three ways of speeding curriculum progress.

Klahn, R. P., "A Report of a Curriculum Study," *National Association of Secondary School Principals Bulletin* 45: 80-84, September, 1961. Consists of an actual report of a curriculum study made in organizing a new school's curriculum.

McNally, Harold J., et al., *Improving the Quality of Public School Programs.* New York: Bureau of Publications, Teachers College, Columbia University, 1960. Contains descriptions of actual curriculum improvement programs in seven public school systems.

Miel, Alice, *Changing the Curriculum.* New York: Appleton-Century-Crofts, Inc., 1946. Describes procedures and methods of promoting curriculum improvement.

Morse, Arthur D., *Schools of Tomorrow—Today!* New York: Doubleday and Co., Inc., 1960. Describes experimental programs being conducted in various sections of the United States.

Platte, DeGroff and E. M. Moore, "Curriculum Improvement, Ltd.," *Clearing House* 34: 153-155, November, 1959. Relates some of the problems and difficulties encountered during a project involving curriculum development.

Pratt, W. E. and D. G. McGarey, *A Guide to Curriculum Improvement in Elementary and Secondary Schools.* Cincinnati, Ohio: Public School Publishing Co., 1958. A handbook of practical techniques and procedures for fostering curriculum change.

Rasschaert, W. M., "A Descriptive Analysis of a Departmental Curriculum Improvement Project in an Urban Junior High School," *Journal of Experimental Education* 27: 37-48, September, 1958. Concludes that teacher values, attitudes, and skills can be changed by the work group-conference method as a means to curriculum change.

Trump, Lloyd, *Images of the Future: A New Approach to the Secondary School.* Washington, D. C.: National Education Association, 1959. Offers suggestions for improvement through reorganization of the secondary school.

Venable, T. C., *Patterns in Secondary School Curriculum.* New York: Harper & Row, Publishers, 1958. Summarizes and appraises the forces influencing the curriculum, the types of curricular organization, and the principles and procedures of curriculum development.

14

ORGANIZATION FOR CURRICULUM IMPROVEMENT

Organization is necessary if curriculum improvement is to be made. Ideas and enthusiasm are not enough. Sources of authority and responsibility must be designated, and channels of communication must be made clear. Members of the staff and community must be informed of ways in which they can initiate and assist the curriculum improvement process. This chapter will explore the roles of various portions of the organizational structure that have been found helpful in inducing curriculum change.

FREEDOM OF A HIGH SCHOOL TO IMPROVE ITS CURRICULUM

The curriculum structure of any high school is dictated in part by state laws and regulations, the requirements of the accrediting association to which the school belongs and in which it wishes to retain membership, the polices of the local board of education, and the curriculum framework established by the office of the curriculum director. The principal is responsible for implementing the rules and regulations in the school that he administers. Each state has a school code which decrees how the school will operate, and in some cases makes a specific requirement of curricular offerings. For example, the 1961 Florida legislature passed a law making it mandatory that each high school offer a thirty-hour course contrasting democracy and communism. Other states have laws requiring the teaching of temperance, conservation, safety, and physical education. The curriculum of a high school must incorporate each legal mandate.

The accrediting association has a major effect on the program of a school. Throughout the past half-century the accrediting agencies have practically determined the curriculum structure of the American high school by the demand for the offering of Carnegie units of credit with a required number of minutes of class time per day to qualify for one. The daily schedule of most accredited high schools has been designed with this requirement in mind. If a school is seeking accreditation, it is told what must be added to obtain it. After proper accreditation is obtained, representatives or evaluation committees from the association visit the school and state what must be added or improved if accreditation is to be retained. The principal, in guiding curriculum development in the school, must help the curriculum leadership to become informed and be guided by accrediting association regulations.

The board of education of the school district in which the high school is located may also make policies which serve as a part of the curriculum framework. The board may, for example, decide that three years of a foreign language must be taught. It may agree to eliminate industrial arts from the curriculum. However, any decision the board makes must be within the state regulations and in line with accrediting agency standards. Usually the board, when making policies that are primarily curricular in nature, adds requirements that it feels are desirable in the community in which the school exists. These regulations apply to all the schools in the district.

The superintendent and his staff work with curriculum development in the school district within the framework described in the preceding paragraphs. They may make additional decisions that further restrict the freedom of choice of the principal and faculty of a high school. The courses to be offered, the manner of grouping, and teaching procedures may be prescribed from the superintendent's office. But the typical systemwide curriculum staff operates by formulating a curriculum framework that consists of broad guiding principles and that indicates the broad areas of content to be allocated to courses carrying certain titles. The individual high school is permitted or encouraged to develop its unique program within this outlined structure. The degree to which an individual school is really free to devise the program that meets the needs of its student body depends upon the nature and method of operation of the member of the superintendent's office in charge of curriculum. The most permissive statement of curriculum policy can be completely restrictive if the person administering it insists that he is the sole source of interpretation and implementation.

Any school system that wants individual school staffs to assume real responsibility for improving the program needs a systemwide curriculum planning and coordinating committee. The committee should have at least one representative of the faculty of each school who will bring problems and promising procedures in his school to the attention of the committee and who will take back to his own faculty issues for discussion and suggestions for programs that it may want to investigate and observe. The committee serves as a clearing house for ideas and practices and a place for identifying parts of the curriculum policy that need clarification or revision. It may be organized to advise the curriculum director, or it may have the function of deciding upon curriculum policies. In any case, it is a channel of communication between the teaching staffs of the individual schools and the systemwide administration.

The curriculum decisions of any school staff are restricted by the legislature, board of education, and superintendent's office. If, however, a staff is in drastic disagreement with a policy it may initiate reconsideration. But until the policy is revised or revoked, the staff may not take action conflicting with it.

The principal and staff of a school may make curriculum changes within the areas not regulated by state and district rulings. If a principal and faculty attempt to infer many applications for existing regulations they will feel that their role in decision-making is very limited. If, however, they assume that any situation not specifically covered in a regulation is open for local school decision, the possibility of the individual school's developing a unique program is good.

THE NEED FOR A CURRICULUM COMMITTEE

In the past, many high schools have left curriculum development to the individual departments. This procedure has resulted in revision of courses, course outlines, and bibliographies within the department, but has not usually led to any major overhaul of the total curriculum. Such a result is to be expected if each department staff has the responsibility of improving only its own program. No one looks at the total high school curriculum.

Each high school should have some group in its faculty organization that has the task of improving the curriculum. Unless some portion of the faculty has this responsibility, the school will probably retain the same curriculum structure that it has.

One of the standing committees of a school faculty should be a curriculum committee. It should be assigned the responsibility of carrying on a continuous evaluation of the results of the present program and then calling to the attention of the total faculty any areas in which the outcomes are not satisfactory.

Some schools have designated all of the department heads as members of a curriculum committee. This practice has two unfavorable results. Each department head feels a responsibility toward the members of his department to maintain the present status of the department or to improve it. As a result, he fights any change that would in any way decrease the size or influence of his department. Secondly, the members of the committee are all status people within the faculty, and their point of view is that of status people. Since these men have usually been on the faculty some time, the result is a tendency to maintain the status quo. Any person who has been in the school long enough to achieve department head status has helped to build the present program and feels a vested interest in retaining it.

A much more effective type of curriculum committee organization is to have a committee elected by the total faculty, with no person representing a particular department. As a result of being elected by the total faculty, the member's responsibility is to everyone, not just to his own department. This shift in the faculty member's responsibility gives him greater freedom to consider change that may lead to a reorientation of the power structure within the faculty. Less likelihood exists that members of the committee will be making decisions in light of their effect on a particular department.

The terms of the members of the curriculum committee should be staggered. To insure continuity of work, not all members of the committee should be elected at the same time. For example, if the committee has six members, it is desirable that they be elected for three-year terms, with two members leaving the committee each year and two new members being added. Under this plan, at least four members of the committee, for a given year, have already served one year and two members will have served two years. Problems are carried over from year to year, and the working procedures of the committee can be maintained.

The chairman of the curriculum committee should be elected by the total faculty. If he is elected by the members of the committee, there is a danger that it will become an in-group and the chairmanship rotated on some basis other than the wishes of the majority of the faculty. To insure that the chairman will have a period of training before assuming the responsibilities of his role, it is wise to have him elected a year in advance of the time he is to take office. During his year of training he should serve as vice-chairman and participate in the operation of the committee. In this way the chairman will not only be the choice of the faculty, but will also have experience with the work of the committee before assuming responsibility for coordinating it.

The curriculum committee should serve as a clearing house for problems. When individual members of the faculty feel that some change is needed within a department or within the total school program, they can make their feelings known to the chairman or to a member of the committee. This question or proposal should then be placed on the agenda and a decision made by the total committee as to whether or not an ad hoc work committee should be appointed to investigate the problem. To guarantee even further that the members of the faculty will have a voice in curriculum change, any member of the faculty should be free to present a curriculum problem to the total faculty even though it has been evaluated and deemed unimportant by the committee. If the total faculty agrees with the individual faculty member and decides that something should be done about the problem, the curriculum committee then has the responsibility of implementing the investigation of the problem.

It should be understood by everyone in the faculty that the committee does not have the authority to make decisions about curriculum policy. The committee is a faculty organization responsible only for making plans for study and for bringing proposals to the faculty. When the proposals are under consideration by the faculty, the curriculum committee should state its position, but it should be prepared to have its thinking reversed if the total faculty holds a different viewpoint.

In brief, the curriculum committee of the high school is a spadework committee. It has responsibility for helping the faculty identify curriculum problems, for developing the means by which problems are studied, for bringing proposals to the faculty, and for helping the faculty to consider all aspects of the proposals under consideration.

STEPS THAT A CURRICULUM WORK COMMITTEE SHOULD FOLLOW

If it is decided that an ad hoc work committee should investigate a problem and formulate proposals, how should it proceed? What types of evidence should be collected? A proposal based on opinion, hunch, prejudice, or selfish interest without collection of data represents a haphazard approach to curriculum change. So does proposing the adoption of the pattern of a prestige school in the region without investigating its results and the extent to which it will suit the needs of the local community. Curriculum improvement is a serious enterprise, and proposals should be based upon as extensive and vigorous a collection of data as time permits.

What steps should the work committee follow? First, it should attempt to discover pupil reaction to the program. Students should be asked to state whether or not they feel that the course or activity being evaluated is meeting their needs, whether they are satisfied or dissatisfied with it. They should be asked to state specifically all phases of the class or activity that they think need improvement.

Second, the work committee should attempt to obtain evidence as to the type of pupil development or achievement being brought about through the activity. What are the types of growth sought by those who direct the activity? What evaluation procedures provide evidence as to attainment of the purposes sought? Does any change take place in student behavior? What indicates achievement? What evidence do teachers or parents have who have observed the situation? Tests, behavior records, interviews, questionnaires, follow-ups are all important techniques for collecting data to use in deciding whether or not the activity is making a worthwhile contribution.

Third, the committee should discover the opinion of parents, and the evidence that they have about the contribution of the activity to their children's development. Interviews in which parents are asked for their evaluation of the activity are an important technique for collecting evidence—especially if the observer listens for incidental observations that the parents may make.

Fourth, the committee should find out what a number of teachers feel about the activity. What does the teacher in charge think? What do other teachers who work with the class or similar classes feel? What do counselors see as an outcome in terms of student growth? What does the principal see? What evidence does any of them have of the success or failure of the existing program?

Fifth, the work committee should analyze the factors that seem to be exerting pressure on the activity. Is there unfavorable parent opinion? Are there certain pressure groups in the community that are striving for a change? What does the traditional concept of education do to produce a feeling of satisfaction or dissatisfaction with the activity? What kind of leadership has been exerted in the activity that has led to dissatisfaction? What does research show about the success or lack of success of the present method in other schools? What do social changes that are occurring imply as far as the particular activity is concerned? To what extent have teachers working with the activity made full use of the resources that are available?

Sixth, the committee should analyze work observed in other situations or reported in literature dealing with this same activity. Do better results seem to be obtained by approaching the activity in a different way? Does research on other programs indicate that more growth is being attained through other procedures?

Not all committees will be able to take all of these data-collecting steps. The extent of the change being considered and the amount of time available before a decision must be made will influence the amount of effort that is put into data-collecting. Unless the evidence is overwhelming in one direction, the committee should probably suggest several alternate proposals with the arguments for and against each. It may indicate its preference in terms of its interpretation of the evidence, but it will assist the faculty more by helping it to see the alternatives than it will by recommending only one course of action. A wide-awake faculty will then ask questions. It will try to discover the extent to which the committee has collected data of the type indicated above.

Some schools make the mistake of leaving decisions concerning curriculum policy to committees. Some unsophisticated faculties think that they should accept a work committee's proposal without hesitation. They feel that to question a proposal means to express a doubt as to the capability of their colleagues. This belief is unfounded and dangerous. The members of the faculty not on the work committee have data that is not accessible to the committee; the feelings and perceptions of the remainder of the faculty are important and must be considered. Unless there is freedom to question and to propose revisions these data are ignored, and this may well jeopardize the success of any attempted change.

The proposals from the work committees should be brought back to the total faculty for acceptance, rejection, or recommended revision. By bringing the proposals to the total faculty, everyone is kept informed. No change is a surprise. Each person in the faculty has a chance to question, to add his opinion, and to play a part in forming the decision.

A work committee should expect revision of its proposal. As it presents a proposal to the faculty, it should expect to get new insight through faculty analysis. Other members of the faculty have had experiences different from those of the committee members. These experiences will be helpful in identifying pitfalls that the committee may not have foreseen. Through joint consideration of the proposal the rest of the faculty will become informed, and the members of the committee will have the possibility of seeing even better procedures than the ones they originally recommended.

A work committee should not expect or want to make decisions for the faculty. It should see its function as one of making a preliminary proposal, which will be modified in such a way that it includes the wishes of the total faculty.

HOW THE CURRICULUM COMMITTEE
FOSTERS EXPERIMENTATION

The curriculum committee in the high school should be responsible for fostering experimentation as well as for facilitating faculty decisions. Although it works within the structure of the district's curriculum improvement plan, in better school systems the restrictions imposed by the district are few. It has been found that, except in the teaching materials supplied and the course and activity labels given, attempts at systemwide changes have very little impact.

Even though a more uniform procedure may seem desirable, curriculum change occurs on a broken-front basis. Teachers, like children, learn at their own speed. A teacher is able to execute only those things that he understands and in which he believes. If he is asked to undertake a core curriculum, for example, when he does not believe in or even understand it, the results prove disastrous both to the teacher and to the youngsters. Because of his feelings of inadequacy the teacher loses his security. Because he is doing something in which he does not believe he loses his self-respect. Because he cannot sincerely back the program in which he is participating he loses his effectiveness in his relationship with the parents in the community. Pupils suffer because of the inadequacies and frustrations of their teachers and conclude that school is a place of mismanagement and incompetency. To attempt to make a systemwide change without extensive study and experimentation is to invite confusion and conflict.

Curriculum development is a gradual process. It is achieved through experimentation with procedures that individuals or staff deem to hold promise. The rate of progress is dependent upon the sincerity and skill of the staff in using the scientific method to achieve intelligent change.

Instead of approaching change on a systemwide basis, it is usually much better to agree within the system on an area in which improvement is desirable and then to encourage individual teachers and faculties to seek to improve that phase of the program in the way that seems best to them. It is not difficult to get a teaching staff to agree on an area in which improvement is desirable. The objective evidence collected can convince all of the need. The difficulty comes in expecting everyone to see the same solution, and the chances for a more desirable solution are greater if many different people within the system have the opportunity to try out the best procedure that they can formulate.

Thus the curriculum committee becomes the basic unit in the coordinating and sharing of curriculum experimentation done by an individual teacher, by a portion of the faculty, or by the faculty as a whole. It has the responsibility for sharing with other schools the results that it has obtained by experimentation and for bringing to its own faculty the results of pioneer work done in other schools.

THE PROCESS OF EXPERIMENTATION

An attempt is often made to conduct systemwide experimentation or research in cooperation with a university research bureau. The problem is carefully formulated, the hypotheses and assumptions clearly stated, the data-collecting procedures tried and validated, and the techniques of analysis described in detail. This procedure is the desirable one, and the results contribute to the development of a more adequate theory of education. But most curriculum experimentation will be much more informal, much less carefully designed and controlled. Its primary purpose will be to increase the insight and skill of an individual or of a small group of teachers. It will be exploratory rather than definitive. Its use to the total profession will depend solely upon the extent to which the results are compared and contrasted with those of similar explorations.

Even though the curriculum experimentation in a school may consist only of a teacher's deciding that he is going to try to improve some phase of his teaching, or of several teachers comparing the results that they get by using different methods or trying new materials, four steps are important.

First, *if an experiment is to be successful the person undertaking it should be very certain as to what the problem is.* He should state his dissatisfaction and the type of correction he wants to make.

Second, *the hypothesis to be tried out should be stated very simply.* Not much time or effort need be expended in elaborating its implications or underlying assumptions. A simple, direct statement that can be understood by pupils, other teachers, and parents is usually most productive.

The hypothesis can usually be stated by simply describing the method that will be used. For example, if a teacher is dissatisfied with the type of achievement students are making in his class and feels that the problem lies in his not knowing the students well enough, he can hypothesize that the achievement will be increased if he visits the home of each of his pupils once during the first semester of the year. The hypothesis is stated in terms of a course of action and an expected outcome.

Third, *when an hypothesis has been established as to the way in which a curriculum problem is to be solved plans should be made for collecting proof of its success.* What type of growth is sought? How can it be detected if it occurs? What are the kinds of situations in which it may be observed? How shall it be recorded? All of these are helpful questions. Even in the informal testing of an hypothesis one needs to think about methods of collecting evidence of its worth.

To collect evidence skillfully, the behavior change sought must be carefully defined. If abstract terms are used in defining it, neither the teacher nor the pupils nor anyone else will be able to tell whether the experimentation has been successful. No one will know for sure what changes have occurred. Only as the changes sought are defined in terms of observable behavior can agreement be reached concerning the results.

Collecting too much evidence should be avoided. Sometimes experimentation is discontinued because the teachers have attempted to record everything that is done or said. If the recording gets too burdensome, teachers will not want to experiment. In planning any experimentation the kind and amount of evidence sought should be determined. The teachers involved should be encouraged to secure the help of as many people as possible. For example, an intern working with a teacher may be asked to assist in collecting evidence. Volunteers from the parent group can be of assistance. Pupils may be used. If any of these individuals knows the kind of behavior he is to observe and has it clearly enough defined so that he will recognize it easily when he sees it, the recording is not a difficult process.

Plans should be made for organizing the data collected. If the hypothesis is clearly stated the evidence to be compiled should be apparent. The headings under which it will be arranged should be developed, and the instruments to be used in collecting the data should be designed to record them under their proper headings. By following this procedure the experimenter has combined the dual processes of collecting and organizing data. As he proceeds he knows at any given moment how much and what types of data he has collected and the areas in which he has little or insufficient evidence.

Some of the evidence to be collected may be found in the feelings and satisfactions of people. Too frequently these are discounted. They are not looked upon as objective, and therefore are not considered concrete or valid. Such data should not be ignored. A person's statement of opinion or feeling is observable behavior. If a method for recording it can be devised, the evidence can be used. To increase the probability that the feeling is honestly reported, the individual from whom the data are collected should be given the chance to state them anonymously.

Fourth, *after the hypothesis has been tried and the evidence collected, the results must be interpreted.* Did the new procedure get
better results? In all areas? In some ways and not in others? Was the
difference due to the novelty of the experimental procedure? Would
teachers with different values and skills have obtained the same results? Are the results significant enough to justify an in-service program
to help other teachers move to the type of program used in the experiment?

Many people should have a part in the interpretation. One of the
shortcomings of much research in education has been that the experimenter alone attempted to interpret his findings. Facts are used
as the basis for judgments, but facts are not decisions. Although all
persons looking at the evidence may agree on what the facts are,
they may not see the same implications for action. An individual interprets evidence in light of his purposes and values. School situations
always involve several types of people—administrators, teachers, parents, pupils, the lay public. If a valid interpretation is to be made,
it should involve representatives of most of these groups. In planning
the design of the experimentation the curriculum committee should,
as part of its function, make provision for procedures by which representatives of the various groups participate in making judgments
about the results obtained.

THE TEACHER'S FREEDOM TO EXPERIMENT

It is important for
individual teachers or groups of teachers within a school to feel free
to experiment. Very few schools are ever in a position where the
total faculty is ready to move at the same time. Teachers, like children,
have different levels of readiness and different rates of learning. To
attempt to hold back the more progressive and enlightened teachers
until their more reactionary and less informed colleagues are ready to
move is to stifle the initiative and creative spark within the staff. The
primary step for those concerned with curriculum improvement is the
development of a permissive atmosphere in which teachers are willing
for others to experiment. Help can then be provided those who are
ready to start.

All teaching is experimental. Since the variables in a teaching-
learning situation change constantly, the results of a given method
cannot be guaranteed. In each class the teacher makes a guess as to

which procedure will secure the best results. Through the years he finds that certain techniques produce satisfactory results most of the time, and he operates on the assumption that these are good. But the wise teacher continually looks for evidence that may cause him to re-examine his hypotheses.

Even the best teacher has certain phases of his teaching that fail to produce the desired results. If he is sincerely interested in teaching, these failures challenge him and he looks for more effective procedures. From his professional reading and from conversations with colleagues he develops hypotheses as to better ways in which to work. If he is secure enough or adventurous enough, he tries them. He may try them in a haphazard fashion, or he may collect evidence to see whether the new methods are more, or less, effective.

All teachers should experiment. None of course should completely change his method all at once. To do so would be to guarantee failure. Each should cling to the techniques that work and every year try a new idea in some area of dissatisfaction. Each should establish some new teaching hypothesis in an area of weakness, collect evidence of the results obtained, and compare them with the results produced by the present method. Change is not made for the sake of being modern. It is meant to decrease dissatisfaction resulting from the disparity between the teacher's ideas and his performance or from poor student reaction and work patterns. But no matter what the underlying cause, experimentation is the means by which teachers can increase their happiness, their self-confidence, and their security in their work.

THE TEAM APPROACH TO EXPERIMENTATION

Although most experimentation in teaching is done by the individual teacher, greater strength is provided if more than one teacher is involved. Each person participating provides support for the others. Because several deem it worthy of their time and effort, the problem seems more important. The work seems lighter because it is shared. Obstacles are easier to overcome because people help and encourage each other. Because of commitment to each other it is less likely that the effort will be discontinued when one individual becomes discouraged.

Further, the team approach provides the possibility of increased validity of the results obtained because the sample is larger. A new procedure may work in one situation, and it is easy to assume that it will work in others. But if several teachers are testing the same hypothesis, greater confidence can be placed in the results of the experimentation.

If several teachers are involved, opportunity is present for establishing controls and for trying out different procedures for solving the problem. Although case studies of individual class activities are desirable and necessary, they can only be exploratory. Before changes are made on a far-reaching basis, the staff should undertake experimentation in which different procedures are tested against each other and against the one that the school has been following. If teachers other than those involved in the experimentation are to be influenced by the results, they will want to compare them with those obtained in classes that follow the procedures to which they are accustomed.

One factor should be considered in the interpretation of the results of experimentation. It needs to be recognized that because of the increased enthusiasm of the teacher conducting the experiment, greater change will probably result there than in situations in which the normal pattern is followed. In designing the experiment an attempt should be made to establish the types of controls that will decrease the role played by this factor.

Another advantage of the team approach is that it makes possible the use of consultants. A school will not ordinarily provide consultant service for an individual teacher who wants to experiment. If, however, a number of teachers are interested in the same problem and want to test hypotheses in that area, the administration may see this as an in-service experience and be more willing to underwrite it. Past experimentation in education leads to the conclusion that one of the most effective ways of promoting in-service growth is to provide access to a consultant who will assist teachers in working on a problem with which they are concerned.

Probably the major benefit of the group approach to experimentation is the result of the interaction. It is usually hoping for too much to expect many teachers to be convinced by the results of research in which they have not had a part. The greatest change that occurs in the curriculum through experimentation comes through growth that takes place while the teachers are experimenting. As men work together the observations they make to each other, the insights they share, and the trials and tribulations they experience promote growth by providing more common purposes, increased mutual understanding, and an expansion of vision of each individual involved.

If the total faculty is interested in the same project, much can be done to increase the benefits derived from experimentation. More faculty meeting time can be used to seek agreement on types of pupil growth sought and ways of promoting it. Through interaction the faculty can come to greater agreement on purposes and procedures. But the possibilities for total faculty experimentation on the same project are much less in high schools than in elementary schools because of the greater diversity of backgrounds and concerns in a secondary school staff. Teachers are more likely to want to experiment in their area of specialization. Persons concerned with program improvement in the high school usually find it necessary to depend upon sharing the concerns and outcomes of a variety of experimental efforts in order to achieve a more commonly held philosophy concerning ways of working with pupils.

THE FUNCTION OF EXPERIMENTATION

The administration and the curriculum committee should look upon experimentation as a process of improvement worked on by many and made available to all. It is not a method of compelling change. If teachers see the administration using the results of experimentation as a club to force change, experimentation will become a threat to be avoided and resisted.

Experimentation should be seen as a way of providing help. People should be encouraged to experiment, to share the results of the experimentation, to examine other experimentation, and then to move ahead as soon as they are convinced that the results indicate a change to be desirable. Under this plan supervision moves from compulsive motivation to extending an invitation and providing assistance and encouragement as the teacher takes the next step.

Innovation should be permissive, occurring when the individual teacher is convinced of the wisdom of the move. Research within the system is a device for collecting data that teachers will deem valid because they have had a part in collecting it or because it has been produced by trusted colleagues.

A major function of the administration and the curriculum committee is making information available. Many devices for bringing the results of experimentation to the attention of the staff should be developed. Opportunities for discussion of the implications of the research should be provided. But any decisions as to steps and strategy should be left with the individual teacher or the local faculty. The school program will move forward as the people who experiment in one area share their results with other teachers. Some will be stimulated by the creative ideas advanced. Others will find suggestions for meeting the very difficulties they are experiencing. But the chief benefit will be the staff's knowledge that the administration sanctions and supports experimentation.

If a portion of one faculty meeting a month is set aside for staff members to describe the new procedures they are attempting, the innovations will multiply. Teachers will hesitate at first because they will not be sure that the administration is sincere, and they will fear that other teachers suspect the motives of those who report. If, however, a few of the respected members of the faculty can be induced to report some of their efforts and the discussion is properly conducted, others will begin to contribute. Descriptions should be heard without evaluation or criticism. No comparisons should be made. No comments should infer that others are inferior because they are not experimenting, too. No pressure should be applied to force experimentation or sharing. The principal's role in the situation is to stress the cooperative approach to improvement and the importance of keeping each other informed. He should demonstrate by his actions the quality of permissiveness that accepts other staff members as professional people seeking to improve their practice through implementation of the best hypotheses that they can develop or make use of.

Some school systems promote sharing of new practices on a system-wide basis. The Marion County, Florida, schools publish a bulletin for the staff entitled *Timely Tips*. Each issue contains a description of a successful new practice from each school. Thus each teacher in the county receives a monthly report of successful new ideas.

To add to the value of *Timely Tips*, the selection of items to be reported is a cooperative effort. No teacher describes his own work. Instead, each faculty decides together the innovation that should represent its school. By using this approach, knowledge concerning what is being tried in each school is spread throughout the faculty. Teachers have an immediate functional reason for becoming informed about the work of their colleagues. More experimentation is encouraged, and members of the staff come to value each other more because they know of the professional contribution that each is making.

SUMMARY

The up-to-date high school is one that is continually changing its program of instruction. When it feels that it has achieved the ideal program and ceases to try new ideas it has started to decline. To keep abreast of current conditions, the high school must continue to make changes.

The intelligent method of change is experimentation. It is never safe to adopt without question the program of another school. Conditions, staffs, student bodies, and communities differ. To have a valid program, each school must develop its own curriculum. Ideas and information can be secured from other schools, but the responsibility for developing the unique program best for that school rests with its faculty.

The ideal program should be sought with the recognition that it can never be achieved. The best that can be hoped for is that the program this year is better than last year's and that next year's program will be better than the present one. Whether this goal will be attained depends upon the faculty's continuing to seek improvement through experimentation.

The good high school is an experimental school. Experimentation is a way of life. The administration and staff recognize this truth and spend a portion of their meeting time evaluating present experiments, deciding upon policy and procedural changes based on evidence obtained from past research, and planning the experimentation that should be undertaken in the future.

The organization needed for curriculum development is one in which the regulations of the state, accrediting agencies, and local board of education are recognized; in which the district administration places primary responsibility for program development on the faculty and provides interfaculty coordination; in which the individual school's faculty organization has a committee responsible for facilitating continuous curriculum study and experimentation; and in which individuals and groups are supported and aided in examining, testing, and improving their instructional procedures and content organization.

SELECTED READINGS

Association for Supervision and Curriculum Development, *What Shall the High Schools Teach?* (1956 Yearbook), Chapter 7. Washington, D. C.: The Association. General discussion of curriculum research.

King, F. M., "A Trend in Curriculum Development," *Education* 80: 433-437, March, 1960. Outlines an organizational framework for promoting curriculum development.

Knapp, D. L., "Curriculum Change: By Drift or Design?" *Educational Leadership* 17: 233-236, January, 1960. Stresses the need for careful planning in making curriculum changes.

Lyda, W. L., "A Suggested Conceptual System for Decision-Making in Curriculum Development," *Educational Record* 41: 74-83, January, 1960. Outlines steps and procedures to use in making decisions about curriculum planning.

Morry, M. A., "The Importance to Curriculum Development of Making Follow-Up Studies of Students in College," *National Association of Secondary School Prinicpals Bulletin* 44: 126-134, February, 1960. Describes the use of follow-up studies in providing direction for curriculum revision.

Olson, A. R., "Organizing a Faculty for Curriculum Improvement," *Ibid.* 44: 94-97, February, 1960. Outlines some principles and practices for involving a faculty in curriculum development.

Pellett, E. A., "A Development in Process: the Science Curriculum in the Whittier Union High School District," *Science Education* 43: 409-414, December, 1959. Describes the use of exploration and experimentation in bringing about curriculum change in the science program of a school district.

Scheffler, I., "Justifying Curriculum Decisions," *School Review* 66: 461-472, Winter, 1958. An examination of the intellectual bases for making curriculum decisions.

Shaver, S. B. and Ragene Farris, "Four-Dimensional Curriculum Development and Coordination for Secondary Schools," *California Journal of Secondary Education* 34: 473-480, December, 1959. Outlines an organizational pattern to insure greater coordination in curriculum development.

Stembridge, A. W., "A Curriculum Advisory Committee," *National Association of Secondary School Principals Bulletin* 45: 75-79, September, 1961. Outlines the work of a curriculum advisory committee.

Taba, Hilda and Elizabeth Noel, *Action Research: A Case Study*. Washington, D. C.: Association for Supervision and Curriculum Development, 1957. Provides an illustration of the techniques and procedures of action research.

—— and Jack Marsh, "Action Research as a Technique of Supervision," *Educational Leadership* 12: 453-458, May, 1955. Suggests that action research can replace or supplement the usual in-service educational program for teachers.

Wagner, G. W., "A Present-Day Look at the American School Curriculum," *Education* 78: 328-334, February, 1958. Stresses the need for basing curriculum planning on a careful investigation of the needs of the school.

Webb, O. C. and S. H. Crawford, "Curriculum Improvement Through Action Research," *National Association of Secondary School Principals Bulletin* 44: 86-93, February, 1960. Describes a program of action research conducted at Miami Senior High School, Miami, Florida, in September, 1958.

Wilkinson, D. H., "Some Factors that Complicate Lay Participation in Curriculum Development Programs," *Educational Administration and Supervision* 45: 173-178, May, 1959. Outlines some of the major causes complicating lay participation in curriculum change.

IV

THE HIGH SCHOOL OF THE FUTURE: A FORECAST

Today's dream is tomorrow's reality. To increase current vision and build future reality each of us must use existing data, frontier practices, and projected social trends to attempt to invent the secondary school of tomorrow.

15

THE HIGH SCHOOL
OF THE FUTURE

All persons concerned with the improvement of the American
secondary school are faced with the task of attempting to
anticipate its emerging pattern. Each must use what he knows
about learning, adolescents, the social trends, the new
technology, to try to see what may be accomplished and the
hazards that may be encountered. Unless professional people
concerned about the welfare of the country, the world, and
adolescents, try to invent the future, the nature of the
secondary school will be shaped by the salesmen with the
most convincing pitch or by political pressure fomented by
irresponsible, sensational presentations via the mass media.

NEEDED RESEARCH

Many of the
present answers to questions about the type of secondary
curriculum needed must be based on inferences made by consulting research data from related disciplines. This approach

299

is not satisfactory. Basic research studies designed to provide evidence concerning the needs of youth and the most effective educational procedures should be undertaken.

Some areas that should be investigated immediately are:

1. How is mental health fostered?
2. How is the creative potential of an individual released?
3. How is commitment to values developed?
4. How are self-direction and the ability to deal effectively with change developed?
5. How is communication accomplished in person-to-person situations? in classrooms? by mass media?
6. How do the perceptions of teachers and pupils differ concerning the curriculum content? the transactions in the classroom?
7. What is the cultural heritage essential for all in our era of increasing specialization?
8. What skills are needed by all who are awarded high school diplomas?
9. What content and skills can be taught by teaching machines and mass media?
10. What type of pupil development can only be nurtured adequately through face-to-face, person-to-person communication?
11. What size and structure of groups most effectively promote the various types of growth sought in the secondary school?
12. How can the pupil growth that the secondary school seeks to promote be measured?

ANTICIPATED DEVELOPMENT

Evidence from research of the type outlined will enable concerned persons to modify the existing program realistically. Until it is available, attempts to anticipate and project the future program must be based on empirical evidence and inferences.

The remainder of this book is the effort of a person who has spent twenty-seven years working in and with secondary schools to predict the development of the next twenty-five years. It is hoped that these hypotheses will help each reader to formulate his own expectations, which may differ from those of the writer, and to plan his work for the type of change he deems desirable.

Values, Skills, Understandings Will Be Fostered

Although it is possible that schools in 1985 will be used as instruments of thought control and social classification, the writer is nevertheless optimistic enough to believe that there will continue to be a social commitment to freedom, creativity, and equality of opportunity. With this basic assumption, an attempt is made to project the changes that technological advances and social problems will produce in the next few decades.

In 1985, as at present, the planners of education for adolescents will hope that each pupil will develop a set of values to guide his behavior; acquire the skills necessary to participate effectively in the culture; gain an understanding of his social, economic, political, and scientific heritage; and become able to make a specialized contribution to the society.

The program of the school designed to promote these goals will be divided into four phases: analysis of experiences and values, acquisition of fundamental skills, exploration of the cultural heritage, and specialization and creativity.

Analysis of Experiences and Values

In the school, each pupil will spend six hours a week in an Analysis Group. With ten other pupils of his own age and a skilled teacher-counselor he will discuss any problem of ethics, social concern, out-of-school experience, or implication of knowledge encountered in other classes. No curriculum content will be established in advance for the Analysis Groups. The exploration of questions, ideas, or values advanced by group members will constitute the primary type of experience.

The purpose of the Analysis Group will be to help each pupil discover meaning, to develop increased commitment to a set of values, and to offer opportunity to examine the conflicts among the many sets of values and viewpoints held by members of the society.

The membership of the Analysis Group will be carefully selected to provide a group composed of persons of relatively equal intellectual ability, but varied social and economic values. The group will remain a unit throughout the high school program of its members. Changes will be made only when a deep emotional conflict develops between students or between a student and the teacher-counselor.

The teachers of Analysis Groups will be emotionally mature people. They will be selected early in their teacher education program because they display a high degree of empathy and are warm, outgoing personalities whom other people like. They will be given special training in counseling, communication, and value analysis. Each will be taught to see his role as one of helping others to feel more secure, to clarify their values, and to communicate more effectively with their colleagues. If a teacher of an Analysis Group attempts to sell his viewpoint, he will be considered unsuccessful and replaced.

Each Analysis Group teacher will meet three groups, or thirty-three students, during the week. His time beyond the eighteen hours in the discussion groups will be for individual counseling with the thirty-three pupils and their parents.

The Analysis Group will be considered the basic element of the educational program. In the late sixties, it will begin to be recognized that unless citizens have values they accept, understand, and can apply, the social structure will disintegrate until authoritarian controls are applied. To counter the danger of collapse of the democratic way of life, the school will be assigned the task of making as sure that each child develops a set of values as it does that he is able to read. The Analysis Group will evolve as the best means of performing the values development function.

Acquisition of Fundamental Skills

Citizens in 1985 will need fundamental skills far superior to those considered necessary in the early sixties.

In the home and in the elementary school, children will learn to read, spell, and compute at their own rate of learning by the use of teaching machines. In the school for adolescents, mathematics, foreign languages, and many scientific processes and formulas will be taught by machines supervised by librarians and a staff of technicians. Machines will teach basic skills as effectively and efficiently as a teacher.

The skills needed by all citizens will be stated, and each student planning a high school program will be told the skills that he *must* master. He will work through the needed programs as rapidly as he can. When he wants to work on a skill, he will go to the librarian, schedule a machine and a program, and go to work.

Some students will complete their basic skills work early in their high school program. Others will work on them until they leave the high school. Certain skills considered vocational in nature will be added to a student's program if he indicates he has college entrance or a specific vocation as a goal.

Two librarians, one to issue programs and the other to help on request, and a staff of mechanical technicians will supervise the work of two hundred students. Disorder will be at a minimum because each person will work on his own level and with his own goals. Moreover, each student will work in a private soundproofed cubicle.

The teaching machines laboratories for the various subject-matter areas—mathematics, languages, grammar—will be an integral part of the Materials Center of the school.

Exploration of the Cultural Heritage

The explosion of available knowledge in the last half of the twentieth century will confront educators with the need for selecting, synthesizing, interpreting, and seeking better methods of transmitting that knowledge. The things that an effective citizen will need to know in 1985 will be a multiple of the knowledge necessary in 1960. Textbooks taught by less than master teachers will not be enough, and ways of bringing each student into a working relationship with the best teachers available will be sought. Basic knowledge from the essential fields will be prepared in the most easily understood media and presented as dramatically and forcefully as possible. This knowledge, from the humanities, the social sciences, and the physical and biological sciences, will be considered the Cultural Heritage.

Roughly a third of the program of each high school student will be scheduled to help him acquire the basic knowledge of his culture. By exposure to the experiences, ideas, and discoveries of the past, the individual will be expected to become literate enough about the basic ideas of his culture to participate in discussions of them or to understand reference to them. For some, it will be expected that the experiences in the Cultural Heritage portion of the program will develop a desire to enhance further the values on which the society is based.

Classes in the Cultural Heritage program will be large. Sometimes as many as five hundred or one thousand will be in a single section. Teaching will be by television, films, or a highly skilled lecturer. No provision will be made for discussion, because ideas that produce a response can be discussed in the Analysis Groups. Only one teacher and an assistant will be needed in each subject-matter field in each school. The teacher will lecture or present the material through an appropriate medium. The assistant will prepare quizzes and examinations and record the marks made on the machine-scored tests. The high pupil-teacher ratio in the Cultural Heritage area, one teacher for each five hundred to fifteen hundred students, makes possible the low ratio, one to thirty-three, for Analysis Groups and highly individual instruction for the exceptional student.

Teachers for the Cultural Heritage program will be selected early in their teacher education program. They will speak well, like to be before an audience, have a sense for the dramatic, and be attractive persons. In addition to intensive work in their field, they will be given work in speech, dramatics, logic, and communication via the mass media.

Specialization and Creativity

The Analysis Groups, the Cultural Heritage courses, and the Fundamental Skills work will constitute the program required of all. But in addition each student will be encouraged to develop a specialization. It will not be required, but the opportunity will be presented.

Shops, studios, and work laboratories will be available for specialized activities. All students will be encouraged to engage in some creative activities, since the Cultural Heritage phase of the program will be essentially a passive one. Writing laboratories, for example, will be staffed to help students who want to develop creative writing ability. School newspapers, magazines, and telecasts will be written in the laboratories.

Other students will select work experience in various industries and businesses in the community. These students will have decided that they will not seek a higher education and will use their specialized program to insure a smooth transition to regular employment.

Special opportunities will be available for the persons who qualify for them in terms of ability and intensity of purpose. Seminars in the various content fields, and some of an interdisciplinary nature, will be available. Students must have displayed unusual ability and show evidence of a desire for individual investigation in a field before they will be permitted to enroll. Seminars will be limited to fifteen students. They will meet for two two-hour periods each week, and the remainder of the time the students will conduct independent research in the library or laboratories.

Small science laboratories will be kept open for full-time use by the individual researchers from the seminars. In fact, students who are not expected to become scientists or technicians in an area will not use laboratory facilities. Laboratory experience will have been abandoned as a general education procedure by the seventies.

In the specialized fields the pupil-teacher ratio will be low, one to forty or fifty pupils. Teachers will give individualized supervision and plan with the Analysis Group teachers the experiences individuals should have.

No longer will the colleges blame the secondary schools for inadequate preparation. Graduation days will have been eliminated. Students will continue to work in the secondary school until they pass their college entrance examinations or move to a job. Most students will enter the secondary school at thirteen, but some will leave at fifteen and others at twenty. A student's decision to leave the program will be conditioned by his completion of the Cultural Heritage experiences, his acquisition of fundamental skills, and his individual goals.

The School Plant

The school plant will have rooms of many different sizes. Buildings with uniform size classrooms will be obsolete. Analysis Groups, specialized education classrooms, studios, and laboratories will be small. Cultural Heritage courses will be held in large halls equipped for lectures and mass media programs. Libraries and shops will be large. Areas where individuals work with teaching machines to perfect basic skills will be divided into small work cubicles.

Basis of Support

The program will be paid for from federal funds. It will be recognized in the sixties that, with a truly mobile population, neither local communities nor the national government can afford to allow the great differences in educational opportunity to continue. No community is immune to poor education in another, and the national government cannot afford thus to neglect a large percentage of its human resources.

The Steps in the Evolution

Many voices arose in the early sixties clamoring for a copying of the European educational system. Some wanted to use tests and allocate the pupil to a specialized curriculum as early as ten years of age and to give him the required courses the experts deemed suitable for him. They proposed restricting the curriculum of the secondary school to the intellectual pursuit of information in certain areas of knowledge. Values and social development were to be left to the home and church.

However, increasing juvenile delinquency, more homes with both parents working, increasing cases of mental and emotional disturbances could not be ignored. The secondary school program had to be made broad enough to deal with values, human relations, fundamental skills in communication, and the cultural heritage, and at the same time offer opportunities for work in a student's special field.

The program described for 1985 will not occur overnight. It will involve a step-by-step change produced by social pressures and technological advance. The steps that will lead to the 1985 program will be as follows:

1960-1965

Increased emphasis on guidance, science, mathematics, and foreign languages, with continuing federal support. The National Defense Education Act has produced desirable results. As more money has been fed into these portions of the secondary school program, better-trained guidance, science, mathematics, and foreign language teachers have been secured, and programs in these areas have been improved because of better facilities and equipment. Little chance exists that the present support for these phases of the program will be decreased.

Increased flexibility in the high school program, with courses becoming available to pupils on the basis of intensity of purpose and level of achievement instead of chronological age. In spite of the arguments by some critics of secondary education for a return to fundamental courses, this change will not occur. The demands of the American society for courses in art, music, family life, psychology, sociology, and even driver training will prevail. Various pressure groups that recognize the importance of each of these areas will stand back of the phase of the program in which they are interested if that portion of the secondary school comes into real jeopardy. They will become as vocal as the advocates of so-called basic education have been. As improved guidance personnel are secured, the fallacy of insisting that certain elective courses be assigned to a given grade level will be recognized. An increased concern for providing for the gifted will loosen some of the fetters that have made the school program unnecessarily rigid.

Increased number of seminars and opportunities for individual research for gifted students. Many high schools are experimenting with advanced seminars and individual research. Some are providing small laboratories where gifted individuals may work on their own outside of class. These efforts are proving so successful that the practice will spread.

Increased use of TV and other mass media and of teaching machines. All of the evidence available indicates that as far as facts alone are concerned, classes taught by a good teacher over TV and other mass media can get results equal to those of regular classes. This knowledge will bring increased use of TV instruction, particularly in the elective courses not available in all schools. Research in the use of teaching machines will lead many schools to use them for teaching skills.

Development of new structural forms for the high school plant. As mass media use increases, the need of some classrooms that are large and other work areas that are smaller will be more apparent. Architects will begin to design more buildings that have classrooms of varying size or more space with movable walls. (See Appendix B.)

1965-1970

Federal support for citizenship education. By the late sixties it will be realized that federal support for vocational education, science, mathematics, and foreign languages is not enough. The nation will become increasingly aware of the need for developing greater commitment to democratic values. Out of the evident shortcoming in this area will come a cry for federal support for citizenship education, even though no one is sure as to how this can best be done. The NDEA will be expanded or some similar bill enacted to provide federal support for the social studies-humanities area of the curriculum.

Use of large classes for teaching the cultural heritage area of the curriculum (literature, social studies, and sciences). Classes will acquaint students with our cultural development by means of lectures, television, and demonstrations. Classes of one hundred to two hundred will not be unusual. Such classes will be developed in school programs that provide seminars. Large classes in these areas will make possible a low pupil-teacher ratio for seminars and creative work. The seminars will provide opportunity for the analysis of information gained in the large classes. Accrediting associations and administrators will move away from the assumption that all teachers should have the same pupil-teacher load and perform the same type of function.

Workshop laboratories provided for the development of individual skills. Reading laboratories and workshops in grammar and spelling will provide individualized instruction permitting students to progress at their own rate. Laboratories will be used extensively in foreign language instruction. Success with the use of teaching machines will lead many schools to do most of their instruction in basic mathematics skills in laboratories where students work individually with machines. Much more of the classroom experience in secondary schools will be in laboratories, whether the field be science, art, foreign language, English, or mathematics.

1970-1980

Guidance and the teaching function brought closer together. It will be recognized during the sixties that, in spite of the money being spent on guidance, satisfactory results are not being achieved. It will be seen that, no matter how well they are prepared, trained guidance personnel whom students see two or three times a year cannot do the job. Recognition will come that, for the typical student, guidance must be performed largely by a teacher with whom the student has long-term contact. A portion of the time provided for guidance will be allocated to classroom teachers. On the other hand, it will be recognized that all classroom teachers are not able to perform the guidance function, that teachers who provide guidance will need specialized training in counseling techniques, group discussion procedures, and value analysis.

The school program for an individual pupil will be organized in such a way that he spends some portion of each week, possibly as much as six hours, with one teacher who has a continuing relationship with him and with approximately ten other students. These eleven students will continue to work with this teacher during the period in which they are in the school. The six hours each week will be spent in discussing the kinds of experiences the group members have encountered in their other classes and in exploring the value conflicts that have arisen. It will be recognized by 1970 that the task of helping students develop values can no longer be assigned primarily to the home or the community. The continued increase in juvenile delinquency will provide the deciding evidence that the school must assume a major responsibility for the development of values to live by. So many value conflicts will be apparent to youngsters that they will need a situation in which they can explore them under trained leadership. Whether this person is called a counselor or a teacher will not be important. But this type of service will be provided by the staff of the secondary school. Specialized guidance personnel will be available as resource people to these counselors, and for referral of problems that the teacher is unable to solve.

Increased concern for mental health. It will be recognized that improvement of mental health is basic to citizenship education in a society in which one or more out of ten spend some time in an institution for the treatment of mental or emotional disturbance. Unless a person is emotionally capable of participating effectively in society he will be unable to use the skills and knowledge that he has acquired. He will be a dependent rather than a contributing citizen. Neither the public nor the profession will any longer be willing to say that the school's function is to develop the intellect alone. Both will recognize that the school must be equally concerned with mental health, and the administration, the teachers, and the program of the school will be evaluated in terms of their effect on mental health.

Revision in the pattern of teacher education. As the school program emerges it will be evident that one pattern of teacher education for secondary school teachers is not enough. The realization will come that some teachers spend their time primarily in the presentation of facts and ideas over the mass media to large groups, that another type of teacher spends the major portion of his time in working with individuals and small groups in value analysis and in counseling, and that still other teachers work with individuals as guides in the development of individual skills, in creative activities, and in vocational experiences. Different patterns of teacher education will be devised for each of these different types of teaching functions.

WHAT THE HIGH SCHOOL WILL BECOME

Change occurs a step at a time. It is stimulated by failure, social conflict, or disaster, which produce fear, frustration, anger, and cries for action. It occurs as a teacher, a school, a school system tries a new method, procedure, organization, or content. It is speeded by success, support, recognition, and approval.

What the high school will become depends upon the degree of dissatisfaction with the present, the range of lay and professional vision, the penetration of the decision-makers' insight, and the public's encouragement of experimentation. The quality of the program will be determined by the wisdom of the decisions made by the public, legislators, board members, administrators, teachers, pupils, and parents—by you and me.

SELECTED READINGS

Ahrens, Maurice R., "Considerations in Planning Secondary Education of the Future," *School Review* 63: 269-276, May, 1955. Discusses

310

the need to re-examine the goals, curriculum design, materials
for learning, methods of teaching, and guidance program of the
secondary schools.

Austin, David B., "Secondary School Program of the Future," *School Executive* 74: 19-21, June, 1955. Predicts that the future program
will be designed to serve the total youth population rather than
a selected few, will be directed toward functional education,
and will be greatly influenced by the improved understanding
of our youth and our culture.

Blanchard, B. E., "What the High Schools Will Be Emphasizing During
1970-80," *High School Journal* 39: 389-390, April, 1956. Foresees the future curriculum as emphasizing general education as
a prelude to specialization; behavior and personality; and social,
economic, and cultural factors.

Bush, R. N., "The High School of the Future," *California Teachers Association Journal* 56: 6-9, October, 1960. Forecasts that the future
high school will have a more clearly defined objective and a
broader curriculum emphasizing inquiry and independent
learning.

Chilcott, J. H., "The Secondary School of 1985," *Clearing House* 34: 371-
372, February, 1960. Anticipates that enrollment will double,
textbooks will be obsolete, electronic devices widely used, and
the curriculum expanded.

Elicker, P. E., "The Next 25 Years in Secondary Education," *National
Association of Secondary School Principals Bulletin* 41: 1-6,
December, 1957. Foresees consolidation of small schools, racial
integration, better staff utilization, and an extended school year.

Fischer, J. H., "High Schools for the Fabulous Future," *National Education
Association Journal* 47: 23-25, January, 1958. Views three forces
as shaping the high schools of the future: the egalitarian, the
demographic, and the technological revolutions currently being
experienced.

Grambs, Jean, et al. for the Commission on Secondary Education of the
Association for Supervision and Curriculum Development, *The
Junior High School We Need*. Washington, D. C.: The Association, 1961. Discusses the functions, problems, and needs of
the junior high school of today and of the future.

Kenworthy, L. S., "Education for the Community of 1985," *Educational
Leadership* 17: 470-474, May, 1960. Predicts that the school
of the future will need to be world-centered, for the community
of the future will be the world.

Mead, Margaret, "The High School of the Future," Symposium, *California
Journal of Secondary Education* 35: 360-369, October, 1960.
Sees a broadening of its functions as the great need in planning
the high school of the future.

Michael, L. S., "New Directions to Quality Education in Secondary Schools,"
National Association of Secondary School Principals Bulletin
45: 11-18, January, 1961. Reviews the contents of J. Lloyd

Trump's *Images of the Future* and *New Directions to Quality Education.*

Morse, Arthur D., *Schools of Tomorrow—Today!* New York: Doubleday and Co., Inc., 1960. Describes experimental programs being conducted in various sections of the United States.

Trump, Lloyd, "A Look Ahead in Secondary Education," *National Association of Secondary School Principals Bulletin* 42: 5-15, January, 1958. Predicts different categories of teachers, specially designed school plants, and the reorganization of the curriculum to identify and teach the basic elements of knowledge and understanding.

————, "The American High School in 1970" in *Frontiers in Secondary Education IV,* Paul M. Halverson, ed. Syracuse, N. Y.: Syracuse University Press, 1960. Describes the school of the future by contrasting it with the school of 1959.

————, *Images of the Future: A New Approach to the Secondary School.* Washington, D. C.: National Education Association, 1959. Presents a plan for reorganizing the school to achieve quality education economically by better utilization of staff.

———— and Dorsey Baynham, *Focus on Change.* Chicago, Ill.: Rand McNally and Co., 1961. Presents in more detail the ideas presented earlier in Trump's *Images of the Future.*

APPENDICES

Most of the efforts during the 1960's to change the high
school program to provide for individual differences have
been confined to provisions for varying the rate at which
a student proceeds through a field or for increasing the depth
of his investigation of a field. An unique program for accomplishing these goals has been developed at the Melbourne
(Florida) High School by the faculty under the leadership of
the principal, Mr. Frank Brown.
Melbourne High School, influenced no doubt by the spirit
of exploration at Cape Canaveral, has increased the flexibility
of the school organization and made it possible for a student
to work at his own speed and to investigate the fields offered at
a level appropriate to his ability. Appendix A presents a
summary of the curriculum offered at that school.
The South Hills High School building and grounds, planned
by H. L. Gogerty Associates (Joseph L. Feil and On G. Low
in charge of design) and the staff of the Covina-Valley Unified
School District, Covina, California, is illustrative of the
imagination that is being utilized in the development of secondary school plants. It is designed to permit a more flexible
program and greater variation in group size and use of staff.
Appendix B shows a blueprint and scale model of that school.

313

APPENDIX A

From *Phase Learning*, a description of the program at Melbourne (Florida) High School:

Under the phase-learning system of nongraded groups, students may be multiclustered for instructional purposes in their various subjects as follows:

Phase 1 .... Basic Education
Phase 2 .... Intermediate Education
Phase 3 .... Depth Education
Phase 4 .... Quest Education

> *The establishment of exactly four phases in all subjects might well create another lock step. The dimensions in the phase system may be increased or decreased for any subject. For instance, clustering in English might utilize as many as six phases. Because of selective grouping, chemistry might require only two phases.*

The four dimensions are designed to group students in relationship to their knowledge of skills: low, medium, high, superior.

This multidimensional grouping of phase learning is designed for more creative development of students as they are scheduled by subjects and depth of subjects, rather than by chronological age level, grades, or a time element. The organization is so sensitive to individual differences in ability that the student may be pursuing one subject in phase one and another in phase four.

Students performing at lower levels of efficiency are guided into a cluster group of basic or remedial education in the deficient area. Average ability groupings, which comprise the great majority of the school, are designated intermediate. Students who demonstrate academic maturity by achieving above the norm are programed into depth education. Those students who are clearly superior are scheduled into quest education and college-level courses. In the nongraded structure, the latter groups are permitted to spend considerable time in independent study and research in their quest for creative excellence.

At the other extreme, the student who is seriously handicapped in basic skills may remain in a basic phase during his entire high school career. If he fails to master basic skills, he does not change phases. In keeping with traditions inherent in American education, as long as he works conscientiously toward his goal and improves his understanding, he receives credit.

An objective of the phase-learning organization is to motivate the student to move as rapidly as he is able from the first to the second, to the third, and to the fourth phases of a subject. In essence, the purpose of nongrading is to give all students basic education skills and provide depth and quest education for those individuals who are capable of a more profound approach.

To make nongrading the challenging and vitalizing force that it should be, each course must be as stimulating and productive as possible within the limitations of time (which should be flexible), space, material, and teacher ability. As a direct corollary of this proposition, it follows that special courses must be geared to the particular potentials of students clustered around the areas of basic, intermediate, depth, and quest education. These courses must give the individual the fundamental knowledge, to the extent that he can absorb it, which he needs if he is to perform in modern society. Confidence originates in accomplishment, and it is vital that all young people enter adulthood fully accepting their dual obligations: to society, as contributing members; to themselves, as individuals of dignity and worth.

. . . . . .

In a multidimensional curriculum, an important facet is a program of independent study for students capable of contemplation, research, and investigation. The important challenge confronting the school is to keep independent study from looking just like homework. If it is no more than this, there is no sense in it, for independent study must be in the direction of inquiry. If the curriculum is to be truly open-ended, units, including all homework assignments, must be left open at the end in order that the student may experience the joys of academic discovery.

The school's most highly motivated students are programed into phase four in the area of motivation and interest. Consequently, the fourth phase of a subject is always left open-ended in order to eliminate all boundaries in the learning process.

. . . . . .

A major objective of phase learning is to induce the student to assume more responsibility for his education. He is encouraged to develop both direction and thrust. As an incentive to greater academic maturity, elevation from one learning phase to another may be initiated by the student as well as by the teacher. This should be preceded by an academic appraisal. Before the student is advanced the evaluation must clearly show an increase in maturity in the subject studied. This is essential in order to avoid the yo-yo effect of returning a student to the same phase. The determination to elevate is a three-way decision involving the counselor, the student, and the teacher, with the latter playing the major role. Once advanced, no student should be rephased to a lower cluster except in extreme and unusual circumstances. Down-phasing has serious implications for the individual in an organization designed for mobility.

The curriculum in motion provides for the elevation of the student immediately upon evidence of improved skills and increased maturity. Prompt acceleration encourages excellence. The usual delays caused by minor details relating to completion of a marking period or an attendance cycle should be brushed aside. These mundane particulars are of dubious value in a climate which projects the limits of learning.

. . . . .

The question arises as to what to do about the student who transfers from the nongraded school to a conventional institution. The answer is an easy one. His record of achievement is simply converted to the traditional grade system and dispatched in conventional form. The procedure is admittedly unorthodox but can scarcely be considered immoral when one considers the immorality of segmenting and restricting learning to a particular grade. A preliminary follow-up of transferring students indicates excellent adjustment to the new school. Some observers attribute this to traits of mobility and flexibility acquired in the yielding curriculum of the nongraded system.

Conversely, students who transfer into nongraded situations adjust easily and with some evidence of increased motivation. The challenge of the phase cluster with its promise of immediate advancement in return for performance seems to be a motivational factor in itself.

Nongrading for phase learning is not a situation in which students will be given credit for courses which they can skip. Students are given credit or units only for work covered—proven ability in a subject does not entitle the student to a credit. It merely permits him to leapfrog into more advanced work. The effect is one of advanced standing but not advanced credit.

Through longitudinal phase learning, the school can provide the student with a well-balanced program which will meet his needs as a citizen and as an individual. The basic skills will not be neglected; they will be dealt with more efficiently because those weak in fundamentals pursue basic work until it is learned. Then, with proper guidance, the individual, whether slow, average, or superior, is academically exposed to the catalyst which may well transform his school experience into one of inquiry and curiosity rather than mere problem-solving.

Longitudinal learning does not imply avoidance of subjects that might require work; rather it entails encouraging the interests which will lead to all of the depth of which the student is capable. The challenge is in the personal and emotional satisfaction which emanates from a feeling of discovery.

Concern for the individual student is basic to the principle of projected learning. The curriculum must provide sufficient variety of breadth in a course offering to provide for the student who wants to be a craftsman, a future historian, or a scientist. Flexible time blocks, efficient use of facilities, and deployment of teacher personnel are prerequisites to this achievement. For the student, a program must be planned which simultaneously challenges him to move ahead and to seek the basic knowledge and discipline necessary to true creativity and lasting accomplishment.

. . . . .

To inaugurate the nongraded organization, each student must be carefully tested with standardized achievement tests in the four basic areas of mathematics, English, science, and history. If the school contains youngsters in grades ten through twelve, students who score below tenth grade level in a particular subject are assigned to classes in the basic-skills phase in the areas of their deficiency. Students who score above grade twelve in a subject, regardless of the age and grade level, are scheduled into the quest phase, where they assume responsibility for their own learning. Here they enter Advanced Placement courses or independent study. For instance, a tenth grade student scoring in grade thirteen on a standardized English achievement test need not go through the stifling experience of studying English in grades ten, eleven, and twelve. Instead, he spends three years in a college-level English course centered around perceptive writing and reading. Care is taken to assure that the emphasis is upon study rather than independence. Highly motivated students may spend much of their time in independent study and research.

In the other extreme, twelfth grade students who read below the tenth grade level are scheduled into the first phase along with students in grades ten and eleven having similar difficulties. In a basic English course, all strive to improve their skills, with attention being given to individual handicaps. Phase placement is not a primary objective in phasing students according to need. The purpose is to accommodate learning in the manner best construed to cultivate the mind.

Students possessing average skills that are traditionally labeled grades ten, eleven, and twelve are programed without reference to grade level into classes made up of those having like achievement. These classes offer the incentive to improve and to grow. Phase organization allows the student to be "unaverage" in his own special way.

The freedom of phase scheduling inculcates academic imagination. An expert in mathematics may find himself joined to a most advanced class in this area while working in a basic course in an area where he has had small success. A student quickly learns and becomes aware that mastery of basic skills will advance him to an average group, while the average has his goal in a higher phase.

The highest phase, a quest for knowledge, is the province of those students with a towering, if not lofty, degree of academic maturity. They are encouraged to embark on a program of independent study and research in one or more areas. This phase is open-ended and the student can advance as far as he wishes.

Independent study schedules are organized in a minimum of two-hour blocks. A student may be assigned to the learning resources center for not less than two hours but to a maximum of the entire school day, depending upon whether he wishes to pursue depth in one or more areas. He sees the teacher only on a consultative basis.

The entire emphasis in the quest center is upon inquiry and intellectual curiosity rather than research, with positive efforts being made to avoid the pitfall of researching everything and contemplating nothing. Students are sought for this group who have a combination of intellectual power and drive. These talents, given proper guidance, can lift the student into a search for excellence beyond anything yet attempted in the high school.

The learning levels, then, which are called phases, are little more than collapsible fences; the curriculum becomes multidimensional as projected learning surmounts the grade barrier. In effect, this exciting new arrangement in grouping disregards the conventional chronological age organization of students and offers intellectual grouping as an improved structure. It permits the school to use rare freedom in scheduling students. They may be programed individually or in flexible clusters. Within this framework, students are phased according to academic maturity into the previously described basic, intermediate, depth, and quest-for-knowledge areas.

Photograph courtesy of Herbert Bruce Cross.

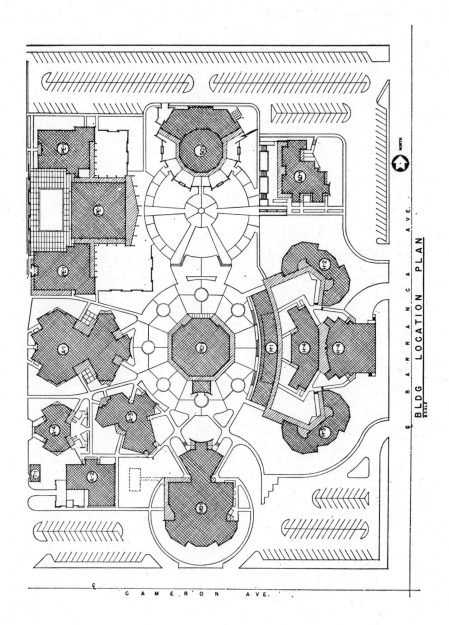

BLDG LOCATION PLAN

APPENDIX B

The buildings in the blueprint (opposite) of the South Hills High School of the Covina-Valley Unified School District may be identified as follows:

RC-1   Instructional Materials Center.

H-1   Counseling offices, first floor; six regular classrooms, second floor.

H-2   Flexible classroom units. Regular classrooms divisible to accommodate small group instruction and classrooms to accommodate sixty students divisible to thirty.

H-3   Same flexible arrangement; seventy-station language laboratory on second floor.

H-4   Most flexible facility on the campus. Will seat three hundred at one time, or two groups of one hundred and fifty at one time. Has stage provisions for drama and stagecraft. H-4 adjoining the large group facility is a unit providing teacher offices and seventy cubicles for independent study.

     Note: The "H" series of buildings is known as the Humanities Center.

MS-1   Math-Science Building, featuring one large group classroom accommodating one hundred students, three laboratories with spaces for independent research, and a complex of divisible classrooms to accommodate groups from sixty to fifteen students.

A-1   Music and Homemaking Building. This building features three homemaking laboratories and a large group space for seventy-five students. Conventional instrumental and choral rooms seat large groups of one hundred.

A-2   Industrial Arts Building. This building features considerable footage of covered outdoor area and the conventional industrial arts laboratories relating to woodwork, metalwork, mechanical drawing, and electronics.

A-3   Business Education Building. This unit features a large group typing room divisible into three smaller laboratory sections. A work education laboratory provides a realistic environment for merchandising and salesmanship. Business education students are adjacent to the large group facilities in the math-science building.

A-4   Arts and Crafts Building. This unit features two laboratories relating to the curriculum in the arts and crafts.

PE-1   Gymnasium and enclosed basketball courts. On either side of the main physical education building are found the dressing rooms for boys and girls.

SC-1   The Food Services Center. This unique facility provides a semi-enclosed area for eating and opens onto a quadrangle for outdoor assemblies, etc.

AD-1   Administration Building. This unit provides for the various administrative services and houses offices and conference space for the student government.

INDEX